CLASSROOM ACTION

Human Rights, Critical Activism, and Community-Based Education

Building on the concept of a "teaching community," Heble and his contributors explore what it might mean for teachers and students to reach outside the walls of the classroom and attempt to establish meaningful connections between the ideas and theories they have learned and the broader community beyond campus. Using a case study approach, the chapters in this volume are conceptually and practically useful for teachers and students involved in thinking about and implementing community-based forms of teaching and learning.

Classroom Action links teaching and research in genuinely innovative ways, and provides a range of dissemination strategies to inspire broad-based outcomes and impact among a diverse range of knowledge-users. It marks a major advance on the ways in which the relationships between pedagogy, human rights, and community-based learning have hitherto been theorized and practised. The discussions in *Classroom Action* prompt radically new ways of thinking about what teachers do in the classroom, and how and why they do it.

(Cultural Spaces)

AJAY HEBLE is a professor of English in the School of English and Theatre Studies as well as the director of the International Institute for Critical Studies in Improvisation at the University of Guelph.

Edited by
AJAY HEBLE

Classroom Action

Human Rights, Critical Activism, and Community-Based Education

UNIVERSITY OF TORONTO PRESS
Toronto Buffalo London

ISBN 978-1-4875-0079-5 (cloth)   ISBN 978-1-4875-2058-8 (paper)

Cultural Spaces

Library and Archives Canada Cataloguing in Publication

Classroom action : human rights, critical activism, and community-based
education / edited by Ajay Heble.

(Cultural spaces)
Includes bibliographical references and index.
ISBN 978-1-4875-0079-5 (cloth)   ISBN 978-1-4875-2058-8 (paper)

1. Community education – Canada.   2. Community and school – Case studies.
3. Social change – Case studies.   I. Heble, Ajay, 1961–, editor.   II. Series: Cultural spaces

LC1036.C63 2017   370.11'5   C2016-907593-1

This book has been made possible with the financial assistance of the Musagetes
Foundation, and of the University of Guelph, especially the Community Engaged
Scholarship Institute (CESI), the International Institute for Critical Studies in
Improvisation (IICSI), the School of English and Theatre Studies (SETS), and Project
Re•Vision. Thanks also to The Guelph Campus Co-operative.

University of Toronto Press acknowledges the financial assistance to its publishing
program of the Canada Council for the Arts and the Ontario Arts Council, an agency of
the Government of Ontario.

Canada Council   Conseil des Arts
for the Arts   du Canada

ONTARIO ARTS COUNCIL
CONSEIL DES ARTS DE L'ONTARIO
an Ontario government agency
un organisme du gouvernement de l'Ontario

Funded by the   Financé par le
Government   gouvernement
of Canada   du Canada

Canadä

for my students

Contents

Acknowledgments

This book has been a long time in the making, and, first and foremost, I want to thank all the contributors for believing in the project, and for their commitment, their encouragement, and their generosity throughout the process. I dedicate this book to my students, from whom I have learned (and continue to learn) so much. I can't say enough about the amazing work that has emerged from our classrooms. If this book offers readers even a small glimpse into the kind of energies that have been activated by your creative thinking, your critical questioning, your spirit of experimentation, and, perhaps most importantly, your extraordinary ability to work with others to achieve positive results, then it will have served its purpose.

There are so many people who have taught, mentored, supported, and collaborated with me over the years. I am grateful to them all, but will only have space here to name a few. I continue to learn from the example of two of my mentors and former teachers, Linda Hutcheon and Edward Said. My friend and colleague George Lipsitz, with whom I've had the honour of collaborating on another recent project, has always been a tremendous source of inspiration. My former graduate students, Jesse Stewart, Ingrid Mündel, and Elizabeth Jackson, remain three of my closest friends and advisors. Their attentive readings and helpful suggestions always improve my work. I'd also like to offer thanks to Frédérique Arroyas, Ben Authers, Christine Bold, Russell Brown, Rebecca Caines, Patrick Case, Alan Filewod, Daniel Fischlin, Julie Hastings, Linda Hawkins, Thomas King, Ric Knowles, Mark Laver, Eric Lewis, George Lewis, Kevin McNeilly, Carla Rice, Justine Richardson, Eric Schnell, Winfried Siemerling, Tina Sorbara, J.R. (Tim) Struthers, Sherrie Tucker, Shawn van Sluys, Rob Wallace, Ellen Waterman, Paul Watkins, and Deborah Wong.

This book wouldn't have been possible without the support of my incredible staff and colleagues at the International Institute for Critical Studies in Improvisation (IICSI) and the Improvisation, Community, and Social Practice (ICASP) project at the University of Guelph. Much gratitude, in particular, goes out to Rachel Collins. I've had the privilege to work with Rachel now on several book projects. Her attention to detail, her support in formatting and standardizing the chapters and bibliography, corresponding with contributors, and preparing the index have been invaluable. I have also benefited tremendously from the support of IICSI's Project Manager Kim Thorne. Kim has been a mainstay of the IICSI and ICASP initiatives for many years, and I have come to count on her in so many ways, for so many things. Kim has recently left IICSI to take on another position at the university. She'll be sorely missed at IICSI, but I know she will thrive in her new role. I am hugely grateful to the Social Sciences and Humanities Research Council of Canada (SSHRC) for their generous support of ICASP and IICSI through their Partnership Grant and Major Collaborative Research Initiatives programs. I'd also like to acknowledge the generous and continuing support I've received for my work through the Office of the Vice President Research at the University of Guelph. Thanks to Malcolm Campbell, Kevin Hall, John Livernois, and Alan Wildeman.

For funding in support of this book, I would like to acknowledge the generous support of the Musagetes Foundation, and of the University of Guelph, especially the Community Engaged Scholarship Institute (CESI), the International Institute for Critical Studies in Improvisation (IICSI), the School of English and Theatre Studies (SETS), and Project Re•Vision. Thanks also to The Guelph Campus Co-operative.

Thank you to the staff at University of Toronto Press, and, in particular, to my editor Siobhan McMenemy, for believing in this project from the get-go, and for her support, guidance, and advice. I'm grateful, too, to the anonymous peer reviewers for their helpful and supportive suggestions throughout the writing and revision process.

There are many organizations and global movements that provide inspiration for a more hopeful future – you can find information about some of these in the webography. All royalties from sales of this book will be donated to Amnesty International, one such organization whose work is making a real difference in people's lives.

Finally, and as always, I want to acknowledge my amazing family, especially my wife, Sheila O'Reilly, my children, Maya and Kiran, my mother, Sushila Heble, my sister, Sucheta Heble, my mother-in-law,

Louisa O'Reilly, and my father-in-law, James O'Reilly (1926–2016), who passed away while I was seeing this book through the final stages of the production process. I continue to learn so much from all of you, and am deeply appreciative of your love, your guidance, your support, and your encouragement. I wish my father, Dr. Madhav Heble, could have been alive to see the publication of this book. Although I grew up knowing that he (and his family) played a role in various activist causes, most notably in India's freedom struggle, my father was always very quiet and humble when asked about his experiences and accomplishments. As a result, the depth of his involvement in these rights-based struggles is something I've only begun to understand since he passed away in 2012. And it's only now, after completing this manuscript, that I'm beginning to understand the ways in which this book has been quietly inspired by his example.

CLASSROOM ACTION

Human Rights, Critical Activism, and Community-Based Education

Introduction: Classroom Action – Human Rights, Critical Activism, and Community-Based Education

AJAY HEBLE

Destinations Out

When Duke Ellington, in a 1957 issue of *Down Beat*, was quoted as saying that he was not interested in educating people, fellow jazz composer and improviser Sun Ra, in the liner notes to one of his earliest recordings released that same year, responded by declaring, "I want to go on record as stating that I am." I've long been intrigued by this statement.[1] In this book, I want to suggest that Ra's pronouncement has a valuable, if unsuspected, role to play in reinvigorating our understanding of the very places where we look for knowledge.

Now, I admit, Ra might seem somewhat out-of-place in a book about community-based learning and human rights education. After all, throughout his time on this planet, Ra insisted that he was ... well, yes, from another planet, that he hailed from outer space. But it's precisely Ra's out-ness (and he may well be the most out-cat in the history of the music) that commands our respectful attention. I've argued elsewhere that outer space functions for Ra as a metaphor for possibility (or perhaps for performing the impossible), for alternatives to dominant systems of knowledge production, and that this was particularly important for aggrieved populations sounding off against systems of oppression and racist constraint.

"If you find earth boring, just the same old same thing," Ra liked to declare, "then come on and sign up for Outer Spaceways Incorporated." Or, in a piece entitled "Imagination," Ra asked us, "If we came from nowhere here, why can't we go somewhere there?" The full poem, reprinted in Ra's book of poetry and prose, *The Immeasurable Equation*, reads, "Imagination is a magic carpet / Upon which we may soar / To distant lands and climes / And even go beyond the moon / To any planet in the sky / If we came from nowhere here / Why can't we go somewhere there?" (206).

All this might seem like flippant rhetoric and offhand space-age futurism from an eccentric and marginalized figure in jazz history. In a recent article ("Why Can't We Go Somewhere There?"), I've argued, however, that it is anything but. Despite being marginalized and summarily dismissed in dominant narratives of the music and all but forgotten in most institutionalized accounts of jazz history, Ra, to my mind, remains a hugely influential and pioneering improvising artist. And "nowhere here," for Ra, was an apt and deadly serious descriptor for the earthbound, dead-end life-situations in which African Americans repeatedly found themselves, a world of systematized and institutionalized forms of violence, oppression, and racist constraint. "Somewhere There," and "Outer Spaceways Incorporated," by contrast, offer a place of hope and possibility, a place of black social mobility. Come on and sign up.

Herein, I'd like to suggest, lies a tale about the resilience, force, and impact of improvisatory performance practices. If, as bell hooks has argued, "African American performance has been a site for the imagination of future possibilities" ("Performance Practice" 220), and if, as another theorist, Stevphen Shukaitis, suggests, "the emergence of a radical future … is almost always necessarily defined by its very otherness from the world as is" (112), then Ra's out-ness, his fondness for blasting off into what other African American improvising artists might have called "destinations out," needs to be seen and heard as a kind of (social and sonic) expression of black mobility. Ra's performances, often featuring a quasi-theatrical improvised romp through the history of African American music, from the early forms of swing (remember that Ra played with Fletcher Henderson) to bebop, free jazz, and far, far beyond into the outer-space noisiness of who-knows-where, were themselves statements about a mobility of practice, expressions both of unspoken, erased, or whitewashed black histories and of unwritten, unscripted futures. The "somewhere there" of improvisation was, for Ra, part of black music's resistance to capture and fixity, its noisiness and clamorousness part of a refusal to give in to the kind of culture of acquiescence or non-participation that resigns itself to the way things are because (or so we are too often told) no other future is possible.

In these pages, I'd like to turn up the volume on some of those earlier arguments to suggest that Ra's interest in educating people might have much to tell us about the kinds of issues that are at the heart of this book. In particular, I'd like to suggest that for education to be a purposeful site for critical social action and engagement, one of our key challenges as teachers, researchers, and educators will be to encourage broader forms of community-based learning and involvement. And this will mean (and this, indeed, is where I take my cue from Sun Ra's Astro Black jazz philosophizing, his own take on what it means to educate) thinking anew about what we do, and about how and why we do it. In short, reimagining the relationship between the academy and the community, I will suggest, ought to occupy a central place in any serious attempt to reflect on what it means to make our work more socially and ethically responsible.

As a teacher of literature, I'm often called upon to account for what I do: just why do I "profess" literature, and why does a study of literary texts matter? In this book, I'll suggest, by way of the principles articulated in the recently concluded UN Decade of Human Rights Education, and drawing on several community-based activist projects initiated by my students, that, no matter what our discipline or our area of study, our pedagogical activities matter because they are connected in complex and important ways to issues of resources, power, and public interest. They matter because they can enable new knowledges and opportunities, and because they can generate alternative ways of seeing (and being in) the world. They matter because of the massive human rights violations and barbarous abuses of power that continue unchecked, this despite the ratification of various international treaties and covenants. They matter because of the tightly controlled, media-manipulated view of the world that's generally accepted, by consent, as a representation of the way things are. In the face of elite control over the way in which knowledge is produced in our society (who controls what gets said, the institutional forces that determine what counts as knowledge or as truth, etc.), and as power becomes increasingly concentrated in the hands of fewer and fewer people and corporations, pedagogy offers one vital place in democratic societies where people should be able to increase their say about decisions that affect their lives. Democracy, after all, is predicated on the ability of ordinary citizens to become aware of issues in their communities and to develop a sense of responsibility for addressing those issues. At issue here is the idea of genuine and open discussion and debate, the encouragement of active participation where citizens can represent their own perspectives and create alternatives to unjust social and institutional structures.

It is thus, I believe, our ethical responsibility as educators to artic-ulate principled arguments about our commitment to advancing alternative forms of social mobilization, new (and more just) ways of understanding, new (and more just) ways of participating in a world of human responsibility. After all, as Samantha Nutt argues in her riveting book, *Damned Nations: Greed, Guns, Armies, and Aid*, "Social change (anywhere in the world) begins with education" (183). It is my contention that pedagogies that are most likely to succeed in produc-ing people aware of, and willing to take on, the vital range of respon-sibilities and rights of citizenship take place not just in classrooms, but also, as Sun Ra's example makes clear, at a variety of sites and in a wide array of settings. In making this claim, I'm following the lead of a number of thinkers, including, for instance, Henry Giroux, who encourages us to think about pedagogy not just in terms of the trans-mission of knowledge within classrooms, but more broadly as "the complicated processes by which knowledge is produced, skills are learned meaningfully, identities are shaped, desires are mobilized, and critical dialogue becomes a central form of public interaction" ("Foreword" xi).

I recognize, too, that, in making such claims for the need to engage in a broadening of our educational priorities, I'm building on a deep and vital history of critical pedagogy and education for social intervention here in Canada. A key part of that history is recounted in Roger Simon's Preface to his book *Teaching Against the Grain: Texts for a Pedagogy of Pos-sibility*. Recalling some of the concerns and conditions that gave rise to the establishment of the Critical Pedagogy and Cultural Studies Forum at the Ontario Institute for Studies in Education, Simon writes, "In 1979 my colleagues and I at the Ontario Institute for Studies in Education (OISE, a graduate school of the University of Toronto) began what we clearly understood was a legitimation exercise. A number of us were developing teaching and research rooted in specific commitments to enhancing the degree of justice and compassion present in our commu-nity" (xv). The pioneering work of Simon, and others such as Deborah Barndt (with her long-standing commitments to activist art, commu-nity organizing, and popular education within social movements)[2] points to how efforts to rethink pedagogical practices and priorities within the context of a university structure can build purposefully on (or be affiliated with) social movement education and histories of social intervention. American Studies scholar George Lipsitz is forthright on this matter: "Academic work," he tells us, can be especially important when connected to activist struggles outside the academy because established educational and cultural institutions are not the only sites from which critical and creative thinking emerge; indeed, these institutions have been greatly enriched over the years by the innovative analyses and arguments about important issues that emanate from social movements themselves. (*American Studies in a Moment of Danger* 287)[3]

In this context, the role of community-based organizations or popular education projects, or what I might call alternative pedagogical institutions such the Doris Marshall Institute for Action and Education (1988–98) and Naming the Moment (1986–96), as well as of unions, grass-roots women's organizations, faith movements, and organizations committed to anti-racist and aboriginal education, needs to be understood as an important part of that history.

The idea for this book emerges, in large part, out of work I've done in the classroom over the last several years, experimenting with community-based forms of learning and teaching.[4] Now, as I have found myself grappling with several pressing, and, indeed, contentious issues – the relationship between theory and practice, between analysis and activism, between the classroom and the public sphere, between academic research and lived experience – I have come to understand that these are exactly the kinds of questions that can redefine (and perhaps reinvigorate) our entire sense of intellectual purpose as teachers, questions that force us to confront the very assumptions informing our teaching and learning priorities. As living traditions of emancipatory hopes and practices, our pedagogical imperatives, in short, are matters of some public consequence, especially in a post 9/11 era in which there's increasing pressure to conform to the narratives promulgated by dominant knowledge-producing elites and in which entrenched (and taken-for-granted) positions crowd out alternative visions and opportunities for change.

In such a context, a central argument this project seeks to advance is this: for education to be a purposeful site for critical activism, one of our key challenges, as university-level teachers and learners, will be to create structures in our classrooms (as well as within the larger institutions in which we work) that encourage broader forms of community-based involvement.[5] Now, lest I be misunderstood, let me be clear that when I talk about community-based education, I have in mind something rather different from the kinds of narrowly defined notions of civic volunteerism or service learning that are frequently offered in response to questions about (and demands for) public accountability. Indeed, rhetoric linking global citizenship to traditional notions of volunteerism too often gets bandied about these days in the service of a marketplace model of education. And as Joel Westheimer and Joseph Kahne point out in their survey of the field, attempts to strengthen democracy and citizen participation through civic education and service learning programs vary widely in their underlying beliefs and assumptions, with many of these programs having at their core a decidedly conservative character. "What political and ideological interests," they encourage us to ask, "are embedded in or easily attached to various conceptions of citizenship?" The critical force of many of the concepts currently in fashion in educational debates – from "learner-centeredness" to "experiential learning" to "citizenship education" – indeed runs the risk of being dissipated unless a commitment to human rights and social justice is central to our efforts and policies.

So what might it mean for us as teachers and learners to reach outside the walls of the classroom, as it has traditionally been defined? Part of what's at stake is the need to produce new criteria of judgment and response (new grading mechanisms, new structures of reward and placement), as well as a broadening of our sense of intellectual purpose. In short, the kind of community-based learning I'm arguing for will mean thinking radically anew about what we do in the classroom, and how and why we do it. This notion of reaching beyond the classroom, or what bell hooks calls "teaching community," must occupy a central place in any serious attempt to reflect on what it means to make teaching and learning more socially and ethically responsible.

As you'll hear from the students who have agreed to prepare chapters for this book, the final "assignment" in my courses often takes the form of a "pro-active, community-facing, collaborative intervention." I challenge my students to move beyond the walls of the classroom in an effort to make interventions in the broader community. I ask also that they use these "assignments" as an opportunity to activate their knowledge and their education, to take the initiative to "do something" about struggles for human rights and social justice. For this book, I have invited some of my current and former students to reflect on the activist community-based interventions that have emerged from our classrooms, and to discuss how such initiatives have shaped and energized their own current research and teaching practices. We'll discuss the opportunities that have been opened up by such community-facing projects, and some of the institutional obstacles and impediments that students have encountered throughout the process. Essays in the volume will, via a case-study approach, be conceptually and practically useful to teachers and students involved in thinking about (and implementing) community-based forms of teaching and learning, and will focus on issues of planning and design, grading and evaluation, and methods and practices.

I understand, of course, the arguments too often leveled against teaching (especially teaching in the humanities) that seeks to be mindful of ethics and political responsibility: that advocacy and political activism have no rightful place in our classrooms and curricula; that such practices are an affront to academic standards; that scholarly rigour and neutrality are being compromised, and institutional structures and protocols are being ignored; that *all* points of view are not being fairly represented, and so on. I am all-too-aware of the risk (a very real one, I admit) that our political claims and efforts will be deemed unworthy, misguided, inappropriate, or unacceptable. In suggesting that we have a responsibility to educate for social justice and human rights, I certainly do not mean to imply that academics have all the answers (clearly, we don't). I also don't want to give the impression that we can, from our position of privilege, save the world by becoming "quick-fix" consultants, or to suggest that academic discourse can be a substitute for activist struggles in the public arena. But I insist that we think rigorously about our sense of purpose. Why do we teach? And how do we (because I think we must) articulate the social and ethical relevance of what we do as teachers and scholars in the humanities? Why does our work matter? Just what's at stake (culturally, critically, politically, institutionally) in research and pedagogy, and for whom? What kinds of critical questions might our work open up about rights, risks, and responsibilities; about the role of artists, intellectuals, teachers, students, and citizens; about truth and interpretation; about histories and communities; and about activism and forms of critical practice?

This book is directed to a broad audience of educators, scholars working across a wide spectrum of disciplines, students engaged in community-based learning and experiential education, and activists involved in struggles for human rights and social justice. It will link teaching and research in genuinely innovative ways, and suggest a range of dissemination strategies to inspire broad-based outcomes and impact among a diverse range of knowledge-users, marking a major advance in the ways in which the relationship among pedagogy, human rights, and community-based learning has hitherto been theorized and practiced.

The Challenge: Calling All Dreamers

As the contributions in this volume make clear, students in the humanities can play a vital role in mobilizing, indeed in *activating*, their knowledges in ways not conventionally associated with their university-level learning experiences.[6] The case studies that follow offer compelling glimpses of some of the innovative ways in which students have sought to set the broader community abuzz with a series of events that have had people (from academic and non-academic communities alike) engaging in lively debate and discussion about a host of vital issues of public concern. These events emerge in response to a challenge I present to the students at the outset of my courses: *Take the initiative,* I tell them, *to do something about struggles for social justice. Imagine moving beyond the walls of the classroom, and building a relationship between academic work and activism in an effort to make interventions in the broader community. Dream big,* I tell them, *and choose an issue you care about.* In responding to that challenge, and in working towards their community-facing projects, the students have found themselves doing things they didn't necessarily expect to be doing as part of a literature or humanities class: working with media, building coalitions, participating in forms of community outreach, learning how to organize a conference, building links and negotiating differences with others across a broad range of constituencies, participating in event management and community organizing, writing fundraising letters and grant proposals, understanding how best to influence policy, learning how to mobilize institutional resources, and so on. They've begun, in short, to rethink their understanding of the places where they look for knowledge and to confront some of their assumptions about what constitutes (and what counts as) research in the humanities.

And just as we need to encourage our students to think rigorously about the assumptions governing their interpretive practices, so, too, I would suggest, do we, as teachers and educators, need to put a fair bit of critical pressure on our own understanding of how we do things in the classroom. In an essay on civic engagement, community-based learning, and the humanities, David Cooper puts it this way: "No longer directing from the sidelines or articulating abstractions from behind a podium," we, as community-based educators, now find ourselves engaged in

a pedagogy that demands a great deal of preparation and planning, but at the same time requires spontaneity and flexibility. We [have] to give up some expectations about what should happen in a college [or university] classroom. In the process, we [find] new ways of thinking about those questions that all of us in higher education ponder: Where does the learning take place, and what do I want my students to take away with them? (15)

Although he isn't referencing jazz or music, Cooper is, in effect, making a case about the community-based educator as a kind of skilled improviser, something I'll return to a little bit later. For now, though, these questions needing to be asked about education, I would suggest, mandate fresh new ways of thinking: they demand a willingness to take risks, to resist orthodoxy, and to trouble settled habits of response and judgment.

All of which brings me to the central argument of this book: the need, put simply, for *classroom action*, for a radical rethinking of our pedagogical practices and priorities in order to cultivate opportunities for students in our classes not only to reflect, but also to act on the connections between what they learn or do in their university classrooms and how they come to understand themselves as socially responsible citizens. The point here is that if the exercise of human rights becomes meaningful not only through the existence of covenants, declarations, and treaties, but also as a result of the broader cultures of consciousness and obligation that might help transform those rules into acknowledgment and action, then a radical reorganization of our priorities as educators seems very much in order.[7] This book thus seeks to advance an argument and an agenda for a pedagogy that is grounded in the struggle for human rights and social justice. While such an agenda is in keeping with the Plan of Action for the United Nations Decade of Human Rights Education (1995 to 2004), as well as with the objectives articulated in the follow-up UN World Program for Human Rights Education, it remains at odds with all too many of the reigning assumptions in current educational practice, particularly those that frame teaching and scholarship within the context of marketplace logics and priorities.

Such an agenda, I must confess, is also at odds with much of what passes for engaged scholarship and teaching in my own discipline of the humanities. Lennard Davis, for instance, has, in his provocative book *Resisting Novels*, expressed concern about how the very act of reading (and, by implication, teaching) novels inhibits social change because we allow our consideration and analysis of the transformations that characters undergo (from blindness to insight, from self-deception to self-revelation and so forth) to become a kind of surrogate for any form of external change. Do texts in an English class, Davis's work invites us to ask, become "sites of resistance" or arenas for dialogue, such that we don't bother to act in the real world? Is there a danger that criticism functions *only* in the classroom, that it doesn't purposefully get extended to those in the broader public arena who are engaged in struggles for human rights and social justice? Does theory (as it has become axiomatic in many humanities classrooms) run the risk of becoming so highly specialized that it may have very little to say to those who don't, by profession, belong to the intellectual class?

Think also of George Steiner's devastating critiques of the failure of the humanities to intervene in a world of barbaric and catastrophic offences. In his essay "The Muses' Farewell," originally given as a lecture in the Netherlands in May 2000, Steiner tells us that

> [i]t may be that the resources of imaginative identification, of the engagement of feeling are more limited than meliorist optimism had posited. It may be that the ability to concentrate on, to respond to abstraction or the fictive, deflects from concrete immediacies, from a confident and "answerable" grasp on surrounding social and political reality. Grief over Cordelia, immersion in a Mahler *adagio*, the world-banishing contemplation of a Vermeer ... stifle the cry in the street. The more alertly vulnerable our affinities to great art, music, poetry, metaphysics or the Siren-songs of learning, the less acute our hearing of human need, of political savagery, the less empowered our reflexes of action. (151)

For Steiner, as Robert Scholes tells us in his 2004 MLA Presidential Address, "The Humanities in a Posthumanist World," "the humanities not only fail to humanize, they may actually dehumanize, by putting a concern for texts in the place where concern for other human beings ought to be found" (726). Such arguments, unfortunately, ring true: we too often, I would suggest, pride ourselves on the fraudulent and misguided belief that an attention to matters of race, gender, class, sexuality and diversity *in texts* offers us sufficient purchase on the urgent ethico-political struggles being waged in the public arena. But I'm not ready just yet to give up on the work that I do: after all, I'm still teaching, I'm still professing literature. I still want to hold onto the conviction – so compellingly articulated in Doris Sommer's book *The Work of Art in the World* – that art matters, that it can function as a vital agent of social and cultural change. In Sommer's words, "interpreting art, appreciating its power to shape the world, can spur and support urgently needed change" (3). Sommer documents how projects that may often begin as works of art don't necessarily stop there: "Instead," she writes, "they ripple into extra-artistic institutions and practices. Humanistic interpretation has an opportunity to trace those ripple effects and to speculate about the dynamics in order to encourage more movement" (7). And the cases discussed in the chapters that follow, of course, give me hope, as do the many students whose projects, commitments, and wisdom continue to inspire me.

As a teacher of literature, I find that one of the things that has been a particular source of inspiration for me is the fact that so many of my students have, in their community-engaged work, chosen to focus, in one way or another, on the transformative potential of stories. Notice, indeed, that many of the chapters in this book emphasize the importance of storytelling, of narrative, and of performance practices in struggles for human rights. This (and the nature of the projects that have emerged from my classes) may well have something to do with the particular literary texts I have asked them to read. Two of those texts, Thomas King's *The Truth About Stories* and Daniel Brooks and Guillermo Verdecchia's play *The Noam Chomsky Lectures*, have explicitly given rise to projects (*Guelph Speaks* and *Haiti Held Hostage* respectively) addressed in the chapters that follow. Moreover, it's interesting to note that King's text and Brooks and Verdecchia's play both contain their own forms of calls to action. King ends each chapter (originally delivered as public lectures) by telling his readers (or listeners) to "take" the story they have just read or heard. "It's yours. Do with it what you will," he says. "But don't say in the years to come that you would have lived your life differently if only you had heard this story. You've heard it now" (King 29, 60, 89, 119, 151). A similar kind of gesture involving the transfer of power happens at the end of *The Noam Chomsky Lectures* when Brooks and Verdecchia, in effect, hand the play over to their audience. They call for the house lights to go down and for the audience to look at one last slide from Noam Chomsky (about Canada's quiet complicity in human rights abuses). Before they leave the stage, they ask the audience to consider the slide and then, when people have had enough, to call out "Lights" for the play to end. In other words, the play won't end until a member of the audience takes responsibility and explicitly calls out "Lights," thus suggesting that he or she has had enough of (literally and metaphorically) being in the dark (about Canada's complicity in rights abuses). Here, as Brooks and Verdecchia would have it, is the challenge: we've seen the play, and now it's our turn, our responsibility, to act.

Any analysis of why so many of my students turn to issues of story-telling for their community-engaged work (and this is so not only with the case studies under consideration in this volume, but also with other community projects initiated by my students over the years) would cer-tainly need to take into account the particular texts we'd read in class that semester, as well as the conversations (and, perhaps, also the calls for action) sparked by those texts. But worth noting, too, is that there is, by now, a provocative body of scholarship that's evolved around a related set of issues. Kay Schaffer and Sidonie Smith have, for instance, written wisely and deeply about the role that stories and testimonies have played as essential catalysts "to affect recourse, mobilize action, forge communities of interest, and enable social change" (3) in rela-tion to human rights and social justice claims. Human rights educator Sherene Razack and critical legal theorist Richard Delgado focus more broadly on the urgent need to engage in what Razack calls "storytell-ing for social change": stories that recast the identities and histories of aggrieved populations and that promote self-representational counter-narratives that enable an enlargement of the base of valued knowl-edges. Indeed, Razack's notion of "storytelling for social change," like King's insistence, via Ben Okri, that "If we change the stories we live by, quite possibly we change our lives" (qtd. in King 153), has proved to be a tremendously powerful source of insight for students engaged in community-based learning. In Razack's words, "For many of us who would describe ourselves as teaching for social change, storytelling has been at the heart of our pedagogy. In the context of social change story-telling refers to an opposition to established knowledge ... [it refers] to the experience of the world that is not admitted into dominant knowl-edge paradigms" (36). In advancing an argument for forms of oppo-sitional storytelling in the context of law, Delgado writes, "The main cause of Black and brown subordination is not so much poorly crafted or enforced laws or judicial decisions. Rather, it is the prevailing mind-set through which members of the majority race justify the world as it is ... The cure," he argues, "is storytelling ... counterhegemonic [sto-rytelling to] quicken and engage conscience" (qtd. in Scheppele 2075). What's at issue here, as the case studies that follow make clear, is the need for human rights educators to present alternative narratives and other perspectives than those promulgated by dominant knowledge-producing elites, to radicalize public understanding by productively unsettling consensual understandings of history, memory, and agency. When the stories that circulate widely in the public domain so often crowd out opportunities for dissent, and when they – in the name of "freedom," "development," "democracy," and, ironically, sometimes even "human rights" – so often fail to serve the interests of the very aggrieved peoples who bear the brunt of human rights abuses around the world, when control over the means of communication is so heavily concentrated in a few elite corporations, there is, I believe, a great deal at stake in our efforts, as humanities educators, to intervene in the popular understanding.

It's perhaps no surprise, then, that storytelling should take on such vital significance in so many of the projects described in this volume.[8] From Canada's complicity in enabling the overthrow of a democratically elected leader in Haiti to access to mental health services for culturally diverse populations to what it means to be a citizen in our home communities, through to stories from marginalized or seldom-heard voices in Guelph and about the barriers (broadly understood) that prevent people from engaging with educational processes, the chapters that follow offer (to quote again from Razack) an "experience of the world that is not admitted into dominant knowledge paradigms." They also, I would suggest, serve to activate diverse energies of critique and inspiration, and in this sense, they remind us that critical pedagogy, as Henry Giroux writes,

is about more than a struggle over assigned meanings, official knowledge, and established modes of authority: it is also about encouraging students to take risks, act on their sense of social responsibility, and engage the world as an object of both critical analysis and hopeful transformation. In this paradigm, pedagogy cannot be reduced only to learning critical skills or theoretical traditions but must also be infused with the possibility of using interpretation as a *mode of intervention*, as a potentially energizing practice that gets students to both think *and act differently*.... Critical pedagogy ... takes seriously the educational imperative to encourage students *to act* on the knowledge, values, and social relations they acquire by being responsive to the deepest and most important problems of our times. (*On Critical Pedagogy* 14; my emphasis)

Like Giroux, I want to encourage opportunities for students to activate their knowledge, to intervene purposefully in the broader communities in which they live and work. In my classes, I draw on the work of Robin Kelley to address "anyone bold enough still to dream" (7). I am intrigued and inspired (as my opening remarks suggest) by the wisdom, the pedagogy, and the lifework of Sun Ra, who remained forthright in his insistence on defining spaces and places of hope. I thus call on all dreamers to experiment, to take on new challenges, to move outside their comfort zones, to act on the conviction (as Portuguese sociologist and human rights scholar Boaventura de Sousa Santos would have it) that "another knowledge is possible."

The notion, as Giroux puts it, that pedagogy needs to be understood as a "potentially energizing practice that gets students to both think *and act differently*"[9] is, as I noted above, consistent with some of the key objectives and principles articulated in United Nations Plan of Action documents dealing with human rights education. For example, "[i]ntroducing or improving human rights education," the Plan of Action for the United Nations World Program of Human Rights Education tells us, "requires adopting a holistic approach to teaching and learning, by integrating programme objectives and content, resources, methodologies, assessment and evaluation; by looking beyond the classroom, and by building partnerships between different members of the school community" (paragraph D18). In the context of working towards such a holistic approach, this notion of "looking beyond the classroom," or what bell hooks calls "teaching community," ought to be central to our attempt to reflect on the key transitions (and, indeed, the most pressing and contentious matters) currently animating the theory and practice of education. At an institutional moment when complacency and careerism tend to be the orders of the day, we urgently "need a new breed of citizen scholars who can identify not only with the institution and discipline but also with community," as Cary Nelson and Stephen Watt argue (37). Indeed, when my students reflect on their own experiences with forms of community-based learning, so many of them come back again and again to how refreshing it is when our classroom work invites us (students and teachers alike) to think rigorously about the relationship between theory and practice, especially when so much of what we do in the university "tends to be about career advancement and competition" (their words), and when so much of what we do in our classes is (again, in the words of my students) "about saying things that we don't necessarily mean or that don't have much relevance to people's lives." Students firmly believe that what they can gain from community-based educational practices, from pedagogy that looks "beyond the classroom," differs markedly from the knowledge they derive from more familiar models of education. In contrast to the passive, compartmentalized, and decontextualized brand of learning (think of Freire's banking model of pedagogy) that gets promoted by rote exercises that call for memorization and regurgitation (only to be forgotten when term tests and exams are over), community-based learning is very much in keeping with key principles articulated in the Plan of Action for the UN Decade of Human Rights Education, specifically that which states that education "shall be shaped in such a way as to be relevant to the daily lives of learners, and shall seek to engage learners in a dialogue about the ways and means of transforming human rights from the expression of abstract norms to the reality of their social, economic, cultural, and political conditions" (paragraph 6). "Looking beyond the classroom," in short, seems to me to be one of the fundamental principles and strategies that ought to define a pedagogy that's mindful of ethics and social responsibility. In times when we're increasingly being called to account for what we do, and when, in fact, we need to find purposeful ways to respond in particular to the anxiety that surrounds current debates about the relevance (and future) of humanities research and teaching (an area too often viewed as having little or no social instrumentality), community-based education for human rights not only offers a resonant opportunity for teachers and students to be explicit in articulating the public relevance of the work we do in our classes, but also productively and purposefully reminds us that learning is an ongoing process of inquiry that is linked in complex ways to notions of democratic citizenship.

Tearing Down the Classroom Walls: The Community as Classroom

The cases discussed in the chapters that follow directly take up key questions about the role and purpose of education. One of the texts referenced in many of these chapters, Paulo Freire's *Pedagogy of the Oppressed*, compels us to think honestly, critically, and rigorously about our teaching and learning practices. If Freire is right to criticize what he famously calls the banking model of pedagogy (and to suggest that it creates passive and unthinking citizens), if he is right to suggest that we need to find ways to resolve the teacher/student contradiction, then how might we do this? What teaching methods can we use to foster democracy in the classroom, to reconfigure the traditional teacher-student relationship associated with the banking model? As we ponder such questions about our teaching and learning practices, it is, I think, worth recalling (as I do in the sample course syllabus that I've appended to this essay) that the United Nations General Assembly proclaimed 1995 to 2004 the UN Decade of Human Rights Education. As that decade has now officially come to an end, we should (to borrow the phrasing that I use in my course materials) take it upon ourselves to ask what such a proclamation has meant (or ought to have meant) for us, as teachers and students. How might it change the ways in which texts are taught, discussed, and written about in the academy? What kinds of pressures does it put on the curriculum, and to what extent does it require us radically to rethink our teaching practices? Clearly, as many critics have noted, a human rights culture and consciousness cannot simply be legislated through government policies. Nor, I would suggest, can human rights be institutionalized simply through changes in educational practices and priorities: social justice, after all, is not likely to be achieved through the inclusion of, for instance, new books on our course reading lists. Yet one of the most compelling, and indeed urgent, challenges for pedagogy has to do with showing how the critical and analytical skills that our teaching seeks to foster are related, in complex ways, to matters of public consequence. And taking this challenge seriously means reflecting rigorously on just how education can participate in the transformation of unjust relations.

In the context of such a challenge, I'm determined, as I've been suggesting, to locate a sense of hope in the recognition among a growing number of educators that human rights education necessitates a commitment to taking teaching and learning *outside* the walls of the structured and formal classroom setting. This is, indeed, one of the central lessons in bell hooks's book *Teaching Community: A Pedagogy of Hope*:

> Teachers who have a vision of democratic education assume that learning is never confined solely to an institutionalized classroom. Rather than embodying the conventional false assumption that the university setting is not the "real world" and teaching accordingly, the democratic educator breaks through the false construction of the corporate university as set apart from real life and seeks to re-envision schooling as always a part of our real world experience, and our real life. Embracing the concept of a democratic education we see teaching and learning as taking place constantly. We share the knowledge gleaned in classrooms beyond those settings thereby working to challenge the construction of certain forms of knowledge as always and only available to the elite. (41)

If we take seriously hooks's insistence that we must attend to the ways in which teaching and learning are going on constantly (and not just in formal educational settings), then we need, I think, to develop a more rigorous understanding of how (and with what impact) alternative pedagogical institutions function in our communities. In re-envisioning schooling as part of our real-world experience, in making the community our classroom, we also, as the essays in this volume make abundantly clear, need to recognize that the privileged research sites of the academy can often be at odds with the situated knowledges, the vernacular cultures, the concerns, and the priorities of the broader community. To what extent, then, do students and faculty at the university have the right to design projects that represent and engage with the community? And, as the chapters on *Guelph Speaks!*, *Haiti Held Hostage*, and *Guelph is Skin Deep* in particular ask, to what degree are university students qualified to take on such projects? To what extent (and in what ways) can they successfully negotiate the right to speak from a place of privilege and to assume the role of change-makers or leaders in the community?

Our case studies suggest that, for all its inspirational value and its real-world impact, the process of community change-making can be messy, complicated, and unfinished, especially when it emerges from the context of a university classroom. The tight confines and institutional constraints associated with university-level coursework – the twelve-week semester format, the need to receive a grade, the protocols around research ethics and so forth – come up as critical pressure points repeatedly in several of the following chapters, as do the more searching and complex questions about issues such as privilege, collaboration, and sustainability. What's at stake in our efforts to tear down classroom walls and to make the community our classroom is the vital need to deepen our commitment to understanding that the sorts of initiatives that have emerged from such a focus on community-based learning and human rights education must be part of a living curriculum. A course on social change, in other words, involves a life-long process of learning. It doesn't (or it shouldn't) simply end when students complete a 12-week course. Nor, for that matter, should we, as educators committed to community-based learning, allow ourselves to become complacent, to settle into (or for) a kind of orthodoxy in our teaching practices.

Tearing Up the Course Outline: Unfinished Pedagogies

In his epilogue to the important anthology *Human Rights Education for the 21st Century*, J. Paul Martin reminds us that "[e]very curriculum in human rights imposes choices and therefore exclusions. The most important step is to make the exclusions consciously" (606). The authors of the chapters that follow all seem to take this advice to heart. All highlight the extent to which (in the words of Elizabeth Jackson and Ingrid Mündel in their contribution on "Access Interventions") community-based pedagogies are "necessarily messy, partial, [and] inadequate." All understand that the teaching methods and learning strategies employed during their projects are very much works in progress, always improvisational, responsive, adaptive, and emergent. Such a recognition is in keeping with Giroux's claim that pedagogy, in its fullest and most realized sense, ought to be understood as being "part of an always unfinished project intent on developing a meaningful life for all students" (*On Critical Pedagogy* 4). Freire, too, makes a related point: "Problemposing education," he tells us in *Pedagogy of the Oppressed*, "affirms men and women as beings in the process of *becoming* – as unfinished, uncompleted beings in and with a likewise unfinished reality … The unfinished character of human beings and the transformational character of reality necessitate that education be an ongoing activity" (84). The fact that several of the projects described in this book have, in one form or another, continued to live on beyond the life of the class – that, in the case of *Guelph Speaks!*, *The Other End of the Line*, and *Haiti Held Hostage*, all have successfully sought ways to ensure some form of continuing institutional support and ongoing replication of their efforts – also speaks to the unfinished nature of such community-facing pedagogies. Moreover, as Gregory Fenton tells us in his chapter, "I walked away from the semester with a sense that my perception of education, my role as a student, and my understanding of community had been radically shaken. But, more importantly, I was able to practice and develop what would become skills that I valued as much as any I had learned before, skills that would continue to inspire and propel me into an ethical way of thinking about work and education." As all the chapters that follow, indeed, make clear, the students who designed and implemented the community projects described in these pages are still exploring, still learning, still asking questions. Living with the consequences of such unfinalizability is not always easy, and it can be tempting to reflect on our projects with after-the-fact rationalizations that seek stability, predictability, and security. Refusing, however, to settle for easy solutions or to glory in a nostalgic or utopian assessment of the impact of the community-based projects that emerged from our classes, the essays in this book offer honest and frank, as well as often hopeful and always inspiring, analyses of what it means to engage in community-facing projects as part of a university-level course.

In an effort to acknowledge some of my own curricular choices and exclusions, and as a way of encouraging students to develop new and even deeper ways of reflecting on the fundamentally unfinished nature of the work that they are doing, I often, towards the end of my courses, ask them to tear up the existing and institutionally-sanctioned course outline that I gave them at the start of class, and to replace it with one their own making. *If you were teaching this course,* I ask them, *what texts would you choose? What kinds of assignments would you set? And how would you grade them?* I ask them to think rigorously about issues such as what we teach (curriculum), how we teach (pedagogical strategies), and why we teach (sense of purpose), and to offer a detailed rationale for their particular choices (of texts, assignments, methodologies, etc.). And, again, wanting them to think about choices and exclusions, about the messy, partial, and unfinished business of community-based education, I urge them to consider, too, the limitations of their efforts.

Having students in these classes design and rationalize their own course outlines is part of my attempt to engage them more fully in the educational decision-making process, to encourage them to negotiate and to test issues such as course design, classroom practices and procedures, and grading schemes. Grading, as I noted earlier, almost always emerges as one of the critical pressure points for students engaged in community-based learning in the context of a university course. And while much of the literature on critical pedagogy is inspirational in its focus on the democratizing of classroom practices, on disrupting conventionally institutionalized notions of our authority as teachers, it tends to be relatively quiet on the subject of grading. How does one grade the kind of community-based learning that happens in these classes? Although I, like many of my students, might much prefer to work with a simple pass/fail system, the constraints imposed by the academic institutions within which we work mandate that I assign a final numeric grade for all students registered in my courses.

Over the years, I've experimented with various grading models largely based, for instance, on self-critiques, on peer-evaluations, or on some combination of the two, along with my own ongoing input into the assessment process. The first time I taught my graduate seminar on human rights and pedagogy, it was, as Elizabeth Jackson and Ingrid Mündel point out in their contribution to this volume, to a large and relatively fractious group of students who decided to work on a single topic for their community intervention. Although they had, to be sure, done a number of other gradable assignments in the course (including in-class seminars and written reports), they chose, as a group, to be graded exclusively on their final community-facing project. And (here's the interesting part) they insisted that they all – all seventeen of them – should receive the same grade. That, as you might imagine, involved a tricky (and, yes, messy) set of negotiations as I prepared for the flak I would be sure to receive from my department, from graduate studies, and (since this was, after all, my first time teaching this kind of course) from who-knew-where-else. The negotiations involved, among other things, working with the class to do an in-depth reading and analysis of the University of Guelph Senate regulations on grading policies, and to facilitate a process whereby they would draft a detailed document of their own that would be used to establish methods and criteria for evaluating their work. Although students, when given this kind of opportunity, are often initially keen to take on the responsibility to develop their own criteria for evaluation, many of them, when reflecting on the process years after the fact, will tell me that never again would they want to go through such a thing. It's so much easier, after all, to fall back on the conventional model and to let the teacher assign the grade.

More satisfying, for me and for students, is a model I've adapted from Ira Shor, a model that allows students literally to make the grade. In his book *When Students Have Power*, Shor describes grading contracts as a way of sharing power, redistributing authority, and negotiating through dialogue (20). I've found that a modified version of such contracts can be a particularly effective way of assessing community-based learning in university classes.

Here's how it works. When students are designing their community-facing projects, I meet with them to discuss their goals and objectives. Once they've adequately negotiated their goals and objectives with me (and this often involves quite a bit of back-and-forth work), I ask them to tell me what kind of grade they feel they should receive if they meet these goals. And if they fall short, in what ways, I ask them, would they adjust the grade? Students, in other words, are, during the planning and design phase for their projects, asked to think carefully about goal-setting, and about how they will measure the impact of the work they are proposing to do. If they meet their goals they will, in effect, make the grade they have set for themselves. I like this grading model for a number of reasons. As Shor suggests, it's a way of sharing power with students and of redistributing authority in the classroom. Moreover, since the goals, objectives, and contractual arrangements are mutually negotiated, it means that we're engaged in a genuinely dialogic process of knowledge-exchange. It also, of course, gives students a sense of their own active participation. And, as Ashlee Cunsolo, Rob Zacharias, and Paul Danyluk point out in their chapter on *Guelph Speaks!*, the importance of addressing and respecting the role of students as active participants in critical, community-facing pedagogy – rather than as its passive objects – is a vital thread that runs throughout this book as a whole. Needless to say, the student-activated achievements reflected in this volume are a tremendous source of pride for me as a teacher: they speak very powerfully to the ways in which university-level work *can* establish a genuine foundation for vital forms of civic engagement. And therein lies a message of hope.

Playing the Changes: Learning from Jazz and Improvisation

My students continue to amaze and inspire me. And this book, I hope, shows, by way of their example, that key changes are happening. One such change that I've sought to highlight in these pages has been the need to create structures in our classrooms (as well as within the larger institutions in which we work) that encourage broader forms of community-based learning and involvement. Think again of "those questions that," according to David Cooper, "all of us in higher education ponder: Where does the learning take place, and what do I want my students to take away with them?" (15). Think of how these questions that need to be asked about research and education, as I suggested earlier, mandate fresh new ways of thinking: they demand a willingness to take risks, to resist orthodoxy, to trouble settled habits of response and judgment. These, indeed, are lessons we can learn from jazz and improvised music, at least in some of its most provocative historical instances. What new theoretical and organizational models and practices might be developed, then, for the development of theories of education and research that embed improvisation itself as a methodology? Cooper's question about where learning takes place is, in effect, precisely what Sun Ra's response to Duke Ellington, with which I began this introduction, asks us to consider. Indeed, I began with Ra's response to Ellington precisely because it issues something of a challenge to the institutionalization of knowledge, because it, like bell hooks's argument about the urgent need for democratic educators to break out of the confines of the institutionalized classroom, asks us to reflect on what it might mean to educate people through something other than conventional academic institutions or traditional educational settings. What Ra has taught us, in other words, is that the *outside* can function as a place of hope and possibility. Ra's example points to the ways in which the locations in which jazz maintains its most salient innovations, its most vital models for social engagement, may well reside *somewhere there*, outside conventional spaces, places, and institutional practices of legitimation. This, it seems to me, offers a vital and enduring lesson for all of us as researchers, teachers, and learners. Come on and sign up.

APPENDIX: Sample Course Outline

UNIVERSITY OF GUELPH
COLLEGE OF ARTS
School of English and Theatre Studies
ENGL 6691
Interdisciplinary Studies
Winter 2012
Pedagogy, Human Rights, Critical Activism: Educating for Social Change
Instructor: Dr. Ajay Heblé
Office: MacKinnon 406
Phone: 824–4120, ext. 53445
Email: aheble@uoguelph.ca
Office Hours: Mondays 10–12, or by appointment

The United Nations General Assembly proclaimed 1995 to 2004 the UN Decade of Human Rights Education. Through selected readings in the theory and practice of pedagogy and social change, this course will explore what such a proclamation has meant and what it should mean for university-level teachers and students of English. How might it change the ways in which texts are being taught, discussed, and written about in the academy? What kinds of pressures does it put on the curriculum, and to what extent does it require us radically to rethink our teaching and learning practices? Clearly, human rights cannot be institutionalized simply through changes in educational practices and priorities; nor is social justice likely to be achieved merely through the inclusion of new books on our reading lists. Yet one of the most compelling, and indeed urgent, challenges for educators has to do with showing how the critical and analytical skills that our teaching seeks to foster are related, in complex ways, to matters of public consequence. Taking this challenge seriously means reflecting rigorously on just how a university education can participate in the transformation of unjust social relations and unequal distributions of power. This course will seek to open up discussion about some of the ways in which a human rights consciousness can and should inform university-level learning and teaching, and will offer students innovative opportunities to reflect and to act on the connections between academic work and broader struggles for social justice, human rights, and a politics of hope.

Required Texts:

- Paulo Freire, *Pedagogy of the Oppressed* (Continuum)
- bell hooks, *Teaching Community: A Pedagogy of Hope* (Routledge)
- Frances Westley, Brenda Zimmerman, and Michael Quinn Patton, *Getting to Maybe: How the World is Changed* (Random House)
- Daniel Brooks and Guillermo Verdecchia, *The Noam Chomsky Lectures: A Play* (Talonbooks)
- Thomas King, *The Truth About Stories: A Native Narrative* (Anansi)
- Ajay Heble, ed. *Class Action: Human Rights, Critical Activism, and Community-Based Education* (excerpts from manuscript in progress featuring essays by former students) (posted on Courselink)

Additional texts may be placed on reserve in the library.

Please note: All required texts for this course have been ordered at The Bookshelf, 41 Quebec Street. Phone: 519–821–3311. http://www.book shelf.ca

Suggested Additional Readings:

- George Andreopoulos and Richard Pierre Claude, eds. *Human Rights Education for the Twenty-First Century*
- Rita Maran, *Human Rights Syllabi for the College Classroom*
- Micheline Ishay, *The Human Rights Reader: Major Political Essays, Speeches, and Documents from the Bible to the Present*
- Noam Chomsky, *Chomsky on (Mis)Education*
- bell hooks, *Teaching to Transgress: Education as the Practice of Freedom*
- Neva Welton and Linda Wolf, *Global Uprising: Confronting the Tyrannies of the 21st Century*

- David Trend, *Cultural Pedagogy: Art/Education/Politics*
- Sherene Razack, *Looking White People in the Eye*
- Edward Said, *Representations of the Intellectual*
- Ira Shor, *When Students Have Power*
- Susan Danielson and Ann Marie Fallon, eds. *Community-Based Learning and the Work of Literature*

Additional Resources:

1. Bibliography and webography – posted on Courselink.
2. Alternative media. For alternative views on world events, I would recommend the following: *Z Magazine, New Internationalist, Utne Reader, The Nation*, CFRU-FM (93.3), Alternative Radio.
3. Some Local Resources:
   - 10 Carden: 10 Carden is creating space for change. For connection. For collaboration. For learning. And most importantly, for incubating new ideas, innovations and approaches. 10 Carden is quickly becoming Guelph's hub for social change and a dynamic place to work, meet, and launch new ideas. It's a shared office and meeting space ideal for individuals, not-for-profits, businesses and groups. The website: http://www.10carden.ca
   - iCAN (Interactive Community Action Network): "iCAN is the product of a collaboration between Leadership, Service and Involvement Programs and Student Volunteer Connections at the University of Guelph. iCAN was originally conceived in 1997 out of a desire to encourage students to take a more intentional approach in choosing a volunteer placement and to begin considering how extracurricular experiences can serve as a valuable complement to the classroom." The website: http://www.ican.uoguelph.ca/
   "This site has been redesigned to introduce University of Guelph students and citizens of Guelph and Wellington County to the wealth of volunteer opportunities and community events available to you. This site is highly interactive – which means that you can conduct searches based upon a range of parameters: the type of volunteering you would like to do, the particular population you want to work with, the length of time you are able to commit, specific skills you would like to develop or enhance, and even the time of year during which you hope to become involved." This site has many links to organizations throughout the area.

- The Human Rights and Equity Office: "The Human Rights and Equity Office of the University of Guelph is dedicated to the removal of all systemic barriers, discrimination and harassment and will engage in advocacy within the university community towards this end." The website: http://www.uoguelph.ca/hre/
- The Guelph International Resource Centre (GIRC): "The Guelph International Resource Centre is a non-profit, non-governmental organization that educates Canadians about global issues as well as their local links. GIRC assists the community in developing awareness, analysis and actions around global issues in order to promote a just and sustainable future. GIRC was incorporated as a non-profit corporation in Ontario on May 23, 1980." The website: www.girc.org
- Ontario Public Interest Research Group (OPIRG) – Guelph: The Ontario Public Interest Research Group – Guelph is a volunteer-driven, non-profit organization based on the University of Guelph campus. Formed in 1976, OPIRG-Guelph addresses social, political, economic and environmental issues of public concern. The website: http://opirg.org/guelph/

Tentative Schedule

Week One: Monday January 9 – Introduction: Teaching for Social Change

- Introductions, Resources, Protocols, Limits
- UN Declaration of Human Rights (posted on Courselink)
- "Plan of Action for the United Nations Decade for Human Rights Education, 1995–2004": http://www.unhchr.ch/huridocda/huridoca.nsf/(Symbol)/A.51.506.Add.1.En?OpenDocument (posted on Courselink)
- Visits from former students to talk about previous community-based projects (and modes of intervention) and to discuss the possibilities and perils of collaboration

Week Two: Monday January 16 – Tearing Down the Classroom Walls: The Community as Classroom

- Paulo Freire, *Pedagogy of the Oppressed*
- bell hooks, *Teaching Community: A Pedagogy of Hope* (see especially Teach 1: The Will to Learn: The World as Classroom, Teach 2: Time Out: Classrooms without Boundaries, Teach 4: Democratic Education)
- Guest: Sandra Auld, Director, Research Ethics, University of Guelph

Week Three: Monday January 23

(A) MEDIA MATTERS
• Daniel Brooks and Guillermo Verdecchia, *The Noam Chomsky Lectures*
• Suggested reading: Edward Herman and Noam Chomsky, *Manufacturing Consent: The Political Economy of the Mass Media*

(B) STORYTELLING FOR SOCIAL CHANGE
• Thomas King: *The Truth About Stories: A Native Narrative*

Week Four: Monday January 30 – Class Action

• Ajay Heble, ed. *Class Action: Human Rights, Critical Activism, and Community-Based Education* (draft of manuscript in progress featuring essays by former students)
• Suggested reading: Kenneth Bruffee, *Collaborative Learning: Higher Education, Interdependence, and the Authority of Knowledge*; Garth Meintjes, "Human Rights Education as Empowerment: Reflections of Pedagogy" (in George Andreopoulos and Richard Pierre Claude, *Human Rights Education for the Twenty-First Century*)
• [Presentation of issues for collective intervention(s)]

Week Five: Monday February 6 – Research as Activism/Activism as Research: How the World is Changed

• Frances Westley, Brenda Zimmerman, and Michael Quinn Patton, *Getting to Maybe: How the World is Changed*
• Some suggested readings: Ariel Dorfman, "Speak Truth to Power: Voices from Beyond the Dark" in Kerry Kennedy Cuomo, *Speak Truth to Power* (Educational and Advocacy package); Daniel Brooks and Guillermo Verdecchia, *The Noam Chomsky Lectures: A Play*; Kalle Lasn, *Culture Jam: How To Reverse America's Suicidal Consumer Binge – And Why We Must*; Noam Chomsky, *What Uncle Sam Really Wants*; Neva Welton and Linda Wolf, *Global Uprising: Confronting the Tyrannies of the 21st Century*; Stephen Lewis, *Race Against Time*; Naomi Klein, *No Logo: Taking Aim at the Brand Bullies*
• [Group discussion on choice of topics for collective intervention]

Week Six: Monday February 13 – Selecting a topic

• [***Deadline for identifying topics for community-based projects***]

READING WEEK (February 20–24)

Week Seven: Monday February 27 – Reality Checks

- Collaborative presentations (15 minutes per group) to a panel of outside "experts." These presentations should concisely outline your topic for intervention, your preliminary ideas about modes of intervention, and ideas about resources available to you and obstacles you might face in moving forward with your work.

Weeks Eight, Nine, and Ten: Monday March 5, 12, 19 – Planning, Progress Reports, and Presentations

- In recognition of the fact that one of the most significant challenges for collaborative work is finding times when everyone is available to meet, we will devote the first half of our sessions during weeks eight, nine, and ten for group meetings. These meetings will be focussed on facilitating productive and purposeful collaborative work. I'll also use these times to hold short interviews/meetings/check-ins with all break-out groups. We'll discuss and identify appropriate modes of intervention, set goals for your projects, and consider how we will evaluate the success of our efforts. We will also consider how an education in English Studies can enable us/empower us to intervene in the public sphere.
- The second half of the class during weeks eight, nine, and ten will be devoted to in-progress seminar presentations to the class as a whole.
- Suggested readings: Naomi Klein, *No Logo: Taking Aim at the Brand Bullies*; Kym Pruesse, *Accidental Audience: Urban Intervention by Artists*; George Lipsitz, *American Studies in a Moment of Danger* (esp. Chapters 9, 10, 11)

Week Eleven: Monday March 26 – Tearing Up the Course Outline: Theoretical Principles and Pragmatics

- Suggested reading: Rita Maran, *Human Rights Syllabi for the College Classroom*, Rita Maran, "Teaching Human Rights in the Universities: Paradoxes and Prospects" (in George Andreopoulos and Richard Pierre Claude, *Human Rights Education for the Twenty-First Century*)
- [Presentation and discussion of alternate course outlines with rationales and self-critiques]

Week Twelve: Monday April 2 – Concluding Remarks, Catch-up, and Action Plans

- bell hooks, *Teaching Community: A Pedagogy of Hope* (Teach 11: Heart to Heart, Teach 16: Practical Wisdom)

Evaluation

This course takes seriously Paulo Freire's claim that equality and social justice are predicated on students playing an active role in the educational process, that teachers and students are both simultaneously learners and knowledge-producers. In an effort to teach in ways that do not reinforce traditional structures of domination and authority, the precise grading scheme for this course will be arrived at through a collective process of negotiation (and interrogation) of various possible modes of evaluation.

Grades for this course will be based on the following presentations and reports:

1. During weeks Two and Three (and depending on the size of the class), we will have collaborative-led student seminars (two per class) on the assigned literary and pedagogical texts. Each student is required to participate in one collaborative seminar during this two-week period.
2. During Week Four, each student will lead a 15–20-minute presentation (depending on the number of students in the class) which identifies a human rights issue which she/he thinks should be the focus of our collective intervention. In preparing your presentation, please identify resources that might be available to help facilitate any interventions we might choose to make, think through the ways in which an education in English Studies (or in the arts and humanities, more generally) might enable us to intervene, and discuss possible ways in which the class might collectively "make a difference" through addressing this specific issue. Please submit to me (and to other members of the class) a written abstract for your presentation (no more than 500 words) along with a preliminary reading list/resource list during our meeting in Week Four. Our task for Weeks Five and Six will be to choose an issue/issues

(from the many that will have been presented to us). This issue/ these issues will become the focus of our efforts at making a collective public intervention.

3. During Weeks Eight to Ten, we will have three (depending on the size of the class) collaborative in-progress presentations (one presentation per week) from each break-out group on projects of your choosing related to our efforts to make a collaborative intervention. I would ask that each of these projects have a public or community-facing dimension: that is, in designing your projects, try to move beyond the walls of the classroom in an effort to make interventions in the broader community. I would also ask that you use these projects as an opportunity to take the initiative to "do something" about struggles for human rights and social justice. The projects should, in some way, attempt to grapple with the relationship between academic work and activism, and to open up discussion around the question of how teachers and students can best "activate" their knowledge in ways that might edge us towards a more just world. How, that is, can we use the tools of analysis that we've developed in English Studies classrooms to work for social change? I encourage students to be creative in thinking through and performing their projects, and to structure their materials in ways which are genuinely collaborative and interactive. Feel free to draw on (and to work in partnership with) local resources and social justice organizations (Amnesty International, OPIRG, CFRU-FM, Guelph International Resource Centre, etc.) in the community. On the day of your presentation, please submit to me and to other members of the class, a 500-word abstract summarizing the project's main interventions and areas of inquiry, and a bibliography of relevant sources. In advance of these in-progress presentations, you will be asked to "pitch" your projects to a panel of outside "experts" who will be invited to class during Week Seven.

4. During Week Eleven, we will have three collaborative one-hour seminars where you will present and discuss alternate course outlines for ENGL 6691, "Pedagogy, Human Rights, Critical Activism: Educating for Social Change." Think rigorously about issues such as what we teach (curriculum), how we teach (pedagogical strategies), and why we teach (sense of purpose). Each group should be prepared to offer a rationale for their particular choices (of texts, assignments, methodologies, etc.) and to recognize the limitations of their efforts.

Please submit your alternate course outline (along with a statement of rationale) to me and to the other members of the course during our meeting in Week Eleven.

5. Final community-facing project. In evaluating this project, I will take into account your response to comments/concerns raised by the class and the panel of "experts," as well as your ability to meet the goals (and challenges) you have set for your group. Each student will be required to write a concluding essay that reflects on the ways in which the community projects might reinvigorate our understanding of the social function of literature and literary study. Use the essay as an opportunity to think through your own rationale for the community projects in which you've been involved, as well as to consider both the anticipated benefits and the limitations of your work. To what extent have the teaching methods and learning strategies employed during your projects been successful? How, in short, has the work you've done in ENGL 6691 encouraged you to rethink your understanding of the places where we look for knowledge, and to think anew about what constitutes research and teaching in the English Studies classroom?

Research Ethics Protocol

Please note that students who propose to use human participants in their research projects must receive appropriate clearance from the course instructor. The potential for risk to subjects who participate in course-based research projects requires that protocol and consent information be reviewed by a research ethics board. For more information, please visit http://www.uoguelph.ca/research/humanParticipants/

Requests for approval of course-based research projects must comply with the following criteria:

- The research projects must be no more than minimal risk.
  - The standard of minimal risk is defined as follows. If potential participants can reasonably be expected to regard the probability and magnitude of possible harms implied by participation in the research to be no greater than those encountered by the subject in those aspects of his or her everyday life that relate to the research, then the research can be regarded as within the range of minimal risk.

- The research participants must be drawn from the general adult population, capable of giving free and informed consent, and may not include vulnerable subjects such as children, persons who are not legally competent to consent, mentally incompetent persons, legal wards or the therapeutically dependent.
- The student projects must not involve any personal, sensitive or incriminating topics or questions which could place participants at risk.
- The student projects must not manipulate behaviour of participants beyond the range of "normal" classroom activity or daily life.
- The student projects must not involve physically invasive contact with the research participants.
- The student projects must not involve deception.

E-mail Communication

As per university regulations, all students are required to check their < uoguelph.ca > e-mail account regularly: e-mail is the official route of communication between the university and its students.

When You Cannot Meet a Course Requirement...

When you find yourself unable to meet an in-course requirement because of illness or compassionate reasons, please advise the course instructor [or designated person] in writing, with your name, ID#, and e-mail contact. Where possible, this should be done in advance of the missed work or event, but otherwise, just as soon as possible after the due date, and certainly no longer than one week later. Note: if appropriate documentation of your inability to meet that in-course requirement is necessary, the course instructor, or delegate, will request it of you. Such documentation will rarely be required for course components representing less than 10 percent of the course grade. Such documentation will be required, however, for Academic Consideration for missed end-of-term work and/or missed final examinations.

Drop Date

The last date to drop one-semester Winter 2012 courses, without academic penalty, is Friday, March 9th.

Copies of Out-of-Class Assignments

Keep paper and/or other reliable back-up copies of all out-of-class assignments: you may be asked to resubmit work at any time.

Academic Misconduct

The University of Guelph is committed to upholding the highest standards of academic integrity and enjoins all members of the university community – faculty, staff, and students – to be aware of what constitutes academic misconduct and to do as much as possible to prevent academic offences from occurring. The University of Guelph takes a serious view of academic misconduct, and it is your responsibility as a student to be aware of and to abide by the university's policy. Included in the definition of academic misconduct are such activities as cheating on examinations, plagiarism, misrepresentation, and submitting the same material in two different courses without written permission from the relevant instructors. To better understand your responsibilities, read the full Academic Misconduct Policy (http://www.uoguelph.ca/undergrad_calendar/08_amisconduct.shtml).

Instructors have the right to use software to aid in the detection of plagiarism or copying and to examine students orally on submitted work. For students found guilty of academic misconduct, serious penalties, up to and including suspension or expulsion, can be imposed. Hurried or careless submission of work does not exonerate students of responsibility for ensuring the academic integrity of their work. Similarly, students who find themselves unable to meet course requirements by the deadlines or criteria expected because of medical, psychological or compassionate circumstances should review the university's regulations and procedures for Academic Consideration in the calendar (http://www.uoguelph.ca/undergrad_calendar/08_ac.shtml) and discuss their situation with the instructor and/or the program counsellor or other academic counsellor as appropriate.

NOTES

1 I first wrote about this statement of Sun Ra's in "Space is the Place: Jazz, Voice, and Resistance," a chapter from my book *Landing on the*

Wrong Note. More recently, I've returned to Ra in a short think piece, "'Why Can't We Go Somewhere There?': Sun Ra, Improvisation, and the Imagination of Future Possibilities," published in a special Improvisation issue of *Canadian Theatre Review*. The current chapter draws, in part, on material from those earlier pieces, as well as from two recent conference presentations: "Scenes of Engagement: Improvisation, Partnership, Social Action," a plenary talk for the CU Expo, "Community-University Partnerships: Bringing Global Perspectives to Local Action" in Waterloo, Ontario (May 2011), and "Destinations Out: Towards a Jazz-Inflected Model for Community-Based Learning," a keynote talk for "Key Changes: Transitions in Our Students, Our Classrooms, Ourselves," at the Association of Atlantic Universities Teaching Showcase Conference, University of Prince Edward Island (September 2010).

2 See, for instance, Barndt's 2011 edited collection, *¡VIVA! Community Arts and Popular Education in the Americas*. The book presents case studies of community arts projects emerging from a transnational research exchange initiative focusing on issues of social transformation. In her Preface, Barndt writes, "This book has been created by and for people who are seeking a more just and sustainable world, who want to integrate education and art into community work, who believe that such synergy can foster greater passion for and deeper commitment to movements for social and environmental justice" (vii). Barndt's collection raises several timely and pressing questions about university-community collaborations, recognizing, for example, how these collaborations have taken place in the context of "troubling trends within the neoliberal university" (100). Particularly worthy of note is "the deepening contradiction of increasingly neoliberal market-driven universities that at the same time promote community engagement and knowledge production for autonomy and social justice" (132). The book also contains a DVD offering an overview of the ¡VIVA! Project and videos linked to the specific case study chapters.

3 Lipsitz's comments are worth keeping in mind in light of several shifts in the global and national context that have, over the last few years, resulted in the strengthening of a number of transformative social movements that offer new ways of thinking about rights, solidarity-building, and pedagogy. These movements, indeed, could well play a significant role as an impetus in shaping future community-based pedagogical initiatives within academic institutions. Idle No More, a powerful Indigenous mass movement that had its origins in concerns about how the Conservative government's omnibus Bill C-45 would erode indigenous rights, has made vital contributions to popular education and political struggles

through teach-ins, performances, protests, and round dances. The calls for change and action employed by Idle No More have generated widespread support across diverse communities, and directly addressed one of the central issues raised by many of the contributors in this volume: How can people work from positions of privilege and across difference to create meaningful social change? Another social movement that has transformed the cultural and political landscape is #BlackLivesMatter. Coalescing largely online through social media, the movement has brought attention to police brutality against blacks, and attributed these incidents to systemic causes. For resources related to (and more about) these movements, please see the webography. For more on Idle No More, see *The Winter We Danced: Voices from the Past, the Future, and the Idle No More Movement*, an excellent collection of essays, poetry, lyrics, art, and images edited by the Kino-nda-niimi Collective. For additional context related to issues of police impunity and #Black Lives Matter, see Ta-Nehisi Coates, *Between the World and Me*. Written in the form of an open letter to Coates's teenaged son, *Between the World and Me* explores what it means to inhabit a black body. "And you know now, if you did not before," Coates explains to his son, "that the police departments of your country have been endowed with the authority to destroy your body. It does not matter if the destruction is the result of an unfortunate overreaction. It does not matter if it originates in a misunderstanding. It does not matter if the destruction springs from a foolish policy" (9).

4 I've already noted that I've been doing this teaching within the context of the humanities, and, specifically, in ways that engage questions of literature, storytelling, performance, and text. This, I think, is particularly worthy of note, for there has hitherto been only scant attention paid to humanities-based, community-based pedagogical efforts. The humanities focus marks an important advance in the tradition of critical education and social activism that I've been describing.

5 The kind of activist, community-based learning that I have in mind is, of course, not entirely without precedent. Here in Canada, for instance, there's the work of Ron Deibert, a Political Studies professor at the University of Toronto. To cite one example of his innovative pedagogy, in 2001 Deibert selected a small group of students from a first-year politics course, and hired them as summer interns with the express purpose of challenging them to make a positive social-change intervention in the arena of public health. Their efforts were chronicled in a television documentary entitled *Activist TV*, in which we follow the six students (and their teacher) as they seek to raise broad public awareness about neglected diseases.

6 While various forms of community-engaged learning and scholarship are becoming increasingly common in university settings, the humanities continue to be relatively absent from attempts to incorporate community-facing projects into the classroom. As Ann Marie Fallon notes in her Preface to the book *Community-Based Learning and the Work of Literature*,

In a 2003 survey ... tenured literature professors reported significant hesitation to incorporate CBL [Community-Based Learning] into the curriculum. Budget constraints, pressure of faculty time, and relevance to one's scholarly agenda all influence a professor's ability to engage in CBL activities. Although numerous useful manuals exist for composition instructors, there are almost no handbooks for incorporating community-based research into the literary classroom. CBL seems to challenge the imagination and logistical preparation of the literature professor. Literary scholars are not trained to be project managers, an important skill in a CBL classroom. In fact, the idea of project management points to another important ambivalence in the literature. CBL implies a sense of practice, of vocational usefulness to one's work. Literary critics have been among the most ambivalent academics with regard to the status of their own professionalization. Reading literature is often regarded as a kind of counterpoint or refuge from professional practice. Finally, literary theory, variously conceived in graduate studies over the past 20 years, has often been intentionally disengaged from the realpolitik of political activism ... [A]lthough literary theory talks a good political line, critical distance often pre-empts real-world action. (Fallon xvii)

For more on the relationship between civic engagement and the humanities, see David Cooper's essay, also published in *Community-Based Learning and the Work of Literature*. Doris Sommer's *The Work of Art in the World: Civic Agency and Public Humanities* offers a fresh and inspiring perspective on humanities education and socially-engaged forms of art. And for a discussion of the vital role that humanities education can and should play in cultivating democratic citizenship, see Martha Nussbaum's *Not for Profit: Why Democracy Needs the Humanities*.

7 Stephen Lewis writes, "It's almost a travesty – no, not almost; it is a travesty – the way in which document after document pours off the presses, especially the multilateral presses, making the same points ad nauseam unto eternity, containing the same figures, positing the same recommendations. In fact, an argument can plausibly be made that the reports have become a kind of Machiavellian delaying tactic. You want action? Wait – here's something else to read" (88).

8 See also Naomi Klein's claim: "Indeed a great deal of the work of deep social change involves having debates during which new stories can be told to replace the ones that have failed us" (461).

9 As I've tried to suggest throughout, I have found the work of Giroux, hooks, Freire, and other theorists and practitioners of critical pedagogy to be profoundly inspirational, especially for their emphasis on the democratization of the classroom, their focus on student voices and dialogue, and their much-needed critique of the banking model of education. However, I'd be remiss if I didn't acknowledge that this work has sparked some provocative assessments. See, for instance, Elizabeth Ellsworth's oft-cited article, "Why Doesn't This Feel Empowering? Working Through the Repressive Myths of Critical Pedagogy," which suggests that some of the "key assumptions, goals, and pedagogical practices fundamental to the literature on critical pedagogy – namely 'empowerment,' 'student voice,' 'dialogue,' and even the term 'critical' – are repressive myths that perpetuate relations of domination" (298). Ellsworth asks, "What diversity do we silence in the name of 'liberatory' pedagogy?" (299).

1 Access Interventions: Experiments in Critical Community Engagement

ELIZABETH JACKSON AND INGRID MÜNDEL

Overview

In this chapter, we reflect on a community-facing project that emerged out of the first iteration of Dr. Ajay Heble's graduate English course entitled "Pedagogy, Human Rights, Critical Activism: Education for Social Change." We share Ajay's understanding of our pedagogical and research practices as "vital place[s] in democratic societies where people should be able to increase their say about decisions that affect their lives" (see the Introduction to this volume). Drawing on the perspectives we have gained through our academic upbringings and life experiences in the decade that has passed since we took part in the course, we turn our now better-informed critical eyes to the project, seeking to draw out some key lessons that are shaping our current efforts to enliven community-engaged projects and research in the work for social change and justice. In particular, we examine our experiences in the course alongside broader reflections on the implications, difficulties, and resonances of critical activism and community-engaged work. We close with a call for critical hope and for continued efforts to implement and create dialogue about community-university partnerships.

1. Access Interventions

In the Fall of 2003, a class of 17 MA and PhD students worked on collectively mounting a day-long symposium, called Access Interventions, that explored questions of access to and access within education. We intentionally chose a set of issues that was flexible enough to lend itself to the convergence of a number of perhaps otherwise disconnected communities (from, for example, public educators and student govern-ments to aboriginal writers and disability advocates): the day's discus-sions hinged on a range of different definitions of the intersection of "access" and "education." The class's decision to mount a conference on questions of "access" and "education" was premised on our desire not only to focus on the constraints and expectations of educational institutions, but also to address systemic issues such as sexism, racism, and ableism that can prevent people from engaging with educational processes. We envisioned the symposium as a site for the discussion of issues of physical (in)accessibility on and around the university cam-pus, struggles around tuition and education expenses, challenges to institutional racism and sexism, campaigns for literacy and affordable housing, and attempts to foster non-traditional educational initiatives.[1] Our hope was that the day would throw into relief the complexity of struggles around access to and within education, and thus highlight possibly-unexplored points of solidarity among various groups in the community.

An interesting by-product of our chosen topic was that, as a class, we were made aware of, and saw how deeply we were limited by, the very systemic (institutional and otherwise) issues that our confer-ence sought to interrogate. While we used Paulo Freire's book *Peda-gogy of the Oppressed* as one of our class texts, the conversations that emerged throughout the class, both before and during preparations for our actual conference, perhaps framed our class more as a laboratory for hashing out the parameters and limits of engaging a pedagogy of the *privileged*. Ann Curry-Stevens points out that at the turn of the 21st century, educators for social change have added a new agenda item to "transformative education's strategic tool kit – one that intention-ally seeks to engage privileged learners in workshops and classrooms and to assist in their transformation as allies in the struggle for social justice" (33). Some of the tensions that surfaced during our class discus-sions were linked to the varying ways in which those of us in the class saw ourselves in relation to the different social issues (and processes for engaging with these issues) that were on the table for discussion. Some were comfortable seeing themselves as actors outside the sphere of the "issue," and positioned themselves as advocates and helpers in relation to "the oppressed." Others argued that articulating and analyzing the construction of our varying subjectivities and recognizing ourselves as complicit with systemic instances of, for example, racism and ableism were necessary precursors to any form of engagement with broader communities and struggles for social justice. The tension between these particular perspectives (and there were many more) was augmented by the constraining apparatus of the course: we had twelve weeks to "resolve" our disagreements, to select a project, to mount the project, to establish guidelines for evaluating the success of the project and of our own efforts, and to learn something along the way.

At the time, we felt huge pressure to perform the course tasks successfully, and trying to do so with a cumbersomely large, fractious, and relatively dysfunctional group of 17 often made the process feel almost nightmarish. However, thinking back to the course now, over ten years later, the endless debates and class tensions – rather than the symposium itself – remain for us the "real" project, a realization that is both troubling and instructive. This realization makes a great deal of sense when we consider that so much of our learning in this class, and indeed so much of what really "matters" and resonates about many projects – educational, organizational, artistic – is the process that creates them rather than the products they create. We learned much more through the process of staging our event, through our struggles and disagreements and flashes of inspiration, than we would have by sitting there being lectured on the ideas with which we were grappling.

Even while acknowledging the importance of privileging process over product, we are left with the lingering question of what we actually accomplished in the course in relation to engaging human rights issues or negotiating a form of critical activism. On the one hand, we wonder to what degree our fragmented process exemplified the kinds of conflict and tension that are often deemed necessary precursors to some form of critical "shaking up," to garnering renewed energy for the ongoing task of challenging injustice. On the other hand, we wonder if the emergent tensions reflected more of our inability to move beyond ourselves and our positioning as bright and privileged graduate students – to actually engage in questions and projects that might have asked us to re-think the whole form, process, approach to *how* we were engaging the broader community (why weren't "they" a part of our conversations)? And even as these questions came up over the duration of the course, what did we do to move them forward?

How, in a classroom context that asks us to step beyond its walls to engage in critical social issues, do we negotiate the tension between the urgency of the issues and the importance of process? Or perhaps thinking about these as a tension is part of the problem. Learning often remains isolated within a kind of utopian classroom space – where important learning happens, but in ways that make participants feel they are "safe" from asking the riskiest questions about our responsibility as citizens and critical thinkers. Were we successful at disrupting the "traditional" classroom space in the ways that we were encouraged to by Ajay? Or did our project – a conference on accessibility and education held on campus with an audience made up primarily of students – remain within the safe space of academic expectation/fulfilment? How were our experiences and capacities shaped and constrained, often invisibly, by our locations within broader systems of power and privilege? How is it possible – if it's possible at all – to do social justice work when the resources we draw upon come to us by virtue of our roles in an institution that continues to perpetuate – and even to benefit from – those injustices? We will return to this issue of systemic location in part 2, in which we will define and critique the ways in which community engagement is discussed, taken up, and often limited by broader systems of power and privilege.

At the same time, if we compare what we did and discovered in this one course with other courses we've taken over the course of our academic trajectories, we know that we learned some very practical things – how to book a room on campus, how to line up conference speakers, how to book community tables, advertising, fundraising, budgeting – that were new to us as people new to Guelph and/or new to graduate work. And in many ways, the questions that were raised through the experience of the course continue to propel us in our work, as academics and as non-formal educators, perhaps lending credence to Peter McLaren's warning that "You can't teach people anything … You have to create a context in which they can analyze themselves and their social formations and lives." Ajay's classroom certainly became a site for learning through experience, for asking tough critical questions about ourselves in relation to broader systemic issues and forces – and, in some cases, for feeling pretty immobilized in the face of the enormity of the questions we were wading through and that seemed to stand between us and the opposite shore of "intervening."

As we have suggested above, the process of this project held, and continues to hold, a great deal more resonance for us than its product – although the colloquium was an energizing and enriching event in its own right, by all accounts. The processes of learning and reflection we were called upon to take part in, the frustrations of getting through our own issues, identifying our varying biases and blocks, and, finally, clearing the way into action, taught us an enormous amount about a range of things: the deeply constrictive and dampening effects of academic regulation and timetables, for certain, and the profound influence of experience and privilege on our "gut" feelings and thoughts – we were undoubtedly products of our circumstances, our identities, our own particular lived realities. Talking as we were about issues of access and obstruction, systemic oppression and privilege, we found that the divisions between our "academic" selves and our "private" selves, never more than a well-strutted illusion, crumbled very quickly. This was a striking realization for us: the rock-solid knowledge that there is no such thing as leaving oneself behind to do one's work, and that the supposed boundaries between ivory tower and real world are, in the end, at least highly permeable. But of course that permeability does not translate into an openness or a dismantling of the very real boundaries that keep academia more welcoming to and inclusive of some of us over others. Another lesson.

For us, the questions that our experiences with Access Interventions provoked have to do with how we can continue to engage with "community" and with struggles for social justice beyond the tenure of a course, a semester, a particular professor, or a student's degree program. Thinking through the sustainability of the "community-facing" project was an important component of Ajay's criteria for us as we embarked on evaluating ourselves and the symposium. And while the project has continued to have a life – in the academic work of at least a handful of the students who were in the course, in a follow-up colloquium on pedagogy and activism we organized at McMaster, and in our special journal issue of the *Review of Education, Pedagogy, and Cultural Studies* – in terms of the interface with particular community organizations or specific issues that were raised over the course of the class and conference, the impact of our intervention is perhaps more muted.

We would argue that thinking about building sustained relationships (rather than "partnerships") with people and organizations beyond the university institution is an important piece of educating for social change. How can we flip from what Randy Stoecker and Mary Beckman describe as an "academic-driven process" to a "community-driven process," in which "an academic-driven process only asks what I can do with my course" (7) while "a community-driven process" involves community members and activists directly in design, project implementation, participatory relationships, and critical engagement? If project sustainability is only about what the student or students continue to do after the course of the semester, how much do these "community-facing" interventions engage the community in a more holistic or dialogic sense?

While the course itself, in terms of how Ajay framed it, explicitly asked us both to consider these "community interventions" in ways that might involve a broader engagement with the community more dialogically and to recognize clearly the systemic nature of inequality, moving beyond the model of "individuals" engaging "the community," how can we actually mobilize/embody/execute such a pedagogy? What are the parameters here? Of activism, engagement, "community"? How do we measure "success" (and do we need to)? And how to do it all in a one-semester course? A lot of the tensions that we felt then, and that we are continuing to notice in our community-engaged work now, arguably stem from working in institutional cultures and climates of inequality and within curricular parameters that run counter to sustained, meaningful collaboration between university classrooms and other sites of knowledge production and learning. We realize that this book, in a way, is an attempt to recognize and articulate that despite all these systemic barriers to broader engagement, despite all these challenging questions, there *are* ways to seed and nurture change even in potentially inhospitable environments. And maybe what we did in our class is a kind of answer – that embodying such a pedagogy is necessarily messy, partial, inadequate, but also provocative and critically engaging, and that what "we" did through the class was perhaps both problematic and an inspired example of critical pedagogy in action. And maybe the answer is that we can't, nor should we, prescribe what "such a pedagogy" looks like operationally – perhaps it needs to be open and receptive to the particularities of the students/participants, to broader community questions and context, to shifting institutional climates, to current debates in the public sphere. In this sense, one can argue that critical pedagogy, engaged pedagogy, is best approached as an improvisatory practice (a notion that Brendan Arnott explores in more detail in his contribution in this volume about *Haiti Held Hostage*). The openness and responsiveness we are advocating line up nicely with the principles of improvised creative expression: instead of heading in with a detailed strategy and a plan from which we must not deviate, we enter instead with hopes (certainly), goals (perhaps), and a lot of willingness to go with whatever flow emerges from our shared work. We listen to our colleagues and participants, taking into account the subtle shifts among us as we move together, and often something unanticipated and quite striking happens. Programmatic pedagogy closes doors before we begin. Improvised, responsive, contingent pedagogy is open, and thus more organic and free.

What's at stake in thinking ourselves out of experiments with community-engaged learning and critical pedagogy? By choosing more traditional pedagogical approaches, what kinds of acts of injustice, of reinforcing status quo notions, do we continue invisibly to perform? There is, of course, a risk to diverging from normative, institutionally sanctioned ways of teaching and learning. The risk is that we might appear to have failed, that our ventures will fall flat; but the risk is also that we might awaken to the injustices that are whitewashed as "normal" and "proper" right under our noses. Maybe we will get wise to the systemic obstacles that keep some of us comfortably at home here and make it nearly impossible for some other people to even get an offer of admission. Maybe we will become angry, or hopeful, or have a good idea and fight to enact it. This is the richness that lies, or can lie, at the heart of this kind of education, and this is why it is so crucial that teachers and students continue to push for new, resistant, change-making ways to do our work.

After term with Ajay had ended, our questions kept percolating. In February 2004, we met up at another conference, where our attempts to engage in conversations about the political implications of academic work were met with silence, deflection, and apparent discomfort. Eventually, our questions were shut down – as though academics and politics ought to be kept separate. As though they can be.

This encounter inspired us to create a conference of our own. Out of a disappointing exchange and over angry coffee, our own conference was born. Thus the connections, experiences, and sense of competence we gained from Access Interventions led, two years later, to three of us from the class (plus two other graduate students) putting on another conference, this one at McMaster. At "Raising Our Voices: Encouraging Academic Activism," we wanted to move the discussion from how, in a particular class, we could engage the community, to asking more broadly what the university's role should be in relation to community engagement. In other words, taking our cue and inspiration from the work we'd done in Ajay's class, we were exploring the responsibility of the public intellectual and the opportunities and constraints that come with academic work. The conference and subsequent journal issue brought a lively range of voices and perspectives to the ongoing dialogue about the relationships – past, ongoing, and potential – between academic work and broader social change.

2. Community-University Engagement: Contexts and Constraints

"Community engagement" is a growing field of inquiry and practice on campuses across North America, a growth that continues to spawn institution-shifting approaches to teaching, learning, and scholarship. While working across the perceived campus-community divide is by no means a "new" academic innovation, its emergence in new configurations and at different sites requires fresh attention both to exactly what *we do* when we "engage" with community and how we can do it in ways that are ethical, contextualized, and responsive. Shifting trends in how universities are being seen and positioned in relation to broader social issues also require a re-thinking of what it means for academia to lead the charge in "prepar[ing] students for responsible citizenship in a diverse democracy" (Butler 52).

Our experiences and work since we took part in Access Interventions have led us to view the course and the event with different commitments and questions in mind. We engaged in the work as graduate students committed to struggles for human rights and social justice, keen to find ways to enliven our work as part of broader work for change. Theorists and practitioners of critical pedagogy, activist-artists, and other politically motivated creative practitioners and educators were highly influential in shaping the lens through which we assessed our project. Now, these commitments hold ground alongside our immersion in the literature and practice of community-university partnerships. We view Ajay's course as an effort to create meaningful engagements between academic and community-based people and groups, and find it productive to analyze the course from this perspective. We are now both committed to investigating the potential of community-engaged work as one of many possible "new, resistant, change-making ways to do our work," as we call for above.

While many conceptualizations of community-university engagement are deliberately and explicitly apolitical, we use "community-university engagement" in a way that draws on the scholarship of engagement, critical pedagogy, and community-based research methodologies to outline the parameters of a pedagogical approach that, in the words of Kerry Strand et al., "stresses collective action, advocacy, critical analysis, and collaboration for the purpose of social change" (120–1). For us, it is imperative that all community-engaged work be motivated by an explicit commitment to and focus upon meeting articulated community needs, and a clear agenda to put research and knowledge to work towards social change and justice.

Given the historical and cultural contexts within which we work, we are mindful of the importance of remaining alert as we plan and enact our projects. The risks of losing focus are too great. For this reason, we recognize that it is important to remain alert to the constraints and challenges inherent in conventional models of community engagement – although, we wish to emphasize, we are not suggesting that most or all community-university engaged work is flawed and terrible. Rather, we are voicing these concerns in order to continue a longstanding dialogue among practitioners concerned that their work not be turned, inadvertently, to negative ends.

Elizabeth Hollander and John Saltmarsh in their article on the "Engaged University" incisively critique institutions of higher education for their lack of responsiveness to social issues. Strand et al. similarly speak to higher education's "inequitable and unresponsive relationship with the community," stressing "the importance of linking knowledge with social inquiry rather than leaving it disconnected from action and isolated and mired in academic culture" (1–2). If a main goal of community-engaged learning, then, is to confront broader social and environmental issues in partnership with communities and to situate ourselves in relation to these broader systemic trends and struggles, the same attention needs to be paid to examining the impact of community engagement on communities – to how and where we may be unwittingly perpetuating systemic injustice. For us, paying attention to these tensions has actually become an important starting point for feeling energized and hopeful about possibilities in/for community-engaged work.

One risk of uncritical community engagement is the production of Otherness in the communities we are allegedly seeking to serve and/or with which we want to partner. Conventional ways of talking about community engagement perpetuate and deepen the imagined division between university and community, placing us in binary positions of have/have not; knowledge/question; resource/lack. While these distinctions are often inaccurate, their effects can take the very real forms of alienation, silencing, and continued lack of genuine communication with community partners. These formulations also ignore the important truth that many of us have allegiances and identify with many of the same groups and organizations that are imagined as distinctly "other" to the university and to our academic selves.

Further, the hierarchical nature of university organizations and the relationships that make up community-engaged scholarship run the risk of breaking down partnerships before they are even established. The relationships among university, funding agencies, faculty investigators, community organizations, and individuals in the community are often fraught and unequal, to say the least, and it can be very difficult to build the genuinely mutual partnerships described on many institutional websites, and in the definition above, when one is embedded in and navigating systems and structures built on hierarchies.

For example, at a recent international teaching and learning conference, a group of faculty and students presented the results of a community-engaged/service learning project. One of their "outcomes" was a film made by students documenting their work "for" partners; another aspect was a website. When asked about the role their community partners had played in shaping the project, the group seemed unable to answer. Eventually they said that they thought the community members had "enjoyed it." When discussion moved to the website, I (Elizabeth) asked, "Did community partners play a role in creating the site? Are their voices part of this project?" Again there was silence; presenters looked to colleagues in the audience, and finally one presenter replied that no, community members weren't currently represented on the website but that it would be great to make some changes to include what she described as "beautiful photographs of grateful recipients."

Grateful recipients. This is the role so often assigned to community members involved in community-engaged projects, whether they are called partners or collaborators or just plain "community members." We do not relate this story to draw attention to this particular project, which had many strengths. Rather, we find the words "grateful recipients" sum up very well the dehumanizing, condescending, disempowering way in which conventional discussions of community engagement tend to characterize non-academic community members. Paulo Freire describes this tendency as "false generosity" and argues that it functions to perpetuate the apparent goodness of oppressors, while relying upon and perpetuating the suffering of the oppressed in order to sustain itself (44).

Amber Dean draws on the work of David Jefferess to articulate some of the possible negative impacts of uncritical community-engaged work. Jefferess, in his critical examination of global education and international voluntourism, argues that the impulse to "do good" (via voluntourism, for example) "constitutes a new form of colonial paternalism and often harms the host communities" in the following ways:

1. Volunteers are often untrained/not competent in the labour they perform.
2. Projects can fuel conflict among and within communities.
3. Projects focus on the symptoms of poverty rather than its causes.
4. Volunteers often take the place of (paid) local labour.
5. Projects often reinforce neoliberal economic policies.
6. Projects risk commodifying Others to give students "an orphanage experience" etc.

(Jefferess 22)

We are not alone in our concerns, and are encouraged by the lively and rigorous discussions we have read and heard in which colleagues work and strive to establish an ethical form of community engagement. We thus want to caution that community-engaged projects, when done uncritically or in a rush, can do more harm than good – or at least enough harm that they should perhaps be paused, reevaluated, and redesigned. We are concerned that this kind of work, however well-intentioned and committed its practitioners, too often serves the greater (neoliberal) interests of the corporate university (e.g. when used as a branding or PR tool to draw students and funders or by encouraging the conflation of "industry" and "community"). Ajay's class gave us a grounded opportunity to work through these potential challenges with a group that shared our principles. We continue to strive to articulate and to protect a position and a space from which practitioners can do community-engaged work in ways that are liberatory, progressive, and genuinely useful to the communities to which we belong and/or to whom we commit ourselves.

3. Critical Hope: Our Emerging Conceptualizations of Politically Committed Community-University Engagement

Having laid out our concerns about some of the possible and real consequences of uncritical community engagements, we want to close with a discussion – even a celebration – of the genuinely radical hope we locate in community-based education. We are mindful that any critique of a socially engaged practice can be readily taken as "proof" that it ought not to be done at all. On the contrary, we offer our criticisms in a spirit of commitment and reflection, so that we can continue to hone this exciting field to be as hope-affirming and productive as it can be. As influential community-based educators Nina Wallerstein and Bonnie Duran caution, "[W]e must ensure that critiques and challenges of CBPR [community-based participatory research] do not play into conservative strategies that dismiss the role of communities participating in change (or that, conversely, leave the work of change to local communities without adequate public government support)" (39).

How, then, do "the public"/broader communities/social struggles benefit from rethinking the role of universities in addressing pressing social concerns? According to a range of scholars and critics, effective community-engaged learning can be a process that allows universities to participate in responding to unequal distribution of political and economic power; to the ways in which gender, class, race, etc. influence the construction of meaning; to the importance of multiple ways of knowing to challenging injustice/the status quo; to the need for collective agency in moving forward a social change agenda; to the impact of global forces and globalization on local communities; to the crucial learning emerging from existing social movements; and to the need to increase social participation in local and global communities.

These broader benefits – that address finding ways of actually shifting social perception – point to the need to consider systemic issues (of race, gender, or economic exploitation, for example) alongside increasing participation in community concerns. If one does not attempt a critical balancing act between conscientious, contextualized community engagement/research and ongoing critical inquiry, it can be easy to lose sight of the purpose of this work. For us, striving to integrate ethical and responsive community-engaged work more actively with ongoing efforts to ask challenging questions offers a way to a kind of tempered or grounded hope – hope that sits in moments when:

- We connect our work to broader histories, memories, and systems in an effort to counter the individualizing and sublimating pressures of neoliberal ideology.
- We give renewed scrutiny to *how* culture is interested and for whom and what – reinvigorating the importance of critical engagement and decision-making that takes into consideration the very interested parameters of the institutions and discourses that we define and that define us.

- We recognize that we are both products and producers of unjust systems, but also, therefore, the ones who can produce and imagine alternative ways of seeing and being in the world.
- We move forward even when everything isn't perfectly theorized – we bring our questions, our stories, our hopes, and our blinders along for the ride in a spirit of openness and improvisation, and of a desire to work out collectively what it means to be here now.
- We make visible the rhetoric/discourse of community-engaged learning as it may be connected to neoliberal projects that work to shift responsibility for collective concerns onto entrepreneurial subjects who are seen somehow to stand outside of history and outside of systems.
- We make normative systems and stories visible, alongside ones that tell a different version of what is "right" and "normal."
- We focus on systemic rather than individualized understandings of change/injustice.
- We develop course-based projects that link explicitly to existing social change efforts (existing networks and collaborations), relationships, research projects, etc.
- We are explicit about defining what we mean by "community," by power, and by knowledge, and where expertise lies.
- We don't pretend that all community encounters are transformative, and are honest about the ways that even our good intentions to trouble good intentions are fraught with re-producing neoliberal logics.

The concerns and commitments central to our class with Ajay and to our colloquium were already and have remained at the forefront of our minds as we carry out work as students, researchers, educators, writers, and community members. What this means is that when we teach a class, analyze a text, or develop a research project with community, we do so with certain questions at the root of these explorations. These are, variously, Who speaks here, and to what end? Who is silenced or spoken for in a particular document or a particular conversation? How might we listen differently and attend to other voices and ideas in order to read our world more fully, more fairly? Thus, from our experiences in Ajay's class, working to engage the broader community in debate and discussion around education, and the conference at McMaster that was about creating a space for academics to think about their own pedagogical practice, to Ingrid's role at the University of

Guelph supporting and developing community-based research projects in collaboration with community organizations, students, staff, and faculty, to Elizabeth's continued efforts to develop ethical and sustained community-university research partnerships and to enliven her teaching and research as elements of movements for social change, we think it's important to recognize, despite its many challenges, that post-secondary education remains what bell hooks would call a powerful "location of possibility" (*Teaching to Transgress* 207). This is, as we have learned, a space that we need to use in ways that actively contribute to work for social justice and critical debates in the broader public sphere. In working across disciplines to find imaginative and community-focused (i.e., sensitive and responsive to community need) ways of engaging students, courses, and faculty with these broader questions, we continually draw on the theoretical musings and both the inspiring and confidence-shaking experiences born out of Ajay's course. Despite the challenges of engaging with work that is explicitly focused on social change, on messy, partial understandings of community, of the classroom, and of who we are or aren't as educators and students, we are often buoyed by encounters with thoughtful, daring, passionate, and compassionate people working away in many corners and pockets of academia. We take heart in knowing that despite the risks and challenges – institutional hurdles, lack of external funding/ support, limited time etc. – academia remains, in halting and renewing and redoing ways, a space for experiments, for improvisations in and for social change.

APPENDIX: Pragmatics

Most broadly, we think our particular class really discovered the difficulty (and eventually the importance) of working collectively (particularly as a collective of stressed-out graduate students), of making decisions together. We all decided to work on one project, and with 17 people involved, it made for some pretty lengthy and complicated decision-making. There was a lot of diversity of opinion in the class. **Solution:** We dealt with this issue by dividing ourselves into four subgroups: fundraising, outreach, publicity, and logistics – which (in general) made negotiating and getting tasks done quite a bit easier.

Because of the indecision and stalling that happened earlier on in the class, however, we weren't ready with our community-facing project until after the course was over. **Solution:** The class agreed to continue on beyond the formal end of the course, and we ended up pushing the date for the symposium into the winter semester.

A more abstract problem we faced was that because we were committed to making the conference accessible on multiple levels, we were forced to examine our own assumptions around accessibility at the same time as we were working to create a space, resources, and dialogue around accessible education. By choosing "education" as our topic, we, in a sense, became our own case-study. **Solution:** In a way, this "problem" became its own solution as we began to realize that learning how to examine ourselves and our own roles critically in relation to the pragmatics and the people involved in creating our symposium was, if not a necessary precursor to engagement, a central "product" of our negotiation with the course's objectives and a key piece in thinking through what our versions of "critical pedagogy" would look like.

Again, because of the lengthy decision-making process (and maybe this doesn't just signal an issue with our decision-making process, but points to the time constraints posed by a single-semester course), the only venue we could find that was available within our price range and for our proposed dates was on campus. Even though this was supposed to be a "community" event, having it on campus posed different kinds of accessibility issues. **Solution:** we tried to deal with this by inviting a number of community members to give workshops and by publicizing across town.

Sustainability of the project. Originally we conceived of the conference as a first step in creating dialogue around injustices within education and hoped to create an "Education and Social Change Collective" that would continue putting on events, raising awareness, creating newsletters, influencing policy at the university, and so forth. Unfortunately, everyone felt pretty burned out at the end, and there was only a small number of people (about six) of the original 17 who even met to discuss possible future projects. As we have discussed, though, some of us did come together years later to dedicate sustained attention to the questions that arose from the class through our follow-up colloquium and special journal issue. Perhaps one shouldn't measure outcomes with a cut-off date: this class continues to ripple its influence into all sorts of areas of our lives and work, even now.

In the twelve years since our colloquium, our colleagues from this course have moved on to new work: raising children, community activism, teaching, launching businesses. We know that many of them continue to be inspired by and committed to the principles we all struggled so hard to articulate together all those years ago. Naava Smolash and Jesse Stewart, for example, have both challenged their university students to put their in-class learning to work in community-facing initiatives. Stewart's students, like us, chose to mount a symposium, focusing their work on the intersections between music and social justice. Rebecca Caines, who is also a university professor, has long dedicated her work to a consideration of voice and self-expression by diverse and often marginalized individuals and communities, and her work throughout her graduate and postdoctoral studies has always remained grounded in questions of lived experience and sociopolitical justice. Our classmate Dave Hudson, who now works as a university librarian, devotes some of his research to the question of the value and valuation of humanities scholarship, and to issues of censorship and intellectual freedom; he is also an accomplished spoken-word poet whose work often tackles systems of power and inequality.

Money was also a problem for us in planning our conference, because we wanted to bring in three keynote speakers, to compensate the workshop participants, and to provide free food and childcare to everyone. **Solution:** We dealt with this by fundraising: we had to apply for grants and ask for institutional and community support (from, for example, a range of downtown restaurants and businesses, internal university funding streams, and the School of English and Theatre Studies, to name a few).

While this tidy linking of problems with solutions is somewhat at odds with our broader theoretical musings above, it nevertheless reflects a brief sampling of the logistical hurdles we encountered in the event planning itself. Given the many years that have elapsed since Access Interventions, we, unfortunately, are not able to provide much substance to the finer details of conference organization. Many of the problems we encountered – funding, time constraints, difficult group dynamics, accessibility, etc. – are not only challenges shared in community organizing and activist efforts more broadly, but challenges we have learned from, even as we continue to encounter them in our ongoing attempts to use the academy as a site for advocacy, community engagement, and public encounter. To some extent, as we have discussed above, each new event or effort must make its own way, stumbling along its own particular path. We heartily believe that most truly responsive and relevant organizing needs to be comfortable working at least somewhat improvisationally; we believe, too, that we learn best by engaging with others who seek to do similar work, learning from those who have worked with and before us, and leaving our marks and musings for others to find later, if they stumble upon them.

NOTE

1 In terms of the specifics of the symposium, there was the "standard" kind of conference fare, with keynote speakers and community workshop facilitators (about 12 formal participants in total) who ranged from Sherene Razack, Professor of Sociology and Equity Studies in Education at OISE in Toronto, to Jaggi Singh, well-known Montreal writer and activist and active member of the No One is Illegal Campaign, to Kathleen Wynne, who is currently the premier of Ontario. We had workshops led by Sabina Chaterjee of "Change Now" (the Guelph youth drop-in centre), Dave Bernans and Sabine Friesinger from Concordia Student Union (who talked about students' right to organize politically and discuss issues such as the controversial Israel-Palestine conflicts and Concordia's blocking of Benjamin Netanyahu), Barry Wheeler (from the Centre for Students with Disabilities at the University of Guelph), Janet Brewster (from College Heights, a vocational high school, speaking on literacy), Wendy Stewart (founding member of Plume Society, an aboriginal multi-media based circle of artists that promotes social justice for Native peoples through the arts), sarah george (who talked about representations of queer folk at and by the university institution), Maria Graham (who spoke to the challenges around pursuing an education while also meeting the demands of being a parent), and Erin White and Dave Sonne from the 2002/2003 Central Student Association (at University of Guelph).

2 The *Guelph Speaks!* Anthology: Storytelling as Praxis in Community-Facing Pedagogy

ASHLEE CUNSOLO, PAUL DANYLUK, AND
ROBERT ZACHARIAS[1]

> The truth about stories is that that's all we are.
>
> (Thomas King, *The Truth About Stories:*
> *A Native Narrative*)

Introduction: From Classroom Seats to City Streets

In January 2007, the authors of this chapter, along with four other graduate and undergraduate students at the University of Guelph, had the opportunity to participate in a community-based, experiential graduate course in the Humanities. Through this course, we were challenged to use our Humanities education to participate in social justice and human rights issues in the community. The authors worked with their classmates to respond to the challenge by creating an eighty-page multi-media community anthology, *Guelph Speaks! Re-Storying the City* – containing thirty written works, fifteen photographs and works of art, and six audio tracks – and to launch the anthology during an evening of music, art, poetry, and storytelling.

Working on the *Guelph Speaks!* project would prove to be an invaluable part of our graduate school experience, and played an important role in defining not only how we approached our academics, but also how we conceptualized the role of academia within community settings. While participating in such a community-focused project within the parameters of a graduate class presented some challenges (which we'll outline in this chapter), it also provided the space to mobilize our Humanities backgrounds to engage in the world beyond the classroom walls. This experience has continued to influence how we approach work at the intersection of academia and community, and has, in many ways, affected how we approach aspects of our professional careers in academia (Cunsolo and Zacharias) and in the non-profit sector (Danyluk).

We continue to believe strongly in this anthology's value (both for our own education and for the anthology's contributors), as well as in the course's efforts to look beyond the classroom walls and participate in the broader community. At the same time, we would not want to downplay the critical issues and challenging questions we faced in undertaking the project: the ethical considerations around "gathering" stories from the community; the fraught terrain of creating and using an editorial framework to select and order personal narratives in the construction of the anthology; and the pedagogical issues raised when assigning, grading, and receiving academic credit for community-based work.

Combining our personal reflections of working on the *Guelph Speaks!* project with theoretical groundings, this chapter will discuss the possibilities that can emerge when graduate students are encouraged to look beyond the classroom walls and into the community. We will consider the importance of mobilizing storytelling to challenge dominant narratives, discuss the opportunities and limitations of undertaking such work within an academic context, and reflect upon both the successes and challenges of our particular community-based project. Finally, we will return to the theoretical texts that framed the course assignment to reconsider, in light of our experience with the project, the praxiological possibilities and limitations that arise from their overlapping, but not identical, arguments around community-based education for social change.

Pedagogy and/as Social Justice: The Beginnings of *Guelph Speaks!*

The graduate course from which this project emerged, "Pedagogy, Human Rights, Critical Activism: Educating for Social Change," was a 12-week, one-semester Special Topics course offering for students in the English and Theatre Studies program at the University of Guelph. Structured to encourage students to find ways to mobilize the curriculum creatively in order to undertake work in the community, this course sought to provide space for students to engage collaboratively as a class and as members of the larger community on issues of human rights and social justice. The group projects were decided upon through a process of brainstorming, class dialogue, vetting, and consensus. Early on in the course discussions, it became clear that a number of us were interested in the relationship between narrative and identity, and excited about and inspired by the political potential of storytelling. As a group, we came together to hone our ideas and interests, and, after settling on putting together a community anthology, we began the process of theorizing and defending our project. After incorporating the feedback and ideas from our classmates and a panel of experts, we sent out a general call for submissions through community resource centres, local businesses, and media for members of the Guelph community to contribute stories, poetry, prose, music, film, painting, artwork, and photography focused on the themes of placement and displacement in the city. Despite a short submission period, we received over 150 pieces from which to choose for the final bound anthology. While submissions were arriving, we fundraised persistently, managing to raise the money necessary to cover our $9,000 production budget fully.

The result, completed just four-and-a-half months after the project began, was 500 copies of a multi-media anthology, professionally published and complete with full-colour insets of artwork and photographs and an attached audio disc. The book's entries reflect a wide range of ages and backgrounds, from elementary students such as Anna Ahmad and Brittany Thatcher to photographers such as Robin Bergart and Trina Koster to poets such as Aislinn Thomas and Melissa Walker to well-known musicians such as James Gordon and The Speakeasies to established authors such as playwright Sky Gilbert and Governor General's Award-winner Jane Urquhart (see Appendix for Table of Contents). The anthologies were given out free to all authors and contributors, as well as to community resource centres and libraries. The rest were disseminated at our launch event and at local bookstores through a "pay-what-you-can" model, with all proceeds going to Action Read, a local adult literacy centre. The project was awarded the University of Guelph's Gordon Nixon Leadership Award in recognition of its "outstanding contribution" to the university. The original assignment had encouraged us to consider the challenge of sustainability within our efforts to intervene in the community; as a group, we had hoped that the circulation of the *Guelph Speaks!* anthology throughout the community would enable our efforts to resonate beyond the timeline and confines of the course. We were thus pleased when two subsequent iterations of the anthology – *Guelph Speaks! More Space* (2008) and *Guelph Speaks! The Onion and the Ivy: Celebrating the Creative Spirit of 40*

Baker Street (2012) – were undertaken by new editorial collectives that drew on the contacts and contents of our project to move it outside the context of a single course, transforming the anthology into a broader community-run initiative.

Storytelling with/in the City

This course was framed by the theoretical work of Thomas King, Paulo Freire, and bell hooks (*Teaching Community*) – a frame we have maintained in this chapter for these reflections on our anthology project. There are, of course, many other studies that theorize the use of storytelling to incite social change and enhance social justice – including Sherene Razack's *Looking White People in the Eye* (1998), J. Edward Chamberlin's *If This Is Your Land, Where Are Your Stories?* (2004), Francesca Polletta's *It Was Like a Fever* (2006), and Rickie Solinger et al.'s *Telling Stories to Change the World* (2008) – but as the work of King, Freire, and hooks established the framework from which our project emerged, we take this chapter as an opportunity to explore the pedagogical benefits of this particular critical paradigm, as well as to test its limits. Our project, conceived in response to the overlapping critical concerns with personal and collective narratives, university/community relations, and pedagogies of political engagement raised by King, Freire, and hooks, sought to gather together stories that expanded our understanding of life within the city of Guelph.

Guelph Speaks! was undertaken, then, in the belief that it is a fundamental human right for people to tell stories in their own voices and from their own experiences – particularly when those stories may not be supported or promoted within the dominant narratives of a given place or time. Understanding the capacity of storytelling to assist with issues of social justice and enhance dialogue around human rights and responsibilities, we argued in the Introduction to our anthology that "storytelling has the ability to bring diverse people, thoughts, and ideas together, and the potential to bring marginalized or seldom-heard voices to the larger community" (Cunsolo Willox et al. 2). With this faith in the transformative power of storytelling in mind, we were hopeful that, in placing these various narratives side by side, readers – including, of course, ourselves – would gain a fuller appreciation for the myriad experiences of living in Guelph, and that the anthology would provide a platform allowing these differing stories to be shared, celebrated, and discussed. The anthology, we hoped, would serve more broadly as a platform for multiple voices, experiences, and understandings to come together and weave a diverse and complex story of life within an urban centre. Looking to expand upon the discourse of human *rights*, we also argued for recognition of the community's larger *responsibility* to listen and engage with such narratives. It is, we argued, both "[t]he act of storytelling – and its necessary companion, listening – [that have] the potential to move us towards a more inclusive community" (2).

Complementing the emphasis on human rights and responsibilities that framed our project, we choose storytelling as our medium because of its ability to share personal conditions and expose underlying currents through the interaction of speakers and listeners. Stories have the potential to invite and encourage us to abstract meaning from the individual ideas, actions, and events shared within, and actively to theorize and connect through the narrative. We discovered, as did the creators of *The Other End of the Line* later in this book, that while stories may be personal, their implications are collective; in this duality exists an opportunity to share our own personal experience while considering the experiences of others, in order better to understand a broader range of lived experiences than is commonly presented through the normative practices of our conventional cultural schemata. In fact, as King argues, our stories do not simply express our experiences in the world; they actively shape us, giving form and meaning to how we experience that world. "The truth about stories is that that's all we are," he writes. "'You can't understand the world without telling a story,' the Anishinabe writer Gerald Vizenor tells us. 'There isn't any centre to the world but a story'" (32). Although we drew heavily from King's *The Truth About Stories* as we worked through the theoretical foundations of our project, we also recognized that the context and politics of particular stories must be respected. King's book is subtitled *A Native Narrative*, for example, and while King's claims about the political possibilities of storytelling move well beyond the context of First Nations, it remains important for us not to lose sight of the particular context and history through which his argument emerged. Part of understanding the power of individual stories, then, is understanding the collective contexts in which they are situated.

Storytelling also dovetailed nicely with the mandates and parameters of our course, for it forms the basis of the community-based, experiential action and pedagogical praxis promoted by Paulo Freire. For Freire, sharing one's own stories and listening to the stories of others is fundamental to the struggle for human rights, and provides the opportunity to subvert the oppressor's process of "stealing" words and stories in order to dominate the minds, values, and circumstances of the oppressed. Following Ben Okri (as quoted in Thomas King), we recognize that "we live by stories, [and] we also live in them. One way or another, we are living the stories planted – knowingly or unknowingly – in ourselves. We live stories that either give our lives meaning, or negate it with meaninglessness. If we change the stories we live by, quite possibly we change our lives" (153). Stories, then, have the ability to change circumstances and understandings, and lie at the heart of what Freire terms "conscientization" – a process of coming to critical awareness and engagement with one's own situation, values, and roles – and the core of his "education as the practice for freedom" (81). In this context, the circulation of myriad voices has the potential to break the perpetuation of dominant narratives simply by sharing and exchanging a wider diversity of human experiences. Inspired by this understanding of the power of stories, we created a community-based work of numerous stories with the aim of collecting and (re)presenting a cross section of the ongoing larger narrative, constantly unfolding, about the many experiences of life in our city – all with the broader aim of raising awareness of diversity within our city and uniting a Humanities education with community-based and experiential learning. We began our project, then, with an understanding of storytelling as a distinctly political vehicle well-suited to the promotion of social justice, even in instances in which the stories themselves might not be overtly political in content.

Working from within an academic endeavour and pedagogical premise focused on gathering stories from across our community, we linked our process to bell hooks's explanation of the power of theorizing and practicing academic discourse in a manner dedicated to making substantial, positive change in one's self and one's community. Creating and conducting academic work that is community-facing and community-focused is one possibility for "linking struggles for justice outside the academy with ways of knowing within the academy" (hooks, *Teaching Community* 46). We identified storytelling – "a significant, simple, crucial vehicle for reawakening, disseminating, and sustaining social justice issues" (Solinger, Fox, and Irani 1) – as having the capacity not only to build new networks and enhance established lines of community dialogue, but also to link the university with these local networks as a means of further empowering the work undertaken by both groups.

As the project began to take shape, however, we quickly came to realize that we needed to think further about what was at stake in our project as an "intervention" in our community. That is, despite our belief in the power of storytelling and the sharing of personal narratives to incite and inspire change – in fact, precisely *because* of this belief – we were also cognizant that working with stories can be both wondrous *and* dangerous (King 9). Taking seriously the power of stories to shape our world fundamentally, King argues that stories "can control our lives" (8); as such, he urges us "to be careful with the stories you tell," and to "watch out for the stories that you are told" (10). What is more, as he notes later, it is not simply *which* stories are told, but *how* they are told, that matters. "[A] story told one way could cure," he writes, but "the same story told another way could injure" (92). And so our project had to wrestle with what we might call the double capacity of stories: the narratives we were collecting had not only the ability to promote change productively and enhance awareness, but also the potential to entrench and further the most damaging aspects of the status quo. In fact, while we were inspired by hooks to take our studies beyond the walls of our classroom, and we drew on King to identify storytelling as a privileged vehicle for undertaking this move in the name of social justice, we found that the actualization of such theoretical material meant not only wrestling with the very particular contexts for our project, but also testing the sometimes-celebratory rhetoric of community-facing research with the practical challenges of its enactment. As we moved forward with the project, we understood that "we must know the limits of narratives, rather than establish the narratives as solutions for the future, for the arrival of social justice" (Spivak 18–19). It may well be true that stories are potentially powerful aspects of social change, but how does the process of "editing" and "compiling" the anthology affect their impact? What do we mean by "the community," and how is it reflected in the relatively small numbers of people who will be willing to share their stories? How and what do these stories, placed within the very particular context of a "community anthology," really signify? And what is the relationship between the difference embodied by these works and their authors, and the academic framework that facilitated their written performance? These were questions that continually troubled us as we went through the process of working on the *Guelph Speaks!* anthology, and, in many ways, these were questions that we realized could never be fully resolved.

Making Space, Facilitating Action

Our concerns with practical engagement and interaction with the community underscored how our own work took place in a space marked by tensions between intellectual traditions and critical differences in how to actualize research and translate classroom-learned skills into a complex world. Our course outline asked us to "make an intervention" into the community, but many of us were wary of the implications of this term, with its connotations of outside interference and unilateral action, and its presumption of authority. Even as we agreed upon the value of stories in influencing a community, members of our group repeatedly expressed discomfort with the idea that we were qualified to "intervene" in the community. Following Freire, we chose to adopt the language (and aimed to adopt the practice) of *facilitators* in the community storytelling process, rather than *interventionists*. As facilitators, we gathered stories within the community, worked on publicity, spoke to people about the project, fundraised so the anthology could be distributed for free, created the publication and had it bound, and attempted to create a space for community communication through multi-media stories. As facilitators, we endeavoured to create a platform for the many existent and ongoing stories throughout Guelph to gain a wider and more concentrated audience through the *Guelph Speaks!* anthology and the community launch evening.

Though the shift from "intervention" to "facilitation" may seem slight, it was important for us in at least two ways. First, it reflected the often-difficult process through which we re-examined our assumptions about the social applicability of community-facing research. Second, and more significantly, it helped us to understand that the purpose of our attempts to establish a link between our academic practice and the wider community was not simply to *apply* our Humanities education to our community, but also to draw on that education in order to create a space in which meaningful community dialogue could occur. After all, recognizing and affirming the heterogeneity of life and experience in our community was at the very heart of our project throughout. Trusting in the power of individual narratives to have an impact – sometimes affirming, other times challenging – on the larger hegemonic narratives of our city, we came to understand *Guelph Speaks!* as aiming to open up such a space, valuing the dialogue in and of itself while striving to be hospitable (in the most open, Derridean sense of this term) to whatever might emerge. The point, then, was not simply to use the conditions of our course to "intervene" in our community, or even to create a bridge between two supposedly monolithic structures that exist beside, and sometimes in tension with, each other – what we might call the two solitudes model of thinking about "the community" and "the academy." Rather, we aimed to take the risk of opening an opportunity for dialogue in which the monolithic nature of these structures becomes exposed as a fiction, and in which – again, directly inspired by Paulo Freire – we worked to spark critical thinking and active dialogue about what it means to live in our city.

As a *facilitation*, we were pleased with the project's success in creating positive spaces – both conceptual/textual, and, at the launch, physical – for meaningful community dialogue. We recognize, however, that *Guelph Speaks!* was also an *intervention*, in the limited sense of that term. Our focus had been on the conceptualization, production, and launch of the anthology as a distinct project; as such, we gave little thought to how we might establish an infrastructure or network that could foster a broader dialogue beyond the project itself. Even if we had the foresight to recognize their necessity, however, the constraints of the single-class context would, for example, have left little room for hosting writing workshops, creating community editorial liaisons, or partnering with the contributors to form a network of local writers. In fact, apart from a seldom-visited website and a comments book at the anthology's launch, we realized we had no way of measuring the success or registering the limitations of our efforts, let alone extending them. This is, we think, a primary example of the ways in which we came up against the limitations of working beyond the scope of our own disciplinary formations: while including follow-up strategies and meaningful assessment tools within the project structure may be obvious to scholars with a background in community-engaged pedagogies, they were beyond the scope of both our expertise and the timeframe of a single-course project. Moreover, as we will discuss shortly, picking up the title of "facilitator" threatened to efface, or minimize, the very real ways in which we *were* intervening in the community – a reality that we could not escape with a shift in terminology. Even as we had gravitated to stories for their power to connect our intellectual work with the lived experience of the city, the isolationist scholarship of text-based literary studies simply had not prepared us to respond fully to the larger social implications of our storytelling project. In participating in a case that aims to stretch the conventional boundaries of Humanities scholarship, we were reminded of the ways in which we as academics are, as Linda Hutcheon and Michael Hutcheon point out, both formed and *de*formed by our disciplinary training (1365). As the field continues to turn towards community-facing research, there will be a pressing need for Humanities-specific research that assists faculty and students in anticipating its particular challenges, as well as for strategies to make the most of its opportunities.

Editing the Community

Looking back with critical reflection at the process, a major lesson we learned from the *Guelph Speaks!* project is how deep a corrective praxis is to theoretical isolation. The ambitious structure of our class, which challenged us to use our training as students in the Humanities to burst through the fictional class/world binary and move outside the traditional Humanities classroom, raised the stakes of our own critical work by challenging us to make a meaningful intervention in the community in the name of human rights and responsibilities. In addition to the project's value as an intervention, it also served as a challenge to live the rhetoric of ethics and justice so commonly (and casually) invoked in contemporary critical discourse. For those of our group in literary studies in particular, undertaking the project proved invaluable not least as a reminder of how strange it is that it is possible *not* to do so. How is it possible, one wonders in retrospect, that it is standard practice for students to complete Humanities degrees without ever having tested the arguments about social justice found in much contemporary theory and criticism by moving beyond the page, never mind outside of the classroom itself? After all, the truth about stories is *not* that "that's all we are," or at least not in a literal sense. The stories we tell ourselves, and which are told about us, are important in large part because of how powerfully they shape the political, social, and economic communities in which we live our daily lives. It would be a mistake, then, for us to take King too literally and restrict our venue of action to stories on the printed page. The truth about stories, we might say, is that in order to understand them we must also include and engage with those who tell them.

We were excited by the possibilities of moving beyond the confines of text-based academic practice, and yet, while we were encouraged to push beyond, or even transgress, its confines, we also came up against the structural limitations of practicing a community-facing pedagogy within the rigid confines of the academic context in which we were working, in which students are forced to negotiate the competing priorities that come from remaining immersed in the larger context of the Humanities – even at the most pedestrian and pragmatic levels. Negotiating the number grade required by the College of Arts at the University of Guelph at the completion of the course seemed to run counter to the broader social justice aims of the course, for example, while time limitations of the semester system had us working through holidays and into a new school year before the project was completed, forcing us to navigate what Gregory Fenton, writing in this collection, has called the "institutionalization of goodwill." The context of a single-semester class could not possibly provide the expansive time or disciplinary knowledge necessary to theorize and thematize our project as thoroughly as we would have liked. While we appreciated and were inspired by the pedagogical freedom of the course and by the ability to think and create beyond standard Humanities courses, we found that administrative realities of academic work, coupled with the structure and expectations of working within an academic institutional context, came with immense pressures. If these pressures do not negate the possibilities of democratic academics within the university system, they certainly complicate them in ways that must be admitted and addressed, for we may bracket the long-established regimens of the university environment in the name of alternative pedagogy, but they remain the immediate context for its practice. The pressures of these contexts operate all the more powerfully in their imagined absentia, for how can we come to terms with these conflicts if our celebratory rhetoric denies their existence?

Many of the anxieties that we faced throughout the project were the culmination of the very practical challenges with which we wrestled throughout the project's duration. The more power we located in the stories we were collecting, the more uncertain we became about our editorial decisions as we put the anthology together. If it was true, as we had argued, that personal narratives are among the most powerful aspects of individual and communal identity, on what authority did we assume to be able to collect, collate, and disseminate such narratives? After all, while the members of our editorial team reflected an array of subject positions, we nonetheless each came to the project from our own particular positions. What is more, all but one of us had moved to Guelph at the start of that semester. What does it mean for us to try to "anthologize" Guelph? As Jeffrey R. Di Leo writes in *On Anthologies: Politics and Pedagogy*, the editorial ideal of inclusiveness and comprehensiveness at the heart of many anthologies contrasts strongly with the necessary work of selection, framing, and omission that goes into their production, meaning that anthologies are "always already implicated in various political and cultural agendas" (2). Moreover, critics of anthologies framed by the perceived communities of their authors have rightly worried that in evincing a politics framed by a call for diversity (rather than pluralism),[2] there is the possibility that they ultimately promote a particular narrative of otherness that works to naturalize a partial portrait of diverse communities, indirectly and unintentionally reifying difference and tokenizing their contributors. Was our own anthology replicating these partial and tokenizing politics? We expressed our anxieties on this matter in the anthology's Introduction, in which we conceded its limitations on this front: "We certainly recognize that there are many Guelph voices not represented in this anthology," we wrote, adding that "it would have been impossible to produce an exhaustive portrait of the city" (3). While we were wary of constructing a simplified portrait of the community and passing it off as a full portrait of its complexity, we remained optimistic about the promise of an even-partial disruption of the dominant narratives of city life, and confident in the significance granted to a collective voice in such an anthology.

Conscious of the limitations of the anthology form but invested in its politics of collective action, our editorial work was completed amid the tensions that underlay our project. We were unable to reach a full consensus on our editorial stance on multiple points, for example, and continued throughout the process to wrestle with competing visions of what it meant to "intervene" in the community through an anthology: should we aim to create a platform upon which a variety of Guelph's stories could simply stand beside each other in meaningful juxtaposition, complementing and contradicting each other, or should we seek out only stories that offered a strong counter-narrative to the dominant story of homogenized urban life? In our often lengthy and occasionally heated group meetings – our record was an eighteen-hour editing session filled with tensions both productive and otherwise – we settled into an uneasy agreement to allow the stories to speak for themselves. The politics of this editorial stance, however, were never fully resolved. Several members of the group remained adamant that since a truly neutral frame for personal narratives is impossible, we ought to release any desire we might have for a comprehensive portrait of the community and focus instead on marginalized narratives. Yet from what position would we determine what constituted a "marginalized narrative"? As graduate students, we were keenly aware of the way in which, as Elizabeth Jackson and Ingrid Mündel put it in their chapter in this volume, we were in danger of practicing a "pedagogy of the privileged" in the name of the "oppressed." And how would we ensure that by intervening in the uneven politics of the community, we would not simply replicate or further the inequity? Our solution was to recognize, accept, and foreground our editorial role rather than attempt to efface it, and to invite a critical analysis of the selection's contradictions. Our Introduction to the anthology reminded readers that "some stories are told louder and more often than others, presenting specific experiences and versions of the city as 'normal,' which in turn alienates and undervalues the tellers of other stories" (1). It also drew attention to the differences between narratives, stating that "[w]hile some stories complement each other, many others seem to challenge each other," adding that "[w]e leave it to you to decide how the stories told in this anthology might inform our continued lives in our changing city" (4).

We were also wary of assuming any authority as objective, disinterested organizers of the collection, and attempted to make the process as clear and transparent as possible, acknowledging the limitations of having a community anthology arise from our course and our group while insisting on its value. We constructed an editorial framework that subordinated the loaded notions of aesthetic or literary quality to stress narratives that showed diversity in both form and content, focusing on stories that spoke to living specifically within the city. We reserved the right to decline "hateful" or "discriminatory" stories, adopting our university's document, *Human Rights at the University of Guelph*, as a guide. We wrestled, however, with how we ought to copyedit the work. When collating community narratives, we reasoned, "cleaning up" or "correcting" grammar was a type of whitewashing of difference; we settled – again, rather uneasily – on a practice of correcting only incorrect spelling and some minor punctuation concerns. In several cases, we adhered to external guidelines; one community resource centre, for example, asked that we edit for spelling, but not for grammar. We looked to send our edited stories back to the authors for approval – although given the time constraints, this was only occasionally possible.

These and related editorial concerns made us painfully aware that the *Guelph Speaks!* anthology was to be a partial and thus limited portrayal of the city. However, our own concerns with the project were immediately challenged by the overwhelmingly positive feedback we received from the contributors themselves. Contributors were thankful for the opportunity to share their work and hear from others at the launch; teachers and literacy resource centre staff reported the anthology had been a powerfully affirming experience for many of their students and members. Indeed, although the collection of feedback was regrettably ad hoc and anecdotal, we found that the community members who participated in the project rarely, if ever, expressed anxieties similar to our own; in fact, many expressed great pleasure and excitement about being part of the anthology and having the opportunity to share their stories and experiences publicly. What is more, we came to recognize our halting (and at times painful) editorial work as reflecting the degree to which we were participants, rather than simply practitioners, in the revisionary work of the anthology. Despite our decisions to adopt an inclusive editorial policy and not to foreground strictly "marginalized" voices, we must concede that this approach clashes with both hooks's and Freire's call for unapologetically political engagement. Nonetheless, we continue to believe that our project afforded us not only the opportunity to hear a fuller component of the community's narratives, but also the challenge to think *with* those narratives, to participate in the difficult process of reimagining the politics of our city.

The Challenges and Limitations of Community-Based Education in the Humanities

For the theorists and the texts with which we engaged throughout this course – Thomas King's *The Truth About Stories*, Paulo Freire's *Pedagogy of the Oppressed*, and bell hooks's *Teaching Community* – words and stories have the potential and the power to lead towards liberation. Connected through their humanist backgrounds, King, Freire, and hooks recognize the power of words, and argue that through sharing, telling, and listening to stories, challenges could be made to dominant narratives and the status quo. In addition to recognizing that words and stories have the potential to liberate and transform, both Freire and hooks suggest that educational environments can and should be places where educators and students partake of the struggle for social justice on the grounds that, as hooks writes, "the more [students] expanded their critical consciousness the less likely they were to support ideologies of domination" (hooks, *Teaching Community* 8). While King's study is not as immediately concerned with formal education as are Freire's and hooks's, *The Truth About Stories* is every bit as pedagogical, and, positioned as it was on our reading list, every bit as much a textbook.

Reflecting back on these materials in light of our own work in this course, however, as students who have now engaged in our own community-based educational endeavours, we are reminded that even when the focus of these theorists is directly pedagogical, their works provide little if any instruction or direction for the *students* who are participating in the educational process. The presumed audience of hooks's and Freire's texts – and, importantly, the presumed animators of its practices – are explicitly educators, with the student experience left largely unaddressed. As students and as learners, we were left to read within the texts and between the lines for examples, cautions, and direction in our own approach to community projects and to engaging in community learning initiatives. While hooks writes primarily from a place of teaching, for example, she still explains how teachers and students can create educational environments and moments for freedom within institutional boundaries, in order to create sites of "democratic education" aimed at struggling against social injustices. "In this space where [educators] offered alternative ways of thinking," she argues, "a student could engage in the insurrection of subjugated knowledge. Hence, it was possible to learn liberating ideas in a context that was established to socialize us to accept domination, to accept one's place within race, sex, hierarchy" (2). For hooks, as for Freire, the emphasis and the strategies are aimed at educators interested in changing their pedagogical strategies, rather than at students who are looking to unite academics with community work.

As aspiring academics, we recognized the value that exploring such pedagogical models would have as we prepared to plan and design courses of our own one day. As graduate students, however – as the presumed "objects" of Freire's and hooks's emancipatory and transformative education – we found little in these particular works that took seriously or sought to address the legitimate and often difficult processes entailed in the project of unlearning within an actively resistant larger academic context. That is, we also looked to these texts for a way to engage critically with the community specifically as students, and found a largely decontextualized methodology for educators; students undertaking a course like our own, informed by this critical paradigm, are largely left on their own to negotiate the structures of academia that, while suspended in theory, remain in force beyond the immediate context of the course. Among the various institutional structures that make such coursework difficult, perhaps none is so pressing as the disciplinary norms that structure the abilities and expectations students bring to a course in community-facing research. To be clear, we feel that much of the pedagogical value of undertaking such a course comes precisely from the challenge it presents to students in grappling with the ethical, theoretical, and practical aspects of animating the critical ideals of social justice. At the same time, however, the pressures of a single-semester course clearly limit the scope of such learning, while the demand that such learning be undertaken in the context of a community intervention raises its stakes dramatically. What is more, we found that the process of transformation that lies at the heart of a transformative pedagogy is never neutral, nor is change always inherently positive. To the extent that these models implicitly frame student frustrations as the painful but necessary experience of learning within a "practice of freedom," many of those anxieties and fears are de-legitimized. Even if they *are* the experience of a necessary emancipatory education, such experiences still ought to be recognized and considered. And if such anxieties and frustrations are *not* a necessary component of such an education, is it not possible they are legitimate critiques of such a pedagogical model? Perhaps, then, the most important intervention made by this collection of essays as a whole will be to begin to address what we see as a lack of critical work that is reflective of, and on, the role and experience of the student within the transformative model of community-based experiential learning and community-facing pedagogy.

While some of the concerns above are specific to the theoretical texts through which our community-facing research was framed, others simply reflect the institutional contexts in which such research is commonly undertaken. Our group spent fruitless hours, for example, struggling with the pragmatics of receiving a number grade for community work. In much the same way, we feel that many of our own anxieties surrounding the politics of our anthology – including questions of voice appropriation, editorial authority, and so on – were exposed, rather than created, by the project itself. These challenges are perhaps best understood as the crystallization of the difficult politics that are always already implicit in the theorization of community-based pedagogies, but are often allowed the luxury of remaining unaddressed without the litmus test of practical application. Part of the real value of such work, then, is this placing of the pressure of actualization against the theoretical foundation of Humanities scholarship.

Concluding Thoughts: Community-Based Education in the Humanities

There is no question as to the pedagogical value of our experience with the *Guelph Speaks!* anthology. The course inspired us to use our Humanities backgrounds to engage with the community in meaningful ways in the cause of social justice, even as it served to caution us about undertaking such work lightly in the future. Our experience with a community-facing curriculum has, in many ways, been pivotal in our development as academics; whether to remind us of the importance of looking beyond our discipline and outside the walls of our institution, or to keep us ever-aware of the power inherent in being an instructor (and the ways in which this power can be shared and mediated), or to encourage us to consider both the very real challenges and the deep fulfilment that come with experiential learning opportunities, we left this experience changed in our pedagogical outlook. While each of us hopes to continue to unite our Humanities training with community outreach and educational initiatives, we remain cognizant of the many academic, institutional, theoretical, and practical hurdles that would need to be surmounted should we attempt to do so. Without question, after going through such a course and a process, we are better prepared to undertake such work in the future – and more inspired to provide a similar opportunity for our students to learn within (albeit with some thoughtful adjustments based on our experiences with this course).

Students and instructors undertaking similar projects might benefit from our own experience by taking seriously the considerable pressures that accompany projects entailing significant financial, energy, and time commitments. In a context in which students are left to define and defend the parameters of a community-facing project, we have found it is difficult but necessary to allow such pragmatic concerns to help delimit the shape and scope of the project. The series of project proposals we produced and defended to both our classmates and the panel of community experts were essential steps towards testing the theoretical and practical limitations of our project. We also found that it was worth negotiating institutional and interpersonal expectations early in the project. In our course, this meant creating a detailed rubric for evaluating both the process and product of our project, and creating an editorial framework to guide our efforts. It was during the establishment of this rubric that we first became aware of many of the theoretical and practical challenges we would face throughout the project. Similarly, while the work of creating a guiding editorial framework for our project was difficult, time-consuming, and contentious, it raised key questions early in our process, sped up later processes of selection and review, and helped us distribute the project's labour among group members.

Finally, the very nature of community-engaged work means that it directly affects lives beyond the scope of the academic course. Looking back upon the limitations of our own project, we would suggest that students undertaking similar work might consider setting aside time to follow up on the project's participants after its primary material goals have been met. In the same spirit, it is essential to establish and maintain a positive rapport with local community groups and individuals in order to generate the greatest value for those organizations and people. Good relations are essential to participation in community-based educational initiatives, and are the key to ensuring that what is created is of value to the organizations and/or the individuals with whom the students are working or endeavouring to assist. Indeed, it is essential to accommodate enough flexibility in the project to allow this interaction with community members to test, shape, and, if necessary, rearrange the nature of the project itself. Furthermore, establishing positive relations with the community will facilitate future connections through which to continue to develop mutually meaningful and mutually valuable community-university partnerships. In our own project, the positive experiences of past partnerships facilitated our own efforts, as many of the university and community groups we approached were already familiar with the goals and scope of our course, due to the work of students in earlier iterations of our course.

We would encourage instructors undertaking similar work to draw extensively from the key texts and theorists from disciplines that have been more consistently engaged in community-based curricula. From our own experience, we have found that a Humanities background is not always conducive to preparing students intellectually, theoretically, and practically to engage in community-facing projects. While the challenges of a single-course model will always make it difficult to offer students the extensive theoretical and practical skills necessary to negotiate the particular challenges of such work, a selective engagement with such readings would be extremely useful. In addition, we found it absolutely necessary for instructors to provide ongoing support throughout the entire implementation process, from theoretical framing of community-based experiential education to practical guidance in such matters as mediating group conflict in productive ways to steering students around realistic time-commitments for chosen projects. While it is admirable for instructors to work towards mediating their authority in the classroom in an effort to move away from the "banking model" of education, it is also important that they continue to work from their particular position of power within the classroom. Our own experience makes it clear that instructors implementing community-facing pedagogy can create a more just and equitable learning environment for the students while continuing to guide and intervene when and where necessary; an active facilitating role becomes more important, not less, as students negotiate what will often be an unfamiliar landscape.

We undertook *Guelph Speaks!* in the belief that our individual and collective actions are directly related to how we understand the world and our position within it, and that these "worldviews" are nothing more nor less than stories. To alter, question, or add to these stories, to interrupt the dominant, normalized narrative with other narratives, has the potential to alter world views, and, with them, actions. Having wrestled through this challenge to create and launch a community anthology that became, if only briefly, an important site of speaking, sharing, and listening for a diverse section of the city, we continue to feel, with hooks, that "[p]rogressive education, education as the practice of freedom, enables us to confront feelings of loss and restore our sense of connection. It teaches us how to create community" (xv). As we gathered, edited, anthologized, and made public the stories in the *Guelph Speaks!* anthology, we attempted not only to add to the community of Guelph, but also, in a small way at the same time, to re-imagine the boundaries of the Humanities community. We continue to believe that an anthology like ours, undertaken self-consciously, without effacing one's editorial voice or eliding the significant problems it exposes, is itself an important, albeit limited, step in the struggle for social justice in our community. And we continue to maintain that participating in such community-focused pedagogical experiences offers important opportunities for students and instructors to begin to work together – and with/in the community – to trouble the university/community and instructor/student binaries, and to begin to work towards more emancipatory learning environments and curriculum.

APPENDIX – Guelph Speaks! Re-Storying the City
Table of Contents

Untitled, by Kristin Demchuk
"Diary of a Moon-Man," by Scott Mooney
Two Photographs, by Heather Pfaff
Diptych, by Ariella Orbach and Andres Ibanez
"Sacred Space," by Rowena Gilbert
Photograph, by Bieke Stengos-Cammaert
"Cherries in the Snow," by Pearl Van Geest
"Scarlet Curtain," by Pearl Van Geest
Portrait of Elizabeth Mooney, by Trina Koster

Audio Tracks
"The Cricket" and "Grey Street," by Brad Woods and The Wooden Trio
"The Good Old Days," by Audrey Pilgrim
"Eclipse," by Guillermo 'g.ives' Yupanqui
"Story and Song," by Bogdan 'Bob' Izdebski
"Hold Out Your Hand," by The Speakeasies
"Another Silver Maple Comes Down," by James Gordon

NOTES

1 The alphabetical ordering indicates equal contributions and authorship. We
 gratefully acknowledge the other four creators and editors of the *Guelph
 Speaks!* team – Allison Dean, Julio Diaz, Colin Holland, and Benjamin Walsh –
 for all their hard work, dedication, and contributions to this project. The
 statements and reflections in this chapter, of course, are the authors' alone,
 and do not necessarily reflect the opinions of the larger group. Ashlee, Robert,
 and Paul would also like to gratefully acknowledge that their work on this
 project was undertaken with support from the Social Sciences and Humanities
 Research Council of Canada. Robert and Paul were also supported by the
 TransCanada Institute while undertaking much of this work.
2 bell hooks quotes Judith Simmer-Brown's commentary on the distinction:
 "Diversity suggests the fact of such difference. Pluralism, on the other hand,
 is a response to the fact of diversity. In pluralism, we commit to engage
 with the other person or the other community. Pluralism is a commitment
 to communicate with and relate to the larger world – with a very different
 neighbour, or a distant community" (*Teaching Community* 47).

3 In Action / Inaction: Political Theatre, Social Change, and Challenging Privilege

BRENDAN ARNOTT

Ajay Heble's Literature and Social Change class came at a time when university seemed both ineffective and impractical to this writer. Exorbitant tuition fees and a curriculum relying heavily on depoliticized settler literature of the early 20th century had me questioning the necessity of post-secondary education. At the time I was in the throes of my "anti-authoritarian" period, living in a communal house with thirteen punks, sustaining myself on dumpster-dived vegetables from the green bins behind supermarkets and discarded café muffins. Reading photocopied zines quoting bell hooks and Susan Stryker seemed to me more useful than the drowsy patriotism of Margaret Laurence, and getting into grassroots tenant advocacy and harm-reduction work while serving free vegan meals downtown felt immediately more practical than anything I was doing in my classes.

The political and ideological interests that accompanied an English major seemed to me to be limited to understanding oppression as something to isolate with a highlighter when reading literary texts: once one identified it in essay form, one could move on without assuming any responsibility for creating solutions. Initiatives to relocate education outside of the classroom or to draw connections among community initiatives felt few and far between, which made me sad, disappointed, and jaded.

Before throwing in the towel on academia, I decided to give Ajay's class a chance. It was a decision for which I am thankful, which allowed me to glimpse and participate in some exciting and productive sites of community practice and education intersecting and informing each other. This chapter will explore how experiential learning has informed and complicated my ideas and assumptions about activism, close reading, allyship, and community-facing projects. I also want to touch on the ways in which experiential learning served as a consciousness-raising exercise that demonstrated how easily one's own privilege can be perpetuated in academia.

As part of our work for Literature and Social Change, Ajay challenged us, as he challenged the other students who've written chapters for this book, to move beyond the walls of the classroom, and to activate our knowledge via what he referred to as a "pro-active, community-facing intervention." Not many restrictions or details were provided, though we were given descriptions of the notable accomplishments previous students in this course had achieved. It was a process that was exciting but daunting, and everyone in the room shot each other worried glances as Ajay listed prior student accomplishments. Often, previous projects had taken on a life of their own outside the class, permanently weaving themselves into the fabric of communities. It was an intimidating introduction, but perhaps because of the restrictive nature of the twelve-week project timeline, our randomly chosen group of seven quickly began discussing content.

Simply put, our idea was to adapt a play based on Noam Chomsky's lectures. Confusingly, this piece of political theatre was titled *The Noam Chomsky Lectures* by Daniel Brooks and Guillermo Verdecchia, but it was not, in fact, a lecture. Instead, it was a play addressing the media's portrayal of the Gulf War using simplified and modernized examples of theories taken from Noam Chomsky and Edward S. Herman's groundbreaking book *Manufacturing Consent*. The 1988 text discussed the way in which systemic biases, self-interest, and propaganda all influence the way in which our news is delivered to us. It used local examples to trace how ownership and wealth within centralized media firms, and the dependence of media on government- and business-produced sources of information, inform the way we process and understand the news.

Essentially, *The Noam Chomsky Lectures* is a play about a book about the ways information is manipulated in its presentation to the public. Got it? Because now it gets a bit more confusing. The characters in the play share the same name as the authors and actors, and are totally inseparable from their real-life personalities, judging partly by their lucid, coherent understanding that they are, in fact, in a play. The set is non-existent, and the only prop is a slide projector used to show different news clippings. I felt an immediate affinity for the way in which the script boiled down Chomsky's complex insights into something a bit simpler, often using current events and news clippings to illustrate the theories presented in *Manufacturing Consent*. It was a serious and dev-astating critique of government, media, and big business, yet was able to change tone effortlessly and turn to satire and parody. The actors would routinely criticize their own method of delivery, mockingly declaring that "if the theatre is to survive, it must become something other than an expensive alternative to television!" (Brooks and Verdec-chia 60) This self-reflexivity felt weird and exciting, with the play using *Verfremdungseffekt* (the distancing effect) to make the audience aware that they were in the position of critical observers.

Our adaption also focused on Chomsky's theories, but we shifted the focus from the Gulf War to the Canadian government's interfer-ence with Haitian democracy. More specifically, our work addressed the role that the Canadian government and media played in aiding the overthrow of Haiti's democratically elected president Jean-Bertrand Aristide, simultaneously cutting hundreds of millions of dollars in international aid and encouraging his replacement with the wealthy minority opposition government of Gérard Latortue. The regime's reflection of North American interests resulted in grossly negligent lev-els of civilian oppression, death, and impoverishment, as well as sweat-shop labour wages being kept at a bare minimum.

The graded portion of our project culminated in a free show at the University of Guelph performed for several hundred people, after which Jean Candio, education and community programs minister in Haiti under Aristide and outspoken critic of foreign interference in Haitian politics, spoke. The project resurfaced periodically over the next year-and-a-half. Long after the course had ended, for instance, we participated in the University of Windsor Media Conference's inter-national "20 Years of Propaganda" event, alongside *Democracy Now*'s Amy Goodman and Noam Chomsky himself.

I was taken aback by how easy it was to obtain the rights to adapt *The Noam Chomsky Lectures* until I remembered that the concept boils down to a fairly simple premise: two people sitting around a table talking about politics. After emailing Brooks and Verdecchia with a rough out-line, we were told we had carte blanche with their script. The following weeks involved our group members all contributing a series of rewrites woven together in ten different acts, each around five minutes in length, focusing on intertwining but different topics. Some touched on Haiti's long history of resisting oppression and colonialism, while others para-phrased Chomsky and Herman's discussions in *Manufacturing Consent*, focusing on the ways in which choice of topic, ideological assumptions, biased sources, quoting out of context, and doublespeak affect the way we process the news.

While we were trying to critique and parody the dissemination and manipulation of information in the media, using Haiti as a focal point, our intention was never to parody Haiti's turmoil. Integrating serious political concepts into theatre was the core of this project, but we wanted to maintain a theatrical narrative to prevent it from becoming a dragging monologue, or a series of impersonal facts rattled off while we stood onstage. Thus, we tried to keep things interesting, incorporating everything from slapstick to a Michael Jackson dance routine into the script. Our hope was that such lighter moments would serve as a satirical contrast to and parody of a situation in which we felt depressed, terrified, and exhausted when confronting all the ways in which Haiti has been taken advantage of by self-serving corporate and government interests. Our employment of humour thus served a double purpose: it allowed us to deliver our content in a way that felt empowering and hopeful for us, and it also resulted in a product that was full of political and social messages without being delivered in a monotone behind a podium. Later in this chapter, I'll get into why this approach was, in fact, problematic.

Aside from high school drama productions, I come from a theatrically bereft background. But since *Haiti Held Hostage* followed in the tradition of *The Noam Chomsky Lectures*, the characters were meant to be indistinguishable from ourselves. Even though we had sketched out a number of detailed scripts within which every line of banter was planned out, the idea was ultimately more important than the wording. Because of this, we had the freedom to improvise within our lines and scripted stage directions. We even began the same way that Brooks and Verdecchia had, milling around at centre stage, reading books and scribbling down notes, oblivious to the audience. When the stage lights went up, we covered our eyes and blinked uncomfortably, as if unexpectedly thrust into a performance. Within the first two minutes, my onstage partner was frantically thumbing through notes arranged on a lone desk in the middle of the stage, asking both me and the audience, "Is there even a script?!"

We tried to challenge theatrical assumptions as well as political assumptions throughout the performance, consistently breaking down the fourth wall, asking our audience to stand up, sit down, and give us money while we stood onstage. Though it feels heavy handed in retrospect, we were attempting to draw attention to their condition: they were the passive observers that theatre performances demand while also being constantly reminded of their autonomy. At one point, I stared into our audience, gesturing wildly, demanding that people who were willing to make a difference raise their hands, and I paused afterward to the point of uncomfortable silence. When someone inevitably put his or her hand up, I would reply that it was all part of our performance, that these were all rhetorical questions, and that we were, in fact, not soliciting audience participation. Aside from potentially traumatizing playgoers, we tried to make a point about discourse, social boundaries, and the limits of acceptable speech. In soliciting participation and then actively denying that we were doing so, our aim was to reveal language as a form of social power in which the conversations in which we believe we are being solicited to participate are, in fact, often excluding us. Recognizing that privilege and power factor into whose voices are heard and who has the ability to present themselves as authority figures is an important part of being able critically to interpret the information presented to us in everyday life.

Working from a pseudo-improvisational background made rewrites infinitely easier because we didn't have to perform rote memorization; this helped us internalize the ideas we were talking about as things about which we could actually have a conversation if necessary, rather than a form in which, if our performance deviated from the script, we'd be left stuttering and clueless about where to go. The nature of the play itself incorporated experiential learning as an improvised practice in the sense that the content in every performance was intended to shift and alter itself, mimicking the way in which the political climate and "truth" of situations are also always in a state of flux.

As new articles emerged and changed or reinforced our understanding of situations in Haiti, our content also changed, giving us near-unlimited revisions, but also providing a critical way of understanding our own relationship with the way in which we consume and use media. Putting on a play and living our lives became nearly indistinguishable from each other over the following few months. Reading the news critically became both an everyday practice and a type of homework, and the revision-heavy process of reworking the play produced a script that involved us "acting" as ourselves and weaving our own experiences with social activism into the fibres of the play.

Organizing performances of *Haiti Held Hostage* also broadened our understanding of "accessibility." A strength of political theatre is its ability to deliver content in a package that holds your attention – instead of a three-hour lecture delivered while the speaker is standing still, we hoped to translate the material into a format that's easily understandable for those outside of academia. Given the density of Chomsky and Herman's theories, I myself was grateful that Brooks and Verdecchia had done the work of simplifying and translating the ideas into accessible concepts.

Considering accessibility in our own play sometimes meant, as it did for the students who put on the Access Interventions project described by Elizabeth Jackson and Ingrid Mündel in their chapter in this book, attending to a variety of seemingly minute details. However, those small thoughts led to larger realizations, such as the fact that the text size in our PowerPoint presentation mattered for those with visual impairment, that we needed to provide sign language support at the presentation, and that we needed to offer childcare for the night to parents who wanted to attend. I credit Ajay's class as the site where a lot of those thoughts about accessibility began, but the experience also revealed the insulated nature of our efforts. Though our performances were always constrained to an academic setting, we truly thought we would draw in a cross-section of Guelph's entire community, whose suburbs and apartment complexes stretched far beyond our campus.

Making a space physically accessible is a great starting point, but as university students becoming versed in anti-oppression practices, we were relatively oblivious to the ways in which our self-identity mediated and hindered the way we engaged with our community. Much of this revolved around our own academic privilege, imagining "community" as a homogenous group that we could pluck out of Guelph and use to fill our lecture halls when it was convenient for us. At the time I was oblivious to the large populations of Filipino and Thai migrant workers labouring in Guelph under the Temporary Foreign Worker Program and the Live-in Caregiver Program. I was unaware that many people had left the educational system for a variety of reasons spanning from implicit and explicit racism to persecution for their sexual orientation, and that these people would likely feel uncomfortable stepping back into an academic setting. Presupposing that our audience had the same needs or expectations as the university was a grave misstep.

We chose to end our production the same way that Brooks and Verdecchia did in the original *Noam Chomsky Lectures*, leaving the stage while a passage from Chomsky's *Language and Politics* hovered onscreen and waiting in silence until an audience member called for the house lights to turn on, at which point we would be finished. The hanging silence of the final moment and the need for the audience to participate by signalling the "completion" of the play felt powerful to us at that moment, but afterwards, it also, perhaps, represented some of our project's weaknesses.

Maybe it was because of the limited twelve-week timespan in which we prepared the project (an issue raised by several other chapters in this book), or maybe it was because only one of our group members was involved in a Haiti solidarity organization while the rest of us approached the issue without the foundational knowledge of the issues we were going to be discussing, but one of the biggest failures about *Haiti Held Hostage* seemed to me to be our contentment at engaging with our issue on a superficial level. While it is impossible to summarize a hundred of years of revolution and opposition to colonialism accurately in an hour-long presentation, we seemed to believe organizing some facts about Canadian culpability in Haiti would serve as a life-changing wake-up call for casual observers. We were engaged in something that retrospectively felt more like a curatorial process than a social justice project, in which aligning facts and statistics would move others to take action, thereby absolving us of responsibility – or, if not absolving us of all responsibility, it relegated our own involvement to that of educators. Elsewhere in this book, Elizabeth Jackson and Ingrid Mündel discuss how their project made them aware that they were participating in "a laboratory for hashing out the parameters and limits of engaging a pedagogy of the privileged," and I believe we were unaware of how we had sectioned off our involvement in a sequestered corner of privilege. Ironically, we had internalized and replicated the model that we were engaged in ourselves: we had regurgitated the structure of a university lecture – positing ourselves as authorities, and our audience as a group to be educated.

In her Introduction to *The Noam Chomsky Lectures*, Joyce Nelson states that "our 'knowing together' may change things, but also … it is less painful to know than to not know" (3). I agree with this statement, and don't want to minimize the importance of those who work on consciousness-raising projects. However, our "community engagement" was limited to several presentations in which we shared our work with an audience – there was never a chance to hear the voices of other attendees or implement them in the work. While the script was technically an open-source project that others could reuse, adapt, and recontextualize, we didn't make this information public to those for whom we were performing (save a small group of editors who made stylistic suggestions). But even if we had gone many steps farther, several well-intentioned white folks doing "outreach" (beginning with our so-called community-building and ending with a call for "content submission") still seems quite problematic.

As well, the total time that we spent showcasing our work in front of an audience was relatively short compared to the amount of time we spent researching. Using three months of preparation time for a little over three hours of "community involvement" seems like a relatively seclusionist way of connecting with the people we claimed to want to engage. As I revisit the project and write about it, I become constantly more aware of lingering brash arrogance in our process, what Susanne Dabulskis calls the danger of reducing others to "peoples who require 'help' in telling their stories" (Dabulskis 2), redirecting the focus back to myself as a "white knowledge producer."

Being a white knowledge producer means that my methodology (speaking only for myself here) for approaching a community-facing project comes inscribed with privilege that is internalized to the point where even recognizing it becomes a murky challenge. Junot Diaz recently addressed this idea in a keynote speech at Baltimore's *Facing Race* conference, stating that "the funny thing about our privilege is that we all have a blind spot ... shaped exactly like us. Most of us will identify privileges that we know we could live without. So when it comes time to talk about our privileges, we'll throw shit down like it's an ace. And that shit is a three!"

Whether this privilege manifests itself through the use of resources that are "written, published, funded, produced, assembled, edited, supervised, organized or facilitated" (Dabulskis xiii) by groups that bear no direct connection with the people we were reaching out to, or through viewing Haitian culture as a resource we could tap into when we wanted to identify with a group of people we dubbed "oppressed," it is, I believe, problematic and needs to be taken into critical consideration. An important question we sidestepped in this process was asking ourselves what qualifications we had to speak on this issue: Why did our voices need to enter the discourse, and what potentially silencing discourses may our voices have replicated?

Reading about Dabulskis's approach to the colonial assumptions contained in our idea of "helping" others made me think much more about my own approach to "storytelling," an issue of significant concern to several chapters in this book. Dabulskis says: "I envisioned myself merely as a 'vehicle' for the telling of their stories, thereby declaring my innocence and neutrality, and assuming not only that the telling of their stories would be beneficial and empowering for them, but that as a Euro Canadian … I could 'accurately' tell their stories" (Dabulskis 9) – a concern echoed, albeit in a different context, by the creators of the *Guelph Speaks!* anthology in the previous chapter.

While the stories we were telling were about Canadian politics trying to control and dictate Haitian politics, fighting to keep sweatshop wages low, and contracting out Haitian public services to privatized Canadian corporations, the question of whether our voices were infringing on the autonomous ability of Haitians to tell their own stories remains a grey area for me. Who decides who is authorized to tell stories? Whom do storytellers select as their audience? By inserting ourselves into the narrative of others' oppression, were we shifting the spotlight back onto ourselves?

While the process of writing and performing *Haiti Held Hostage* was a constant negotiation among ourselves, a group of professors, members of Canada Haiti Action Network, and a select group of incredibly patient friends, another area in which we identified opportunities for improvement came from how our project seemed content to move only in circles in which its message was already accepted, if not already actively practiced. People at the University of Windsor Media Conference were interested in our message because it related to the perpetuation of propaganda in the media, and the Canada Haiti Action Network wanted our play because its tone fit an evening of similarly political programming.

This isn't to say that it's ineffectual to reach out to people close to you. I'm sure that we conveyed some things about Chomsky with which many people in those auditoriums and conference rooms weren't completely familiar. But what I lament now is how it all amounted to nothing afterwards: we wiped our brows and felt accomplished because we'd shifted the burden of focus onto the viewer, as if we were saying, "Well, now we've given you the tools – it's your fight to take up!" There is a distance and safety in advocating for open-ended change in Haiti without having to worry about what implementing that change means, physically or theoretically. The open-ended cry for change is important, but working towards effecting that change is infinitely messier.

Elizabeth Jackson and Ingrid Mündel, in their contribution to this book, address the difficulty of characterizing one's pedagogical content when they speak about their own work, stating that

> embodying such a pedagogy is necessarily messy, partial, inadequate, but also provocative and critically engaging … what "we" did through the

class was perhaps both problematic and an inspired example of critical pedagogy in action. And maybe the answer is that we can't, nor should we, prescribe what "such a pedagogy" looks like operationally that it needs to be open and receptive to the particularities of the students/participants, to broader community questions and context, to shifting institutional climates, to current debates in the public sphere.

Though our pedagogy with the *Haiti Held Hostage* project was, at the very least, "open" to the input of anyone in the community who was aware of it, consulting people outside of the spectrum of Haiti-related academia in Guelph would have been a great way to receive more input for our project, and to help determine the opinions of others regarding how we could work towards being useful "vehicles" for these narratives instead of thrusting our own research into the spotlight and congratulating ourselves on "effecting change" without the confirmation of other communities. Though engaging in activism is partially about seeing your choices and decisions linked to the status of others and making the changes necessary to work with those people, we had a responsibility to seek further avenues of community collaboration before stepping onstage. The gut-gnawing nervousness that I felt before each performance might have merely been stage fright, but it might have coursed deeper – we were both physically and discursively putting ourselves in the spotlight, and in the process, excluding others.

I'd like to talk for a bit about the way that Ajay graded his class, because I think it touches on some more of the strengths of his approach to community-based education, as well as more of our group's own weaknesses throughout. When it came to marking, this class integrated self-evaluations and grading contracts initiated by students into the process, and this allowed us to give our own thoughts on our contributions, shortcomings, and hesitations about the project. In addition to adding a degree of self-reflexivity that I was unfamiliar with in English Studies programs, this method prompted a strange honesty and self-criticism. After filling out the evaluation, I spoke to classmates about how they'd scored themselves; everyone admitted to being fairly self-critical. No one gave him- or herself a perfect score or claimed that he or she was faultless in his or her efforts. While doing so would've been pretty self-absorbed (Yes! I win at activism!), I think part of the reason was also due to the way in which our participation in this project complicated the notion of "completion."

Once our project made the jump from a theoretical essay to a living and breathing initiative with which other people interacted, it took on a more obvious inherent incompleteness. With the process of grading ourselves came the acknowledgment that we were in a perpetual state of revising and improving our information, as well as the knowledge that the project was open to criticism or adaptation from a number of sources. A "final draft" of *Haiti Held Hostage* felt impossible because the project now existed in a constantly changing world: revisiting this project years later, I was immediately overwhelmed by how much new information about Canada's relationship with Haiti would need to be included if we were to present the play today.

For students approaching a text such as Brooks and Verdecchia's *The Noam Chomsky Lectures* as a resource for community involvement, some of the questions I've raised so far probably feel daunting, discouraging, or unanswerable, but having a flexible grading system is an important pedagogical step towards engaging and attempting to move beyond these feelings. Engaging with the community will often inevitably mean getting things wrong, stepping back from assumptions you weren't aware that you were making, being open to hearing others' opinions even when they drastically differ from your own, and keeping your goals elastic and flexible. When a curriculum takes these experiences into consideration as valid educational content, there is more incentive to break away from traditional methods of learning.

Ajay's class was a stark contrast to other university-level courses, which felt framed by students frantically moving towards their degree as something quantifiably achievable: a definitive mark on a transcript for grad school, a final stamp of approval, a piece of paper signifying success and finality in our hands.

My post-classroom experiences of activism have provided a contrary viewpoint; there is rarely a sign of "completion" in sight, and friends who've immersed themselves in community mental health, Indigenous solidarity, and anti-G20 protest initiatives are constantly struggling with seemingly insurmountable odds, and there is rarely a point at which the struggles they're undertaking are easily resolved or routinely completed.

Ajay's class felt very different from anything else I was doing in university at the time, and essays required for other classes that lacked community-facing initiatives began to feel slightly less important to me. Advocating for the abolition of homophobia, racism, classism, sexism, and ableism seemed less challenging, perhaps less urgent, when the process of critical analysis could simply end at theorizing, and I felt many times as though it were easy enough to write essays without having to leave the library, both mentally and physically. I began to feel a disconnect from a genre of theoretical writing that could detach itself through what Martha Nussbaum calls a "hip defeatism" that can only highlight why things are wrong, and then finally mention at the end that we should absolutely take some steps to remedy the situation, without giving much more information about how tangibly to work towards a solution.

Another regret about our project is that I have been intensely guilty of embracing the very tactic that Nussbaum describes, and the idea that employing words subversively will form some concrete political resistance. Even writing a paper critiquing my own failures still falls victim to this problem. Or, phrased differently: Does this essay stop becoming a sob story about my own shortcomings and start becoming useful for others who are reading it, others interested in community-based forms of learning and teaching? Is being intensely critical of my own involvement in pedagogical initiatives actually going to help *create* a critical pedagogy? Too often in our play, after addressing inequality, we'd treat it with what Nussbaum might call a "lofty obscurity and disdainful abstractness" that ultimately replaces the need for legislature or social movements because "these symbolic gestures, it is believed, are themselves a form of political resistance" (Nussbaum, "Professor of Parody" 1).

I acknowledge that many scholars have arguably sparked a lot of change through their work. I certainly don't mean to disparage the work of those scholars, nor am I wanting to foster an unnecessary dichotomy between theoretical and practical activism, but my time away from *Haiti Held Hostage* does, I must confess, make me feel somewhat guilty of being a writer dealing in the genre of what Nussbaum criticizes as "mystified symbolism," of, that is, continually moving further into abstraction rather than addressing any semblance of a more concrete political project. Of course, defining a "concrete political project" feels impossible. Ultimately, thinking about the way universities grade us on our experience made me realize how much I had invested in talking theoretically about injustice while remaining hesitant to engage with real-world solutions. It made me realize the necessity of a curriculum that emphasizes the vitally configurable and integrated connections between theory and action. To see our abstractly worded essays as adequate resistance in themselves denies the potential for social movements to accompany them.

Haiti Held Hostage continued for roughly a year-and-a-half after we finished Ajay's class, and, throughout this time, we had a chance to revise and present the play several times in Toronto at small fundraisers for Haiti organized by the Canada Haiti Action Network. A broadcast of our performance went up on a website called Guelph Social Justice, which made it accessible to folks in other areas and also included subtitles. However, a lack of infrastructure eventually plunged our project into disarray. The Guelph Social Justice website eventually lost its domain address, our group members moved on and inevitably split up geographically, and our correspondence became less frequent. We've continued to discuss the future of *Haiti Held Hostage*. In an ideal situation, we would've loved to coordinate a workshop around the content of the play and to source theatrical input and feedback from others, as well as to engage focus groups in a critical evaluation of our content. This would not only have created more of an open-source format for sharing the play when we performed, but also treated the script as just as important as the performance. At the moment, *Haiti Held Hostage*, despite its ability to live on well beyond the frame of the original class assignment, exists in a strange but perhaps not indefinite political limbo. As I was situated in Osaka during much of the time I was writing this chapter, I've removed myself from involvement in the project completely in any performing sense. However, every few months I forward the script to someone else who has expressed interest in revising it, but no concrete plans for continuation are currently active. Still, I remain hopeful that the future of the project might continue to mutate and transform into new things, if only because Brooks and Verdecchia have essentially created a template that can be reproduced with infinite variations.

When Peggy McIntosh tells us that "one who writes about having white privilege must ask, 'Having described it what will I do to lessen or end it?'" (McIntosh 189), she perhaps identifies the core problem with me writing this paper. Having addressed what I see as my own personal shortcomings working on *Haiti Held Hostage*, what good will come of it? Should this chapter exist to urge you to do better than I did, or to push yourself outside of your comfort zone when working on community-facing projects?

Throughout this chapter, I know that I've been contradicting myself quite a bit. I feel critical of what I see as a university-based static approach to social justice and community interaction, yet when a unique project such as Ajay's class provided the possibility to move outside of that traditional framework, our group chose to remain under the wing of academic comfort, which provided us with a crutch of sorts to avoid community-facing interactions. Even with all of the shortcomings I've listed about our project (which is by no means an exhaustive list), Ajay's class helped broaden the possibilities of how academia can interact and integrate with social movements, and for that I am absolutely thankful.

Still, there are many unanswered questions that I am mulling over in the aftermath of this class and my academic career. For example, can you accurately acknowledge privilege when you're in a university structure that's sustained by, and to a degree responsible for, perpetuating class privilege? Even with the generous help of Haiti Action Guelph, the Canada Haiti Action Network, and professors at the University of Guelph, did this project nevertheless descend into a classist attempt at representing a group we defined as "oppressed"? Did our geographical distance from Haiti alone relegate us to the position of advocates for a people for whom we hadn't been asked to advocate? Would the time and energy that I put into *Haiti Held Hostage* have been more effectively allocated to things happening in my own city, in my own community? Would running the free vegan community kitchen space downtown that I mentioned at the beginning of this chapter have ultimately outweighed the benefits of the theoretically based project that we put on? Is there any way to address the contradiction of spending over two thousand dollars a semester and perpetuating class privilege while talking about poverty and human rights violations as if I am doing something helpful for those whose rights have been infringed upon? Is there any way to write a paper on a community-facing project without it feeling unfinished and fractured?

One important step towards addressing these questions is realizing that as university students, we are in a bubble much larger than we realize, and our decisions are more often than not the result of an upbringing that values the interests of the academically well-endowed as of primary importance. And this really is one of the core challenges of a community-facing initiative – to wrestle oneself and one's efforts away from the grips of institutionalized privilege, to use the discursive tools that academia provides in a way that chips away at the tradition of armchair activism that academia often unwittingly perpetuates. Still, there's an underlying incompleteness to both this paper and my own feelings about my participation in it. An experiential learning class offers an excellent panorama of the bridges that need to be mended between the practice of transformative social work and the texts students are reading, and I would advocate for its implementation in universities everywhere until my voice goes hoarse. At the same time, we need to beware of the ways in which our community-facing projects can continue to perpetuate the privilege that being university students undeniably affords us, and while theoretical concepts are a great starting point for knowledge and inspiration, we also need opportunity to take this knowledge and inspiration into our own communities and let them grow there.

Looking back on *Haiti Held Hostage* several years later, I now feel a mix of happiness for having had the opportunity for that unique experience, and (perhaps inevitably) regret and sadness about the shortcomings of our project. I feel embarrassed when my mind plays back images of myself on stage, naively self-assured in my mission at that time. I feel regret for all the communities that our narrow vision of community excluded, and while it did mark a political awakening in the way I looked at how ideas are presented to us in media, I also can't help but feel that it was inadequate in terms of making the leap from theoretical to practical, or concretely improving the condition of the Haitians for whom we advocated in our presentations.

Ajay's project significantly redefined the way I think of social work, community involvement, and activism in my own life, and the lessons I learned through his Literature and Social Change course, while sometimes painful, have informed multiple areas of my life. Now (post-Osaka) as I'm on the cusp of finishing my Masters of Social Work, I find that the lessons I learned all those years ago resonate louder than ever. Seeking out relationships between texts and the world to which they speak, striving to change our roles from those of passive participants to those of active community members, and always questioning, deconstructing, and challenging power remain integral tasks to this day. There is much work to be done in the classroom, but even more outside it.

4 Is This Project "Skin Deep"? Looking Back at a Community-Facing Photo-Art Initiative

GREGORY FENTON

> To speak of beautiful dreams and grand ideals is safe – you could go on forever. But to realize them through action is dangerous.
>
> (Ai Weiwei, "With Regard to Architecture," posted on his Sina blog, January 22, 2006)

On June 22nd, 2010 I set foot on Canadian soil after over three hundred days abroad in the People's Republic of China, the first of two years working as a public school ESL (English as a Second Language) teacher in the city of Tianjin, affectionately referred to by some locals as "the world's biggest village." Within the confines of this bustling, yet, from district to district, disproportionately developed metropolis, I made a journey of self-discovery that involved transplanting my whole notion of self across a great boundary: not the Pacific Ocean, although that is indeed a great and politically significant expanse. I refer here to the challenging transition from student to teacher. For four years prior I had struggled – through debt, essays, exams – to come to some semblance of an idea about pedagogy, my community, and myself. Walter Benjamin wrote, "There is a secret agreement between past generations and the present one" (Benjamin 254), and I had, in my own engagement with society, culture, and history, come to realize that critical pedagogy means setting oneself against the path that has been set out before us and working against the grain.[1]

In his seminal text *Pedagogy of the Oppressed*, another transplanted educator with far more pedagogical experience than I, Paulo Freire, points to a model of liberatory education that is constructed on models of teacher-students and student-teachers and opposes the power binaries of a "banking model" of education. *Pedagogy of the Oppressed* accompanied me in a physical and ideological sense across the Pacific Ocean and into the classrooms of the school in which I taught. While Freire's text carries a canonical significance in my educational work, its material limits became all too apparent as I attempted to form community in my classrooms in Tianjin, and then beyond those walls into the city. As the days passed, I encountered boundaries and borders that fostered intersections of alienation, rediscovery, displacement, and affective turmoil. All of these borders were put into play with the subject constructions of teacher-student and student-teacher. I knew before long that I had moved way outside of the space(s) of the university classroom in which I began to acquire the tools of my pedagogical trade. The hybridity of my subject position as a foreign ESL teacher in China played havoc with my ideas about entering a classroom and working as an educator. I became acutely aware of the politics enunciated by my presence in front of each group of students. At the same time that I articulated my own pedagogy through classroom interactions, the realities of global neoliberal capitalism, the internationalization of education in both West and East, and the politics of race, gender, and class all weighed heavily on much of the dialogue both inside and outside of the classroom. Citizenship and its many modifiers – including, although not limited to, Canadian, Chinese, North American, Western, communist, global, international, *lǎowài*[2] – assumed an unexpected place of prominence in day-to-day work and life in my capacity as a foreign teacher.

But the shifting of language around citizenship, as well as the erecting and falling of borders, was something I had explored before in a much more controlled setting – to be specific, the winter semester of my second year as an undergraduate in 2007. At that time, I had the chance and good fortune to take the second half of a two-part English course with Professor Ajay Heble called "ENGL 2130: Literature and Social Change." We were instructed to do something simultaneously challenging and profound: we were given the assignment of developing a community-facing project that would move the values of social justice and social responsibility from the fruitful work in which we had been engaged in the classroom since the beginning of the fall semester into the community. Several of Professor Heble's previous students were brought into our classroom to entice and inspire us with their stories of community-facing projects from the past; I was equal parts awed and terrified. It should be written in stone somewhere as a reminder for university educators that even the most open-minded and socially aware undergraduates can cower in fear and anxiety in the face of what experiential education can demand. To accept a traditional grading system as the framework for a university classroom; to leave human rights concerns and discussion of the ethics of pedagogy to the interests of campus and community organizations with their significant resources and contacts; to think about my career more than my social responsibilities – all of these things are commonplace, easy, and well-supported by the traditions of the Canadian education system and its emergent corporate values. As I witnessed all too clearly, neoliberal policies and attitudes that students and students' grades serve the greater purpose of enhancing and feeding the free-market system and its apparatuses are in vogue in far too many classrooms in Canada today. I needed to move from what I perceived as accepted (if not acceptable to my own beliefs) and comfortable into something genuinely uncomfortable and unusual.

In some ways, what I perceived then and now to be a radical awareness in Professor Heble's approach is what led me to embrace what Freire terms "libertarian education" (72) and accept the challenge that was posed to me in class to transgress the false borders of the university classroom and choose an approach of love and hope instead. While engaged in the struggle to redefine classroom labour and reposition ourselves as progressive students, we affirmed Sara Ahmed's perspective that "Hope anticipates a happiness to come" (Ahmed 181), a dictum that recognizes the limits of our present and mobilizes unhappiness towards a more just future. At least in the initial planning of our projects the challenge of community-facing education rarely seemed elitist, nor did it seem a task that demanded exclusive literary knowledge, hipster connections, or a lot of money. Professor Heble's instruction was in the category of what Freire terms "an act of love," a pursuit of social justice that "stops regarding the oppressed as an abstract category," and asserts that "[t]rue solidarity is found only in the plenitude of this act of love, in its existentiality, in its praxis" (50); our projects would demand from us a solidarity with community members outside of academic circles and in the broader *community* (a term we were forced to engage with continuously). For our work to succeed in its pursuit of meaningful political action or social justice or egalitarian goals required nothing short of love – love set on a determined path for more equitable tomorrows. Such thinking might seem hyperbolic or, at worst, trite, but this sort of honesty and affective consciousness seemed, to me and to other students in the class, atypical of our prior pedagogical experience – and liberating in its dissent.

For students in this situation, the guidance and support of a creative and open-minded educator is a critical precursor to the leap into the mindset of experiential education. A diversity of talents, political viewpoints, interests, class status, enthusiasm, degree of free time, social standing, identity markers, and social circles must be embraced in a dissonant whole for a classroom – or student project group – to function in solidarity with the community, and, of course, with each other. The acceptance of dissonance in the classroom prevents the creation of hierarchies and homogeneous thinking that can debilitate otherwise ambitious students and the possibility of critical thinking. It was as important for us to "get the authority out of the room" in order to acknowledge the agency we had as student-activists as it was for us to formulate a coalitional, or collective, politics in the classroom, where our first impulse was to strike down the radical individualism that runs through the neoliberal rationale of today's institutes of higher education. By simply working together in a collaborative community-facing project, dissonant viewpoints and all, we were already subverting the structures of power behind the immensely popular and highly individualized discourses of innovation, entrepreneurialism, and self-actualization that too often rob universities of their potential to produce critical knowledge and pursue goals of social justice.

With warmth in the classroom at the start of the winter semester and a fiery hope in our hearts for what our projects could grow into by the semester's close, we formed our groups and began to develop our plans. The assignment required students somehow to include literature – the study of, the interpretation of, the application of – into our work. Accomplishing this feat required a radical perspective on the signifier "literature," and a careful reflection on its symbolic currency. One needed only to turn to *The Economist* to see one example of the growing reach of alternative/non-traditional/non-canonized "literatures" in global culture: an online article posted August 4th, 2010 documented hip-hop mogul and philanthropist Wyclef Jean's intentions to run for President of the Republic of Haiti ("Making a run 'til November"). The article explained that even though Jean possessed questionable ability to speak either French or Creole to the Haitian population in his capacity as leader, "as Leslie Voltaire, Haiti's envoy to the UN, puts it, the world's most famous Haitian '*speaks rap*'" (emphasis mine). With globalization and advances in the usage, proliferation, and availability of technology (particularly Internet technology) redefining the meaning of a "text" while hip-hop and jazz culture make their ways into the annals of academia,[3] the malleable field of literary studies generated a practical and pluralistic praxis for traversing the many gaps between academic discourse and the public sphere. While some might question the logic of traditional disciplinary practices of literature juxtaposed with a course that focuses on community-based/community-facing projects, I argue that the inclusion of conventional forms of literary study encouraged a critical reflection on media, rhetoric, and textuality in an era of neoliberal globalization. The ability to engage critically with a text reflects our ability to engage critically with the rhetoric of public policy, global capitalism, and political discourses as we encounter them through our work as public intellectuals.

The second significant criterion that was presented to us as we began to brainstorm project development ideas was that our criteria for grading were to be designed by our groups at a date prior to the eventual launch of our projects. We were to explain how success could be quantified and then, post-launch, submit rigorous peer reviews. Although our goals, whether in terms of attendance numbers or desired media coverage, would necessarily fall outside the usual boundaries of a 100-point grade scale, the end of the semester would still require our professor to assign grades for our work. There wasn't to be an absence of grading; rather, the process of reaching a final grade was to be atypical of the traditional, banking-model classroom. The great pedagogical theorist and educator bell hooks writes, "Grading has become even more stressful in a world where students determine that they need to make a specific grade to be successful and want to be awarded that grade irrespective of their performance" (*Teaching Community* 16). One of our roles in the experiential learning model was to rethink the process of "making the grade." The "performance" that hooks writes of was exactly what we, as students, were required to qualify, quantify, and then analyze critically as we pushed forward and developed our projects. This focus on "performance" rather than "result" was, frankly, liberating for those of us who reject the typical university semester as either a redundant lead-up to an all-important final examination or an exercise in uncritical regurgitation for periodic instructor evaluation – as in the case of classrooms centred around "teaching to the test"; either way, the shift in formal evaluative structure required an honest and self-critical creative output not usually demanded of undergraduate students, at least not to this degree. Students motivated purely by careerism or a neoliberal drive for that ultimate commodity of scholars, the university degree, were satisfied by the presence of a final mark, while the rest of the class was assured a greater independence and focus on the *process* of the course. And there was no doubt in our minds that we were going to make that process mean something special.

Four other students in the class and I collaborated and came up with a rough outline based on a zany art project I had dreamt up over the winter holiday. Eventually, this project was collectively transformed and translated into something we called *Guelph is Skin Deep*, a photo-art initiative exploring constructions and limits of citizenship in a local context. As University of Guelph undergraduates who, with the exception of one group member, studied in a community away from our hometowns and in a place where all of us were unsure of our status within the larger community of Guelph, we wanted to know, just as the editors of *Guelph Speaks!* did, how and when we qualified as citizens of the city. If not, what prohibited us from "acquiring" full citizenship – the transient nature of being a student, our status as individuals who lived and worked in a community within a community, or our own ambivalence about venturing off campus for any extracurricular work or genuine community participation? At first, our project was meant to be self-serving, even as we worked towards promoting social justice and education through an exploration of citizenship. Our goal in this regard was, at least in part, to avoid the construction of what Donna Haraway refers to as "a conquering gaze from nowhere" (581), a perspective that uncritical researchers all too often embody in order simply to observe a project's subjects from unnamed, unobservable subject positions. The nature of the *Guelph is Skin Deep* project, after all, required a blunt methodology of representation of the individuals involved with our work and of their ideas that we intended to record. Instead of trying to explore questions of citizenship through scientifically objective methods of representing a community, thereby leading to claims of statistical universality, we wanted to make clear from the outset that the voices to surface in our work would be nothing more or less than *some* in *many*. Haraway explains that in order to "become answerable for what we learn and see" we need to offer a representation of "elaborate specificity and difference and the loving care people might take to learn how to see faithfully from another's point of view, even when the other is our own machine" (583). We would not exclude voices that were offered to us, and we would be always and completely transparent about our methodology for selecting project participants; this is one of the mantras that led to the success *Guelph is Skin Deep* ultimately achieved. For an additional take on questions of representation in community-facing work, Elizabeth Jackson and Ingrid Mündel's earlier chapter in this volume speaks to the ethical and political responsibilities of representation as politics and history enter into the classroom when you adopt the role of tellers and re-tellers of others' stories.

In order to explore questions of citizenship, we decided to narrow our exploration to one very simply worded question that would inevitably lead to complex, loaded answers: "Who is a Guelph citizen?" The formulation of this question was actually a time-consuming process, a laborious effort to ensure each of those words was stable enough to procure interesting and provocative answers without setting up too many limits (or ignoring necessary ones); our initial prompt used the interrogative pronoun "what" as part of an admittedly misguided attempt to solicit responses focused more on qualities (engaged, artistic, etc.) than individuals (working poor, refugee, etc.), thus avoiding difficult questions of identity that we were anxious to confront. As we found during the course of our research, our right to explore citizenship was quite eagerly questioned by many members of the community, and rightly so. The project was operated from the safe and privileged position of the university and its apparatuses, and yet, at the end of our deliberations, we decided to proceed with the word "who." Our decision came down to the desire to acknowledge the confrontational nature of discussions about citizenship. Ultimately, we didn't want to operate under the assumption that our own intended goodwill could somehow soften this confrontation. We could not simply assume the transcendence of our own privilege as university researchers and ignore the impact that our positions and identities could have on those responding. We were questioning our own citizenship just as much as any participant in the *Guelph is Skin Deep* project could hope to, and we wanted to ensure that participants could both identify with our intentions and feel comfortable enough to question our subject positions openly as we carried the project through. The spatial signifier "Guelph" outlined the geographical borders of our research; for our purposes, this included people whose time in Guelph was transient, from those holding temporary employment to students like us.

The idea for a photo-art project was moulded to suit our desire to interrogate notions of citizenship, a fusion that crafted a unique voice for the answers of our participants and a vibrant means of expression for the project. We chose to paint the answers that we received on the skin of those who provided them. The use of skin as the message's medium was an attempt to connect the physical body with the words that were being enunciated; a second, related meaning was to connect the physical body with the broad question of citizenship, a subversive commentary on the alienation of and from our bodies in the material relations of contemporary capitalist society. These statements were then photographed with input from project participants, tweaked with digital photo editing software, and printed onto high-quality five-by-seven-inch photo-art papers. The use of photography was linked with the desire to capture these voices in a permanent record, a static exclamation and meditation on the shifting notions of citizenship inside the city of Guelph. The photo editing software – Adobe Photoshop CS3 – was used to crop the photos, administer minor touch-ups (mostly cosmetic adjustments to enhance picture clarity), and render the photographs into black-and-white. The use of black-and-white was not a political decision, but rather a financial one; it was cheaper for us to make black-and-white prints than to print in colour. It was our goal that after we collected and printed all of our photo-art pieces we would be able to distribute them at a public launch event, an occasion that would invite members of the community (and beyond) to collect and take home one or more of the printed *Guelph is Skin Deep* works. All of the printed works would be available for free, our hope being that these ideas on citizenship would infiltrate the community in some way and inspire those who viewed and read them. To complement the messages written on participants' skin, we asked each project participant voluntarily to provide a name and a position within the community (results included "music teacher," "princess," and even "occupationally challenged," among others); if provided, these were added alongside a transcription of the message painted on the skin and a logo we developed for *Guelph is Skin Deep* (all added afterwards by computer). (See the end of this chapter for a sampling of images from the *Guelph is Skin Deep* project.)

Part of my desire to explore citizenship through our work in *Guelph is Skin Deep* stemmed from a concern about the state of human rights at home and abroad, the troublesome nature of rights discourses, and a firm belief that white supremacist and market-centric, neoliberal models of being are held dear at the heart of Canadian society. Within Canada, the recent occurrences of police brutality and the suspension of basic civil liberties during the 2010 G20 summit in Toronto were poignant and fear-inciting truths not only about how the definition and application of citizenship is in flux, but also about how interpretations of citizenship can be disseminated in different ways among individuals of different identities, class statuses, and political ideals. Policies that oppose funding women's rights to abortions in developing countries,[4] eliminate $45 million dollars in funding to arts and culture programs, and introduce censorship in the form of denied funding for so-called controversial film productions[5] are all recent examples of the previous Canadian government's attempts to isolate those expressing ideological dissonance from the hyper-conservative, white-centric, and undemocratic values that have surfaced in the Conservative Party's rhetoric and public policy. Outside of Canada, in the United States, the topic of citizenship is a popular headline in media outlets of all political stripes across the country, particularly with the rise of Donald Trump, but few discussions in recent years have been as terrifying as the implications of Arizona's recent immigration law SB-1070, advocated by that state's previous Republican governor Jan Brewer, which allows police to detain any individual suspected of being in the country illegally.[6] Criticism has abounded, accusing Brewer and the immigration legislation of racial profiling and the privileging of a model of citizenship that is white supremacist at its centre; the law would de facto force people of colour in Arizona to carry identification at all times or face potential prosecution and persecution. By the time this essay is read, it is possible – one hopes – that Bill SB-1070 will have been overturned and buried by the forces of social justice and activism against white-supremacist thought and hateful prejudice. Nevertheless, these discourses that perpetuate hate have become such a commonplace part of Canadian and American life, particularly for people of colour, immigrants, and the poor, that a specific bill passing or dying has little effect on the material realities of citizenship for millions of North Americans.

One of the most salient examples of citizenship, its status in contemporary urban Canadian society, and its relation to skin – a linkage critical to the aims of *Guelph is Skin Deep* – is documented in the fictional account of Dionne Brand's character, Oku, in her Toronto Book Award-winning novel *What We All Long For*. In Brand's book, a keystone now on my bookshelf and a common text in my undergraduate studies at the University of Guelph, where Brand is a professor in the English department, Oku is a young black Torontonian, one of several multiethnic protagonists. A short scene describes him as an eighteen-year-old boy, travelling home in the "quietness of the city" (Brand 164) when he is faced with an unprovoked "perverse fondling" (165), physical inter-rogation by two police officers who stop him for no other reason than, one assumes, his blackness. While the fact of racial profiling by police officers in Canada is not an uncommon narrative, Oku's response to it is startling:

> Two cops came out of the car. He can't remember if they called him, if they told him to stop. His arms rose easily as if reaching for an embrace. One cop reached for him. He can't remember what they said or what they wanted. He only remembered that it was like an accustomed embrace. He yielded his body as if to a lover, and the cop slid into his arms. (164-5)

The "accustomed embrace" of the police poignantly demonstrates the intersection between the significance of race in connotations of Cana-dian citizenship and the dominant discourses of criminal justice, power relations, and biopolitical control in the city of Toronto. Although it may be well-known as one of the most culturally diverse cities in the world, in Toronto (and in the nearby city of Guelph) this label does not exist without opposition and without barriers. This is about more than individual social relations; the relationship between race and citizen-ship is both historically and currently linked to the operations of the dominant capitalist mode of production. David Theo Goldberg sum-mates what this implies for our globalizing environment: "Race is a foundational pillar of modernizing globalization, both shaping and col-oring the structures of modern being and belonging, development and dislocation, state dynamism and social stasis" (Goldberg 330).

Earlier, in *What We All Long For*, Brand describes a TTC subway car on a typical Toronto morning: "Mornings are like that on the subway trains – everyone having left their sovereign houses and apartments and rooms to enter the crossroads of the city … Anonymity is the big lie of a city" (3). Whether this crossroads about which Brand writes is oppositional, as in the case of Oku and the police officers, or positively generative, it was something that I desired to learn more about in rela-tion to myself and my country, having grown up in a small town in southwestern Ontario where I didn't have access to the crossroads of urban Canada and knew so little about it. And why not be fascinated? Within global crossroads, both for teachers working abroad and for those living in urban centres like Toronto, it can be tempting to embrace an anonymity that leads to the sort of hopelessness that was behind our own motivations for *Guelph is Skin Deep*. Paulo Freire writes, "If I do not love the world – if I do not love life – if I do not love people – I cannot enter into dialogue" (90). The opportunity to develop a community-facing project and pursue the positive goals of social justice allowed me, the other group members, and witnesses at the launch event who would hopefully carry the photo-art pieces home with them an opportunity to build our own crossroads at which ideas could enter into dialogue with each other, directed by us but uninhibited, locked down in the physical borders of each photo-art piece but unhinged from the liberal notions of individual moral and political autonomy that constrict the voices of our cities and inhibit our attempts to mobilize collectively.

The gift that emerged from the experiential education of the undergraduate students producing *Guelph is Skin Deep* and the other projects in Ajay Heble's course was dissonance and difference – clear and uninhibited; hostile, resilient, and unforgiving. As in Brand's fictional Toronto, the dissonance in experiential learning environments is a source of creative energy that provides a forum for marginalized voices and ideas based in a coalitional politics of collectivity and heartfelt insistence on establishing democratic public spheres. The colour of our skin, the nationality indicated in our passports, and the political ideologies to which we subscribe – all of these differences and the borders they erect are at constant risk of privatization and depoliticization by neoliberal deployments of tolerance discourse, colour-blind articulations of liberal multiculturalism, and claims to a post-racial society; I argue that these differences and borders of race, class, gender, and nationality need to be reaffirmed and repoliticized in order to recognize our own subject positions and social responsibilities when we proceed to speak to and act towards and with others. This is critical in a community-facing project, when teaching abroad, and when an individual reflects on the meanings of citizenship. The challenge, for us, was simultaneously to engage with and acknowledge these borders while trying to move *among* those that threw up barriers to effective dialogue. This became more difficult as our project began to expose the global nature of conversations about citizenship.

And we do need to recognize that experiential education, by definition, must engage with a globalized world. After my first year of teaching, I was able to feel the pride of seeing my students travel abroad to universities in Canada and Japan, their presence as international students affirmation of the difference between people and the global structures of power that permeate higher education, youth culture, and new paths of global capital. The physical presence of thousands of Chinese students who travel to Western universities (127,628 students came to the United States for the 2009–10 school year) is shifting the dynamics of higher education in the West and foregrounding the engagement with voices and ideas that emerge from different historical, social, cultural, economic, and political points of reference.[7] As a student in a Canadian university, I too often felt as if theorizing about race, class, and globalization failed to acknowledge the physical presence of bodies moving across borders as international students, tourists, and second-language teachers. The fact is that while pedagogical models of experiential education attempt to encourage movement outside of the classroom, that which is outside of the classroom will contrapuntally move inside, particularly from the rising economies of the developing world; more attention, for example, needs to be given in the humanities to the shifting state of higher education globally now that China is officially recognized as the world's second-largest economy (Barboza). What remains at risk in an uncontested discourse of race, citizenship, education, and globalization is perhaps best typified by the barely contained racism and xenophobia of "journalists" like Stephanie Findlay and Nicholas Köhler, who, in their 2009 "Too Asian" article, proclaim that "many white students simply believe that competing with Asians – both Asian Canadians and international students – requires a sacrifice of time and freedom they're not willing to make."

These changing social dynamics are significant for classrooms that use experiential models of education as they attempt to push outwards into the broader social community and simultaneously and necessarily redefine what that community includes. It seems that in the few years that have passed since the inception of *Guelph is Skin Deep* in 2007, it has become more imperative that intellectuals recognize the influence of the rising academic discourses of the developing world and the rising number of international students who join our pedagogical spaces. The exploration of citizenship in our community-facing project was short-sighted on this front. It is the responsibility of future scholars who seek to foster community-facing initiatives in their classrooms to consider more carefully the international networks of the university classroom in terms of student demographics, economic ties, and ideology.

In a recent art installation at the Grand Army Plaza in Manhattan (and in 2013 in Toronto), renowned Chinese artist-dissident Ai Weiwei reconstructed twelve animal heads representing the traditional characters of the Chinese zodiac, bronze representations of which were among items looted by European ransackers of Beijing's Yuanmingyuan (Old

Summer Palace) in the 19th century; most have not been recovered. Much has been made of his choice to display the sculptures in the United States under the shadow of a widespread demand by the Chinese government and its citizens (via the Chinese media and the blogosphere) for stolen Chinese relics to be returned to their homeland. At the same time as this sculpture straddles the issue of national ownership of art and historical artefacts, Ai's own freedom has become the subject of international scrutiny and analysis. Detained on April 3rd, 2011 while attempting to board a plane to Hong Kong at the Beijing International Airport, Ai Weiwei was the "most high-profile detention yet" in what Evan Osnos, long-time Beijing resident and blogger for the *New Yorker*, described at the time as "the Big Chill, an ongoing sweep of Chinese writers, activists, lawyers, and others, which constitutes the most intense crackdown on expression in years" (Osnos, "Detained"). Ai, the foremost example of a mainland Chinese artist who is outspoken about expressing his political views through popular social media outlets, particularly Twitter (despite its censorship in China), also exemplified the power of explorations of citizenship via the skin when he posed for a widely published photograph on the 20th anniversary of the Tiananmen Square Massacre in 2009. In the photo he stands, hands on his hips, with a blue button-up shirt open to proclaim, in large block-letters across his chest, "FUCK";[8] Mao Zedong's portrait on the Gate of Heavenly Peace is clearly visible in the background. The internationalism that has come to characterize Ai's role in contemporary art – *Art Review* recently named him the top artist in its annual "Power 100" rankings of the world's most important art-world figures ("The Power 100") – has a different interpretation depending on where it's discussed.[9] Individuals like Ai Weiwei, who move across borders both real and imagined, force responses to be enunciated in ways that take into account citizenship, nationality, and other political factors, all dependent on our own subject positions. As an example of a site of difference that conflicts with borders and the people within them, Ai's body, both in the photo from Tiananmen Square and as an object detained[10] by the Beijing government, underlines the fact that issues of art and politics are richly complex and in need of an astute understanding of subjectivity and the biopolitical modes of power that regulate the production of subjectivities in increasingly transnational societies. It is this theoretical complexity, and this intersection of the real body and the bodies of theory and art with which intellectuals engage, that informed the methodology of *Guelph is Skin Deep*, and, I believe, must inform the actions of students who take part in models of experiential education. After all, the global nature of Ai Weiwei's role as artist reflects the global nature of citizenship itself in a world in which borders are being drawn, being erased, and shifting continually.

For the *Guelph is Skin Deep* project, we collected responses from politicians, writers, community volunteers, students, and even a priest as our group moved into the community of Guelph. This was painstaking work, and responses were sought in places that varied from participants' homes to a farmers' market. As we attempted to gather responses from the community and represent them in our photo-art pieces, we found that a fog was lifting on a city that was still largely unknown to our group members. A positive aspect of experiential education is the opportunity for students to gain access to the outside community for themselves, a process that removes the strangling sense that school is an island in the centre of a forbidding ocean. However, the degree of access once outside the university varied from student to student. The obstacles to being in the community, even while part of a community-facing project, are partly the result of what I term the *institutionalization of goodwill*, the way in which community outreach projects and charitable causes are delegated and distributed by educators and undergraduate students as a commodity in the education system. Experiential education is hip (not to mention potentially profitable), and its popular aesthetic can sometimes create barriers for well-meaning students who don't move in circles (or occupy the subject positions) that allow access to artists' collectives, volunteer opportunities, and community groups. While the *Guelph is Skin Deep* project certainly provided an opportunity to build partnerships with groups doing positive social work outside of the university, those already in certain circles, or who fit a certain archetype within the broader community, were better able to access these opportunities; in many ways, aspects of experiential education did not privilege everyone equally. I suggest a continued interrogation of *community* that considers the global merging of ideas, cultures, and politics – and the differences that are emphasized by this merging. A goal of experiential education, to go beyond the classroom and learn in conjunction with the world outside, necessitates a release from our own obsession with self and, instead, the embrace of a need to promote the resolution of global concerns that may not affect us directly or may be beyond our ability to comprehend. Experiential education demands the development of questions rather than an expanded terrain upon which we can simply categorize and divide new subjects of our knowledge.

Perhaps by the time our community-facing project reached its climax at a launch event on March 30th, 2007, we had not managed to create something as open and accessible as we would have liked. The shortcomings stemmed from our restricted capacity to give as much work as was needed, our limited access to community resources, and the challenge of creating genuine interest in the project from within the community. No matter how hard we tried to pull together our own "act of love," fissures in the group formed as project members fought over responsibilities and time constraints, deadlines slipped past, and the simple act of billing a "photo-art project" as something that community members should check out on a Friday night proved to be a huge challenge. Probably our biggest exposure for the project came almost by accident, as Thomas King, the award-winning Canadian writer whose work is discussed elsewhere in this volume, prepared to accept a nomination to be the New Democratic Party representative in the 2008 federal election the same night as our launch event. The local newspaper, the *Guelph Mercury*, picked up on the coinciding events and published a short write-up about our launch in an article about the nomination: "If King does secure the NDP nod, one of his first campaign appearances will take place very shortly thereafter. He hopes to attend the launch of the Guelph is Skin Deep project at the Guelph Youth Music Centre on Cardigan Street" (Tracey). Our hopes skyrocketed as the rumour spread, with the assistance of the same newspaper article, that Jack Layton, then leader of the federal NDP, might also attend our launch event after King's nomination meeting. And, indeed, the night of the launch at the Guelph Youth Music Centre, both King and Layton shared the stage with us as we presented the project to the community. In our mind it was a triumph, a coup for the group; however, our jubilation was met by the more significant fact of many empty seats. And that really is the most difficult thing for positive, energetic students in a community-facing project group: the silence that meets your efforts. In the launch speech that I gave that night, I quoted the musician and activist Paul Robeson: "Friends. I am deeply happy to join with you in this appeal for the greatest cause which faces the world today. Like every true artist, I have longed to see my talent contributing in an unmistakably clear manner to the cause of humanity. I feel that tonight I am doing so" (Robeson 118). Robeson was speaking in 1937 of democracy in Spain, but I felt at that moment that the human desire for positive social change that we sought through our project was in sync with his words. In the end, we felt joy at the pursuit of honest ideals as we attempted to enrich our community, and we felt sorrow that we couldn't possibly meet all of our goals and assumptions about success, especially the need to infiltrate the community to a greater degree.

Perhaps 75 or 80 people attended the launch of *Guelph is Skin Deep*. The final photo-art pieces were stunning, as we had hoped, and those who had the chance made an attempt to take home each one of the 37 unique postcards. Word-of-mouth after the launch suggested that people had seen the pictures and were interested in the motivations of the project, with some even making inquiries about spin-offs for new "Skin Deep" projects. Nearly up until the point when I departed to teach abroad, friends and community members from Guelph asked me if there were plans for the project to continue in the future.

But how is success measured in experiential education models? Why does it matter for us to pursue this model of learning? Certainly, we received a fair number grade for the project at the end of the semester, but our peer-reviews tended to be more divisive than instructional. Our launch turnout was lower than expected, but the project evidently survived in the memory of the community after that semester's grades had been calculated. Incalculable, however, was the emotional aftershock of working on a community-facing project, the toll of all that was invested over the course of a semester. Inevitably, groups within a class compare project outcomes with each other, and each member of the group claims responsibility for such a far-reaching project to different degrees. I walked away from *Guelph is Skin Deep* with the sense that I had boldly scratched the surface of a great, but flawed, endeavour. While I had searched for clarity throughout the project in my exploration of that word, *community*, by the end I felt as though the whole experience was a great rush to the head, and I was left disoriented. In fact, my sense (and this echoes a sentiment expressed by contributors of several other chapters in this book) was that the process really was the point, and the outcome was somehow intangible, as if it hadn't really completely concluded.

In this sense, experiential education in the form of *Guelph is Skin Deep* had been a profound awakening of sorts. I wasn't left empty-handed; I had discovered a mode of public engagement that demanded struggle and the pursuit of a greater self-awareness (as well as the strength to relinquish that obsession with self that dominant pedagogies propagate in higher education today). Wherever the project came up short marked an opportunity for learning in the future, and I began to understand the importance of the public intellectual's role: to pose questions about issues of social justice and class struggle, while hoping, against the depoliticizing language of the new corporate mode of higher education, to engage in a meaningful way with political and cultural resistance.

The duty of the student in an experiential learning environment is to encourage and engage in dialogue with our social world, among other things. I remain unconvinced, as I feel is appropriate, that we were able to reconcile the gap between the university classroom and the community outside of it; after all, that task could never be ours alone. In the globalized world, with its classrooms of students who arrive from around the globe and its movement of people both *within* and *beyond* all sorts of borders, the task of reconciling such a gap must be undertaken by those who move *in between* the classroom and the broader community. Another scholar of critical pedagogy, Henry Giroux, explains that as "education turns to training in the public schools, higher education willingly models itself as a business venture, and the wider corporate culture becomes the most powerful pedagogical force in the country, while 'democracy becomes dangerously empty'"[11] (Giroux, *Youth* 65). The act of resistance to this neoliberal conquest of education must not only be a movement unified from within our Western academies – a movement that must overcome the many barriers mentioned in this essay that inhibit student involvement in community-facing projects – but also one that is aware of broader developments in national and transnational milieux. This may include the influence of contemporary artists like Ai Weiwei as they struggle with regimes that "[have] decided to silence him in the most brutal fashion" (Rushdie), or it may simply mean a recognition of broadening alliances in the form of the bodies – students, teachers, writers, tourists[12] – who are living and working *in between* nations. It must also mean concrete alliances with workers, union activists, and social justice organizations.

Discussions of citizenship, the motivation behind *Guelph is Skin Deep*, must be at the heart of experiential education and critical pedagogy. Recognition is due to the fact that almost all – or maybe, indeed, all – of the issues prevalent in the humanities classroom are now global issues, from discussions of race and class to debates of great literatures and philosophies. I walked away from the semester with a sense that my perception of education, my role as a student, and my understanding of community had been radically shaken. But, more importantly, I was able to practice and develop what would become skills that I valued as much as any I had learned before, skills that would continue to inspire and propel me into an ethical way of thinking about work and education: how to fight, to struggle, and to pursue acts of love.

frank valeriote
lawyer
"social justice
integrity
ingenuity"

social justice integrity ingenuity

Guelph is Skin Deep

committed passionate active engaged

jan hall
university professor,
activist and host of
royal city rag cfru
93.3fm tuesdays 7-9am
"committed, passionate,
active, engaged"

Guelph is Skin Deep

james profit
director of ignatius
jesuit centre
"open, socially
ecologically
committed"

Guelph is Skin Deep

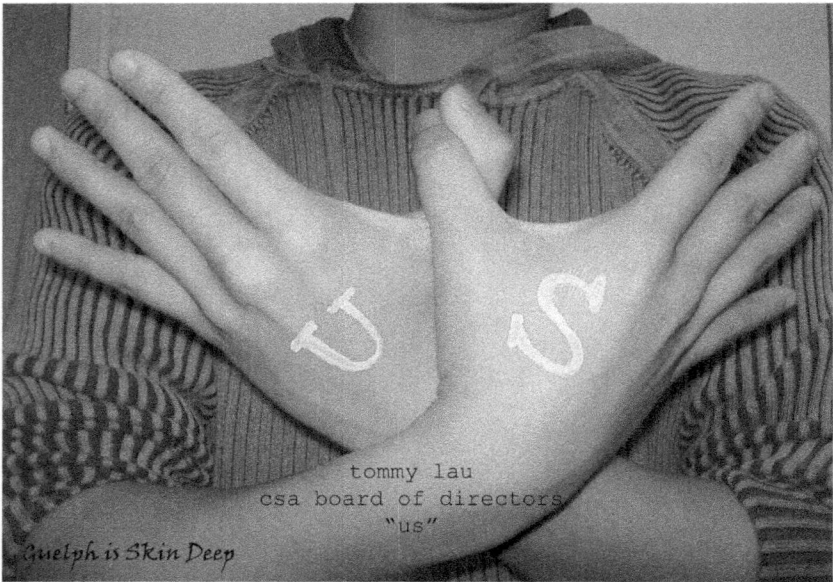

tommy lau
csa board of directors
"us"

Guelph is Skin Deep

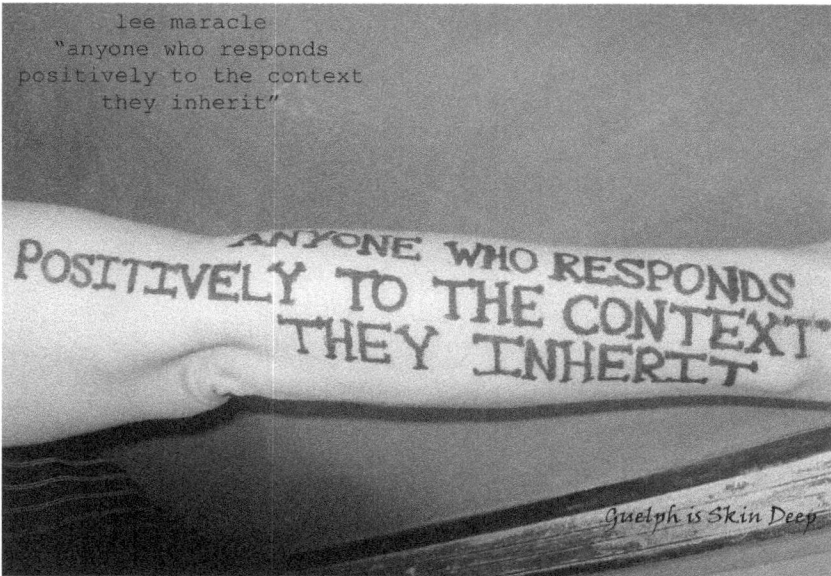

lee maracle
"anyone who responds
positively to the context
they inherit"

Guelph is Skin Deep

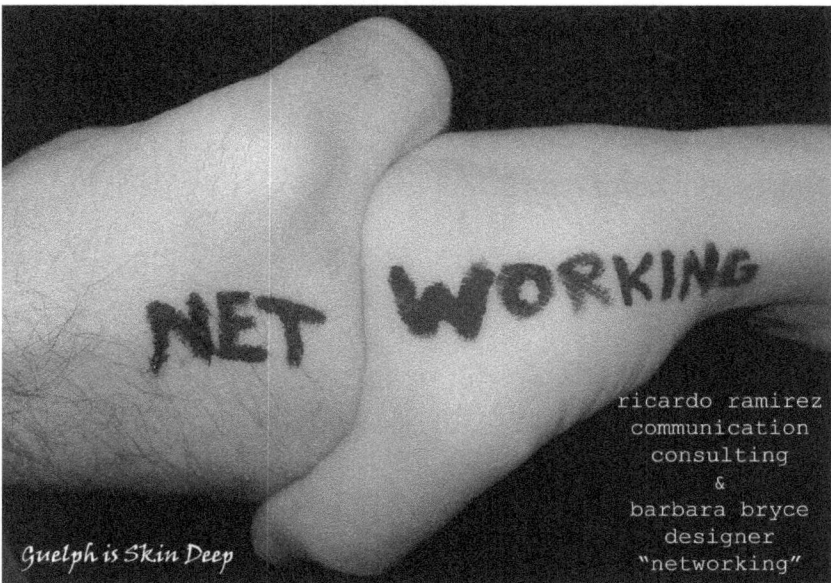

Guelph is Skin Deep

ricardo ramirez
communication
consulting
&
barbara bryce
designer
"networking"

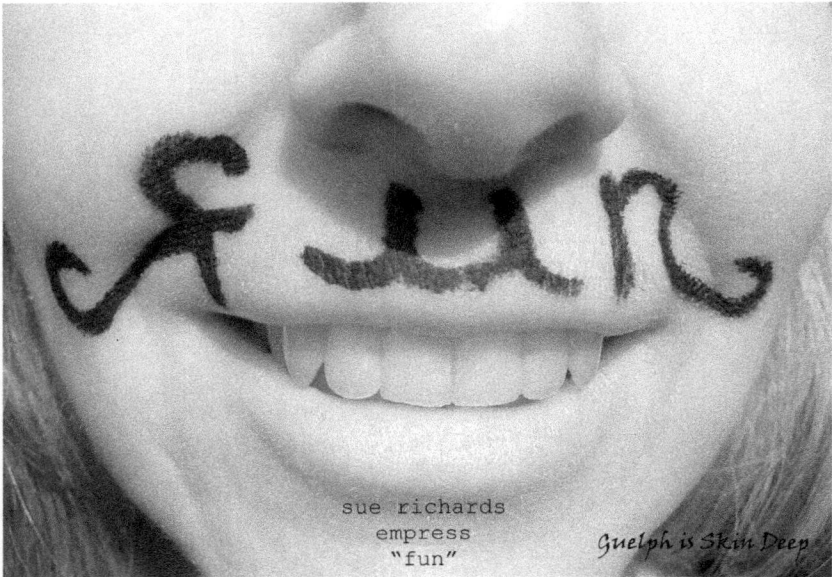

sue richards
empress
"fun"

Guelph is Skin Deep

marva wisdom
community advocate,
volunteer mentor,
liberal
"diversity"

Guelph is Skin Deep

NOTES

1 Most of this paper was written in 2009–2011 while I was working and travelling in East and Southeast Asia. While I am currently working towards a PhD in English, I have (mostly) preserved the state of this paper and its arguments from the time it was originally composed. I believe it is important to capture the sentiments I had in my transient state of international expatriatism as a debt-ridden, geographically displaced recent graduate reflecting on my relation to these ideas on community-facing education.

   While the arguments and reflections presented above are my own and may not reflect the opinions of other group members, the *Guelph Is Skin Deep* project was a collaborative effort that could not have been successful without the hard work and dedication of Katy Butters, Bethany Dekorte, Ryan Porter, and Jen Roberts. I am also grateful for the inspiration of Professor Ajay Heble, whose lessons of hope and perseverance for the cause of social justice have stayed with me from those first undergraduate classes at the University of Guelph to my own job as a teacher in China. Finally, as in all of my endeavours, this never could have been completed without the inspiration and support of my partner, Stephanie Cheung.

2 *Lǎowài* (老外) translates from Chinese to mean, literally, "old foreigner." The term is commonly used to describe individuals of non-Chinese nationalities, although it is primarily directed towards Caucasians.

3 For one example of what undergraduate students can use and are using to study culture, media, politics, and literature through an alternative lens, see Chang.

4 See "No abortion in Canada's G8 Maternal Health Plan."

5 See Benzie, Campion-Smith, and Whittington.

6 See Archibold.

7 For a further analysis of these numbers see Lewin.

8 The original source of this photograph, Ai Weiwei's blog, was shut down by the Chinese government in 2009 and is no longer accessible.

9 For more on Ai Weiwei's disappearance and its broader social implications, see the authoritative *New York Times* Op-Ed by Rushdie.

10 As of May, 2011.

11 Henry Giroux is quoting Sheldon S. Wolin, *Democracy Incorporated: Managed Democracy and the Specter of Inverted Totalitarianism*. Princeton: Princeton UP, 2008. Print. 261.
12 For a recent example of the role of tourism in transcending traditional understandings of borders, see Osnos's "The Grand Tour."

5 Reflections on Dialogic Theatre for Social Change: Co-Creation of *The Other End of the Line*

MAJDI BOU-MATAR, BRENDAN MAIN, MORVERN MCNIE, AND NATALIE ONUŠKA

In a true dialogue, both sides are willing to change. We have to appreciate that truth can be received from the outside of – not only within – our own group ... We have to believe that by engaging in dialogue with another person, we have the possibility of making a change within ourselves ...

> Thich Nhat Hanh (qtd. in hooks,
> *Teaching Community* xv–xvi)

We are all storytellers. We recall, create, and recreate stories through musing, meditation, reflection, imagination, song, dance, poetry, live performance, written documents and spoken word recitals, and day and night dreaming. Whether the stories we tell are drawn from personal experience or from narratives we have heard or received,[1] in sharing these accounts, we become storytellers. Storytelling, as the chapter on *Guelph Speaks!* elsewhere in this volume also makes clear, is a means of communication that occurs in a variety of social contexts, including those that are familial and communal. Moreover, storytelling shapes identities and ideologies, both individual and collective. Each one of us carries stories in our memories and, in certain ways, these stories mark our physical selves. Stories serve as intricate maps: they trace where we came from, stretch back across ancestral histories, root us in the present, and point us towards possible futures.

Stories are alive; they serve as a connective tissue among our family members, our communities, and ourselves. They function as a vital life source, and, like blood, they provide sustenance. They inform, nurture, and sustain identities, and when told with love, they have the profound potential to effect transformative processes, perhaps even small miracles of sorts.

The project we discuss in this chapter, *The Other End of the Line*, is a special kind of story: a live theatrical performance that has now been (re)told several times over. As a play that outlines the difficulties immigrants to Canada face when navigating the Canadian mental health system, it invites audiences to occupy the position of story-receivers and to enter into a larger ongoing dialogue in and with the communities in which they live and work. The processes of the play's creation, realization, and (re)realization gesture towards questions about what live performance can accomplish within an academic conference setting that so-called regular conference papers or conventional academic discourse might not be able to achieve. What are the advantages and disadvantages of disseminating information through live performance? In what ways does live performance invite a more involved response from the audience, and what may result from this?

The creation of *The Other End of the Line* is the outcome of a collaborative partnership between The Centre for Community-Based Research (CCBR) and their participation in a Community University Research Alliance (CURA) project, The MT Space, and a group of graduate students from the University of Guelph in 2006. The authors of this paper were among those students, and we were tasked, as part of our work in Ajay Heble's course "Pedagogy, Human Rights, Critical Activism: Educating for Social Change" (ENGL 6691), with undertaking a project of community-based education, as informed by the current state of critical activism. What follows is an account of some of the key theoretical discussions, practical considerations, and artistic decisions that informed our process. We discuss our intent and perspective in taking on such a project, our responses to specific challenges of craft and collaboration, the criteria by which we would judge its relative successes and shortcomings, and the current and ongoing presence of *The Other End of the Line*, a project that continues actively to live beyond the scope of our class in 2006.

The Start of "The Line"

Professor Heble's class began with a frank discussion of the complex ways in which social change is brought about in the world. In time, we would discuss philosophies of action, bodies of theory, and critical pedagogies, but Heble opened with a series of simple questions regarding activism and change. For example, "Can a book change the world?" There was, of course, considerable room for a discussion of the impact of social writers and a tradition of satire stretching back to antiquity, but one of the marked effects of such questioning was the range of answers it produced from the class: some passionate, some ambivalent, but all representing a breadth of ideologies and aesthetic traditions about the vital role of art in society. In other cases, humanitarian questions were asked: "In what ways do we expect to influence the world through our activism, our critical practice, our research and teaching? In what ways can hegemony be effectively challenged?" Our difficulties in articulating a coherent answer served as further evidence of our unease at the thought of involving ourselves in the pursuit of demonstrable change. It was, after all, uncommon, at least in our own education, to see such emphasis on our own agency, on the practical results and impacts of our learning. In the space of this particular class, we would, indeed, be pushed towards examining the possibilities for turning our learning and skills towards social change, and charting the progress of such an endeavour in the months to come.

With this practical focus in mind, we spent some time with a popular, rather than a conventional, academic text, Catherine Hyde's *Pay It Forward*. This novel was adapted into the 2000 film of the same name, which had recently repopularized the notion of "paying forward," a relatively new phrasing of a very old idea concerning the constant perpetuation of chains of random reciprocity. Rather than take this idea as an ethical parable, however, our class examined its viability as a hypothetical continuing project, and opened up consideration of its perpetuation as well as its ability to exist independently of those who devised it. One major objective for our own project, in fact, would be this very element: How, with limited funds and in a limited span of time, could we produce something that would disseminate itself? And, in approaching such a project, how best could we make an impact? Such a discussion moves away from the utilitarian abstractions of quantified good, towards our own idiosyncratic set of abilities and philosophies. Put simply: Charged with "paying it forward," what would "it" be?

As it turns out, "it" found us. One of the members of our graduate class was Majdi Bou-Matar, director of Kitchener's MT Space, a theatre troupe. The CCBR had contacted MT Space and requested that a short dramatic presentation be performed at a conference entitled "Taking Culture Seriously in Community Mental Health." The conference was to be held at Wilfrid Laurier University in Waterloo, and would bring together research experts, social service providers, cultural leaders and organizers, mental health practitioners, and those affected by mental illness for a discussion of the current state of mental healthcare in Canada. Bou-Matar was comfortable with most aspects of the process, including direction and casting, but was still in need of writers to workshop and solidify the script. As a project involving a social cause, combining the practical aspects of relaying a message with the aesthetic aspects of theatre, and in need of writing and editing skills that we could provide, this initiative was easily voted in as one of the projects a section of our class would tackle.

With our project in hand, we immediately turned our attention to a number of concerns and obstacles. Along with our frank discussion of the minor challenges we would have to solve, there were three major concerns that were most apparent to us, and all of these seemed fundamental enough to upset or invalidate our project before we had even begun.

The first was a question of authorship and craft: How could we represent the experiences of others? More specifically, how could we, as mostly white, middle-class students and academics, produce a document that legitimately spoke about the experiential realm of others: other perspectives, other ontologies, other lives lived? "Stories are wondrous things. And they are dangerous," as Thomas King states (9). Herein was the heart of the problem. If the story – in this case, a live performance – misrepresented those who are mentally ill and racialized, not only would we *not* be helping to bring about positive change, but we would be running the risk of fostering damaging assumptions, and, despite our best intentions, further perpetuate power imbalances. It would be the height of pretension to imagine that we could say something that others could not, or lend some insight into the deep-reaching implications of either an immigrant experience, or an experience with Canada's mental health system. How could we help to produce a finished play without serving as artistic autocrats, dictating what did, or didn't, get expressed in the final version?

Furthermore, feedback from the expert panel that later visited our class to comment on our proposed projects highlighted our own doubts and insecurities. The panel asked: Who are you to undertake this project from your position? Since you have not lived those experiences (of being mentally ill and marginalized racially), how will you act so that you do not stereotype? If there's even a glimmer of stereotyping, we were told, you will be attacked for it.

If the first concern centred around authenticity and power, the second hinged on authority. How were we, as students in the humanities, to produce something valid and insightful to various leaders and professionals in their respective fields? As non-professionals, our own experience with the state of the issue was marginal at best. How could we outline the dimensions of an issue without offering some prescription, some suggestion of the best direction in which to progress? We recognized that this very absence of authority lent us a narratological problem: how best to articulate the emotive aspects of a crisis without trying to contain it, narratively, through a dramatic resolution of some kind.

Finally, there was the matter of craft, and the medium itself. Since we were tasked with the creation of something that could self-perpetuate and mimetically evolve, the conventional bounds of traditional theatre were inadequate. Theatre, more so than other media events, is an art that exists within its time, lacking the broad ability of film and radio to be reproduced and disseminated at will. One performance at one venue would not be enough, if we followed the spirit of our humanitarian challenge. But the alternative – that an identical play be put on in many venues, by many troupes – seemed insufficient, as well. If we were going to turn away from conventional authorship to produce a script that better reflected the experiences of our actors and audiences, it wouldn't suffice to produce a single, unchanging work that would be merely reproduced as occasions saw fit. Rather, we would have to aspire to a play that could be mutable, an alterable document with a living history; one that, like Brooks and Verdecchia's *The Noam Chomsky Lectures* (a play that gave rise to Brendan Arnott's project, discussed elsewhere in this book), might actively encourage further adaptation, and one that relies more upon the improvisational strengths of its actors than on any predetermined narrative arc.

These fundamental challenges to our process each contested an element in the hierarchical relationships present within the creation and reception of art: the relationship between author and finished work, between performed work and audience, and even between a finalized play and its relationship with a larger audience in the world. It is through our approaches to these challenges, as well as through the practical experiences of organizing meetings and incorporating feedback, that we come to this chapter, listing both the occasions on which our process overcame or partially assuaged our concerns, and the areas in which the difficulties of producing and maintaining such a project caused us to fall short, at least from our perspective. We offer comments about the relevant pedagogy and theoretical arguments surrounding such pursuits, and the ways in which we laboured to inform our project with the spirit and values of our original assignment. Finally, we chronicle the unforeseen difficulties, concerns, and obstacles we encountered in setting out on such a project, those that caused us to renegotiate and re-evaluate both our theory and our praxis.

We offer this chapter, then, as a case study, and we note that our project now has some history – that it can be examined, in effect, as an entity in itself. Our methodologies are offered up not so much as a "how-to" lesson that guarantees certain results, but rather as part of an honest discussion of the conflicting forces at work when undertaking such a project, and of the ways in which we approached and negotiated these conflicts. Our bias here is obvious: our authorial involvement in this project means that we have very specific ideas about what we meant to accomplish, and these will, we recognize, fundamentally influence our assumptions about what we find in our analysis of *The Other End of the Line* as a finished (albeit always an in-progress) work.

Putting Theory into Practice

Our graduate course, "Pedagogy, Human Rights, Critical Activism: Educating for Social Change" (ENGL 6691), as Heble's Introduction to this book tells us, explored the United Nations General Assembly's proclamation of 1995 to 2004 as the Decade of Human Rights Education[2] and what this proclamation means for university professors and students. Within this context, the coursework invited students to challenge the ideological boundaries drawn and actualized by institutionalized education;[3] to examine current teaching and learning practices within academia, including curriculum development; and most importantly, to use what transpires within academia to work for positive change in the world in terms of unjust social relations and unequal distributions of power. As students, we were given the opportunity, as expressed in our course outline, "to reflect and act on the connections between academic work and broader struggles for social justice, human rights, and a politics of hope." Thus, one of our main objectives as a group was to enact the marriage of theory and practice; we looked for ways to take theoretical knowledge out of the so-called ivory tower and actualize it in a practical and tangible manner, to concretize it in the real world, and more specifically, in our local community.

The process of constructing our theatre piece, *The Other End of the Line*, was largely informed by the texts we'd been reading in class, in particular *Teaching Community: A Pedagogy of Hope* by bell hooks and *Pedagogy of the Oppressed* by Paulo Freire. The creation of our play was based, via the insights of Freire and hooks, explicitly on a dialogic model. This meant that we, as graduate students, would not go through the conventional process of writing and finalizing a polished copy of the script (to be "the writers," "the narrators") and then deliver this script to our actors to memorize and act. We wanted the play and the process of its creation and development, from inception to delivery, to follow a genuinely dialogic model, one that is, as Freire would have it, *co-creative* in its collaboration. If we wrote the script and had the actors memorize lines we had written, we would be occupying what Freire refers to as the role of the narrating Subject (the conventional teacher) and the actors would become the listening Object (the conventional students) (71). Freire argues that

> [n]arration (with the teacher as narrator) leads the students to memorize mechanically the narrated content. Worse yet, it turns them into "containers," into "receptacles" to be "filled" by the teacher. The more completely she fills the receptacles, the better a teacher she is. The more meekly the receptacles permit themselves to be filled, the better students they are.
>
> Education thus becomes an act of depositing, in which the students are the depositories and the teacher the depositor. Instead of communicating, the teacher issues communiqués and makes deposits which the students patiently receive, memorize, and repeat. This is the "banking" concept of education model. (71–2)

To be clear, we were graduate students involved in a project, not teachers or professors. Yet we would be taking on (or at least approximating) the role of a teacher, one who has knowledge (in this case the script, the narrative) to bestow upon the actors, who would not be acting, but "puppeting" our script with us. The question, then, was how we might move out of these prescribed and institutionalized roles of "teacher" and "student" or "writer" and "actor." If we followed the "banking" model of pedagogy critiqued by Freire, wouldn't we simply be perpetuating an oppressive dynamic by depositing the script into the actors, by, in effect, treating the actors like empty containers to be filled with our knowledge? To do this would oppress the actors and position them as unknowledgeable: "Projecting an absolute ignorance onto others, a characteristic of the ideology of oppression, negates education and knowledge as processes of inquiry ... and the students never discover that they educate the teacher" (Freire 72).

In order to co-create (co-"author") within our group and our community, we followed a process of collaboration and inquiry that emphasized the *co-* in co-creation, allowing parties to exchange knowledge in ways that would be an exercise in agency for all. For certain, maintaining a balance of power was critical in the creation and production of the performance. Dissolving the subject and object position or the conventional oppressor/oppressed opposition was not simply a matter of having the actors co-create the script with our group. This was only one important step in moving forward along the spectrum from oppression to empowerment. Another significant part of the process was having focus groups meet with our team to give us feedback at rehearsals. These responses proved to be extremely valuable and very much informed the final production.

In terms of addressing the problem of how to approach power imbalances, Freire offers something of a solution through his concept of problem-posing education. "In problem-posing education," he writes, "people develop their power to perceive critically *the way they exist* in the world *with which* and *in which* they find themselves; they come to see the world not as a static reality, but as a reality in process, in transformation ... Hence, the teacher-student and the students-teachers reflect simultaneously on themselves and the world without dichotomizing this reflection from action, and establish an authentic form of thought and action" (83, emphasis in original). Freire further explains that problem-posing education "enables teachers and students to become Subjects of the educational process by overcoming authoritarianism and an alienating intellectualism; it also enables people to overcome their false perceptions of reality. The world ... becomes the object of that transforming action by men and women which results in their humanization" (86). Thus, the Object in the anti-dialogic model is humanized and no longer objectified.

Performance and After Life

On December 7, 2006, *The Other End of the Line* was put on stage for the first time. The first performance, as we've indicated, was designed to be part of the "Taking Culture Seriously in Community Mental Health" conference held at Wilfrid Laurier University in Waterloo, Ontario. This conference was part of a five-year Community University Research Alliance (CURA) research project led by the CCBR in Kitchener. The purpose of the research project was to look at the best ways in which to provide people from culturally diverse backgrounds with community-based mental health support systems, and to study the barriers that prevent racialized and marginalized groups from accessing existing mental health services in Canada.

The room was filled with over 150 delegates, made up of mental health care professionals, social workers, settlement agencies, and multicultural community associations. The space was designed as a traditional large-scale conference setting with a large carpeted room, round tables, small stage, podium, microphone, screen and power point projections. The intention of the conference organizers, as well as the theatre troupe, was to disrupt this institutional setting, and to intervene in the conventional proceedings of the familiar conference model.

Directly after lunch was served, the play started with the sound of an African djembe played live by local drummer Garima Harvey Fletcher, accompanied by Indian classical chants performed by local artist Priyanka Sinha. Five actors rushed through the main doors behind the audience, streaming in multiple directions towards the stage while putting on their white lab coats. The actors occupied the small stage instantly, and for the next twenty minutes, presented a series of vignettes interwoven with movement, dance, drum beats, and high-pitched chants. (See the end of this chapter for two photographs from the performance.) While one could sense the uncompromised attention of the audience as the play commenced, as well as laughter at certain moments, it was difficult to know what the final reception of the piece was going to be. The impact, however, became clear when, as soon as the piece ended, we received an instant and a resounding standing ovation.

On the last day of the conference, participants were asked to fill out a conference evaluation form that included, among other assessment questions about proceedings, a request to "share [their] thoughts on the theatre performance." These comments proved to be a valuable resource in assessing the impact of the performance on its target audience, and to stimulate the next steps for this project. We learned, through audience responses to the evaluation form, that the twenty-minute theatre presentation "captured the true essence of what the conference is about," as one comment explained, and that our play, as another delegate wrote, "nailed the purpose of this research project."

In their comments, people clearly expressed that the presentation was a "great educational experience" and "an important teaching tool for everyone," and that it was "better than an academic presentation." There was also a feeling that the theatre piece had the ability to "connect the audience and the people at an emotional level," and that at the same time it "raised the energy level of participants" and was a "nice change of pace from PowerPoint presentations."

Most importantly, the evaluation forms revealed to us that the performance "needs to be shared with the greater public as [part of an] advocacy/awareness campaign." One comment suggested that the play should tour to "hospitals and medical schools," while another asked "[our] group to go outside of this workshop and educate the community."

Subsequent Performances

Our partners at the Centre for Community Based Research (CCBR) (representatives of the larger Community University Research Alliance partnership) had commissioned this play based on their research. Because of the play's positive reception, the CCBR immediately started looking at ways to expand on the play's success. Together we looked for additional funding sources and opportunities to present the play in new contexts. And before long, the production became an organic part of many other presentations by the CCBR researchers; the play was presented to mental health professionals at smaller conferences in Kitchener, Hamilton and Guelph. As of this writing, the performance continues to thrive, and to resonate with new audiences.

Formalizing Theatre for Social Change

The MT Space is a company that was founded in 2004 in the Kitchener-Waterloo area with a mandate to create, produce, and present theatre that draws upon, reflects, and ultimately assists in building Canadian contemporary community. MT Space artists have always emphasized theatre as a community-building tool. The company was created in response to professional immigrant artists' need for a space to practice their profession in Canada. The company allows immigrant artists a space in which to engage in theatre activity, interact with their Canadian peers, and integrate themselves into this virtual community of artists that constitutes part of the cultural landscape of Kitchener-Waterloo, and, eventually, into the wider community.

The MT Space's main activity, however, is focused on creating new theatre productions using a long creation process and extended local run of performances, while touring occasionally when the opportunity arises. While such productions have achieved various results and produced significant kinds of cultural work for the community, they have tended to be confined within the limits of the traditional theatre space and experience. For the most part, they have attracted those who are interested in watching a live performance and are willing to make the effort to come out to see a play.

The MT Space produced *Seasons of Immigration* in 2005, a full-fledged production about the immigrant experience, and this production attracted a lot of attention, triggering discussions about the importance of theatre in settlement programs and diversity training (the City of Kitchener went as far as commissioning one performance for their staff as a training tool in cultural awareness and sensitivity). However, the play was, like any traditional play, presented in a conventional theatre setting, with seats and lights, and of course with all the inherited assumptions of power built into such an experience.

The Other End of the Line project, on the other hand, allowed the MT Space team to realize the extent to which theatre may be even more socially engaging and effective if it succeeds in disrupting conventional assumptions about space, and consequently, in subverting the power differentials associated with conventional theatrical venues. This, as our experience in ENGL 6691 taught us, can be achieved by creating and presenting issue-specific pieces in collaboration with those who are struggling with such issues, or are most concerned with resolving them.

Drawing on the experience of *The Other End of the Line* at the CURA Conference, the MT Space started looking for a model for creating theatre designed specifically to push forward and to spark social change, a model we knew would entail a process that was different from, and more flexible than, that of the main-stage productions we were used to creating. This model built on our consideration of the ways in which the CURA event was organized, and took into account our reflections about how research findings about cultural diversity in community mental health, in effect, gave us the very topic and focus of our play. The key stakeholders gathered at the CURA event provided us with a sense of urgency to move forward with our theatrical interpretations of this issue. The material for our creation was, in short, provided by the conference resources and research findings. Researchers and community leaders from different cultural communities that were subjects of the CURA study were engaged in the act of creation from the very outset. Focus groups met with our team prior to starting the workshop, and also attended rehearsals at which they provided valuable feedback that directly informed the final production. Hence, the play built its "engaged" audience and pre-set the conditions for its success at the early stages of its development.

We were also aware that such plays need to be much shorter in length than our usual theatre presentations: 15 to 20 minutes as opposed to the more standard 60 to 75 minutes for our main-stage productions. The shorter length allows the play to be inserted productively and purposefully into the dense agenda of existing events, and allows time also for discussion and reflection on the show immediately after it has been performed.

Moreover, we felt that such productions should have the capacity to be presented anywhere, without any specific spatial needs or technical requirements. Therefore, the plays have to depend solely on the performers' bodies and voices, with minimal need for set elements and props, and with no need at all for stage lighting. We wanted to create plays that could easily be performed for people at conferences, annual general meetings, community forums, and town hall gatherings in order to intervene in proceedings, stimulate discussions, and influence deliberations. And, since people in such forums are already engaged in discussion of specific topics that are of social relevance and urgency to them, the presentation of such theatrical works hits home and complements what they are already trying to achieve. With all these ideas in place came the MT Space's new, aptly titled program, Theatre for Social Change.

Theatre for Social Change was, as we've been suggesting, created by The MT Space as a result of *The Other End of Line*'s success. It is designed to allow for the commissioning of issue-specific short plays by those who are looking for new and creative ways to raise specific questions, discuss certain topics, or present their research findings. Partnerships with social service organizations, settlement agencies, and social interest groups were sought. The program gained quick exposure and generated significant interest.

Ontario Council of Agencies Serving Immigrants (OCASI)

The Ontario Council of Agencies Serving Immigrants (OCASI) is one of the largest organizations that has invited our Theatre for Social Change productions to participate on an annual basis. The Toronto-based charity represents the "collective voice" of its 200 members. Its membership is comprised of agencies from across Ontario that provide services for newcomers to Canada. OCASI's mission "is to achieve equality, access and full participation for immigrants and refugees in every aspect of Canadian life." At its biannual Professional Development Conferences, OCASI brings together staff from its many different member organizations for training and professional development sessions as well as networking and the sharing of new initiatives and programs. These conferences are usually attended by over 300 delegates, representing over 150 different organizations. There couldn't have been a better marketing and outreach tool for us.

The MT Space's first participation in an OCASI Conference was in spring 2009 with a performance of *The Other End of the Line*. Not long after the performance started, we realized that this crowd was the perfect target audience for this kind of work. The audience was culturally diverse, and they were the very people who were totally immersed, in their own lives, in the challenges that the play seeks to address.

The MT Space was invited to perform at the OCASI conferences three more times. Different pieces devised through the Theatre for Social Change program were presented. Most importantly, these conferences have exposed the project to almost all of the agencies that serve immigrants in Ontario, and many of these later invited us to their own events.

Tour: *Leaders Mobilizing Change Workshop and Theatre Series*

On April 1 2009, the CCBR launched a new project titled *Leaders Mobilizing Change Workshop and Theatre Series*. Funded by Citizenship and Immigration Canada, this project planned to tour *The Other End of the Line* to 14 cities across Ontario, accompanied by a training session for mental health practitioners, settlement workers, and cultural minorities aiming at producing a "commitment to organizational change" (CCBR website). The project's core objective was to incite "institutional change by eliminating systematic barriers in the mental health system."

It took a year for the tour to be organized; the theatre troupe was on the road in the spring of 2010. Due to financial and logistical difficulties, the program visited 10 cities (Hamilton, Toronto, Markham, Mississauga, Windsor, London, Ottawa, Sudbury, Kitchener, and Waterloo) instead of the 14 originally planned.

The Other End of the Line II

A few months before *The Other End of Line* went on tour across Ontario, a group of MT Space artists, many of whom were participants in the original production, created *The Other End of the Line II*. This second version was directed and supervised by actress Pam Patel and playwright Gary Kirkham (who helped develop the script), neither of whom was a member of the original ensemble. The play was also commissioned by CCBR, but this time for the closing conference of the CURA project held on December 4, 2009. The objective of the commission was to look at the same issues but from an "opportunities" standpoint rather than just in terms of barriers. While *The Other End of the Line II* served its purpose that day, however, the original play created in 2006 remained the main performance on tour and continued to be offered as part of the Theatre for Social Change program. This, we would suggest, is mainly because theatre as a medium gains its social force and efficacy from presenting problems rather than by offering solutions. It is worth noting, though, that one of the newly created scenes in the second version has permanently been added to the first version of the piece due to its relevance and creativity.

Inspired Performances: *Across the Veil, Volunteering Eh*

Following the same method of creation used for *The Other End of the Line*, and through another commission from the CCBR in partnership with the Somali Canadian Association of Etobicoke, the MT Space created *Across the Veil*. This performance piece was based on research conducted by the CCBR detailing personal incidents of hate crime in Canada as experienced by members of the Somali community of Etobicoke. The play premiered on July 12, 2008 at the Somali-Muslim Hate Crime Summit held at Thistletown Multi-Services Centre in Etobicoke. Using a theatricalized style with movement, live music, and vocals, the play presented a series of vignettes highlighting incidents of hate crimes against those who tend to be marginalized and racialized in a multitude of ways (women, black women, black Muslim women, and black Muslim women wearing hijabs). Also, it looked at relationships between Somali youth and, more specifically, young Somali men and the Toronto police; participants recalled numerous accounts of both obvious and subtle discrimination because of preconceived notions of the "black man" or "Muslim man." On that day, the play received a thunderous standing ovation from a packed audience, which included political dignitaries, the Staff Superintendent of Toronto Police Services, and other distinguished community leaders.

Across the Veil continued its journey to other forums; it was performed at the Multicultural Inter-Agency Group of Peel conference, Bridging the Gap with the Muslim Community, and at the Communities Working Together against Hate Crimes Public Hate Crimes Forum at the University of Waterloo.

Inspired by the process, methodology, and success of *The Other End of the Line, Volunteering Eh* was another play that was brought to fruition. This play was commissioned by the Kitchener-Waterloo Multicultural Centre as part of a larger project funded by the Government of Ontario in order to understand the volunteer practices of newcomer youth to Canada and the challenges they face when volunteering. The project was also set to come up with strategies that would facilitate access for, and deepen the engagement of, newcomer youth in volunteerism.

Both *Across the Veil* and *Volunteering Eh*, alongside *The Other End of the Line*, are still being offered to the community via the MT Space's Theatre for Social Change program, and have been in demand for the five years since the program was originally launched.

An Analysis of Success

What factors contributed to the success of this project? How do we measure success and impact in community-based learning initiatives? We believe the *particularities* of this case indicate the *potential* that exists for those who are interested in creating partnerships that respond to the needs of individual communities.

Most of the challenges we faced were, we feel, addressed and overcome, and the ongoing challenge of how to create an ethical representation that balanced a sharing of information with creative expression was resolved on the day of the performance. The overwhelmingly positive response to our final product indicated that we had, in fact, met this challenge and succeeded.

In this chapter, we have adapted the form of a case study to position ourselves as participant observers. As "case writers," we are able to view our project as a whole, which has led to an assessment of its value. Arguably, an examination of *The Other End of the Line* as a "success" points to its value as a resource for future theatre-based community projects.

The Problem of Omission

Leaving our claims about the success of our project largely intact, we would, however, like to draw attention to a particular omission that raises questions about collaborative work. In outlining this omission, we hope to engage further discussion on university-community partnerships and the goals of collaboration. The CCBR in Kitchener, one of the CURA partners, offered us a mentoring relationship as well as a space in which to hold meetings during the production phase of the performance. Their input, along with that of three representatives from different cultural-linguistic groups who had participated in several focus group sessions, greatly shaped the content of *The Other End of the Line*. Since reaching consensus was a consistent goal for each of these meetings, we believed that we had established a strong collaborative relationship with CCBR, but a perception of our project after the fact has put this into question. On the CCBR website there is a page devoted to the Taking Culture Seriously Research Project, in which *The Other End of the Line* is referred to as being performed and produced by the MT Space; however, the page makes no reference to a group of Masters students from the University of Guelph having helped to produce the play. Is this an unfortunate oversight? Or a technical error? Or does it reveal a particular problem that can arise from collaborative work?

This omission raises a number of questions: What might such an omission signify within the framework of a live performance that attempts to create and open up a space for those who are often marginalized, "unheard," and rendered "voiceless"? In terms of co-creative processes, who was thought to be collaborating with whom? Was the perception that CURA was collaborating with the MT Space but not with us? Were we collaborating with the MT Space and not with CURA? While we see this omission as an oversight rather than an intentional exclusion, it does raise questions about the functioning of hierarchies within collaborative work, and it also emphasizes how varied contributions may be valued differently. As university students who were committed to a dialogic method for collaboration, and as advocates for future university-community partnerships, we leave these points open for further discussion.

Markers of Success

Any analysis of the success of *The Other End of the Line* needs to account for the presence of the MT Space as a collaborative partner. As a theatre space that "exists to explore cultural intersections amongst people, their histories, and their forms of expressions," The MT Space invokes cultural exchanges to create innovative theatrical performances. In response to a visible *lack* in the Canadian theatre community, The MT Space is dedicated to an artistic vision that is more reflective of the experiences of culturally diverse communities. As such, its commitment to culture through an innovative practice was an ideal fit for this particular issue and the goals of the conference. Again, this points to the foundational strength of our project. But even with these ideal conditions for potential success, the challenge of creating an ethical representation of the issue was, as we mentioned earlier, an ongoing and primary concern. To ensure that we did not misrepresent the research, or the voices of the people we would be portraying (health professionals or members of specific cultural-linguistic groups), we initiated the dialogic process we've described in this chapter.

As students, we intended, among other things, to respond to our professor's challenge to put theory into practice. As we've suggested, our engagement with Freire's text developed our understanding of how we might apply dialogic dynamics because of the opportunities they create. The dialogic model was realized not only within the creation of the very performance (between "actors" and "narrators/writers"), but also within the scope of the larger community, as the CURA partnership was responding to a need for dialogue and collaboration between and across diverse communities.

Our meetings and discussions with a representative group of CURA partners – some members of this group were from specific cultural and linguistic communities – helped us to distill a large body of research, and, at the same time, offered us further insight into the emotional registers of particular cultural-linguistic groups. When we were working with actors from diverse cultural backgrounds, exchanging ideas was an integral part of our creative process. The understanding and personal experiences that the actors brought to the issues supported the research, and this confirmed their emotional connection to this project. In effect, this motivated the integrity of their performance. By adopting a dialogic process, we *enacted* collaboration through respectful dialogue and consensual agreement regarding the content of the performance. Yet we discovered that too much dialogue can endanger productivity. After one particularly discussion-focused day during the workshop period with the actors, we realized that we had not given enough consideration to the actual performance, which would be presented at the conference in under two weeks. A new approach to our dialogic practice included specific daily goals, which allowed us to balance discussion with action.

Another factor to consider for future projects is funding. Although many theatre-based community projects do not rely on professional actors, the particular circumstances from which our project evolved made professional actors a requirement rather than an option. We were a group of Masters students working in collaboration with both the MT Space, a professional theatre company, and a CURA project, an existing university-community partnership of 140 partner groups. CURA's original offer to the MT Space (to commission a theatrical performance) ensured sufficient funds to engage a group of professional actors for a month-long period. Although one of our group members is the artistic director of the MT Space, he did not receive payment for directing the show, nor did the rest of us, as producers, receive payment. In our case, it was mutually decided that the actors, as working artists, needed to be paid for their contribution to this project.

Depending on the particulars of any project, funds will be allocated where they are deemed necessary, but having access to funds is almost always a necessity for most community-based projects. What an appropriate context, shared intentions, and sufficient funds provide is a level of confidence that generates enthusiasm for the project and its success. Despite our growing confidence and focused energy, we knew that the greatest indicator of success would be the audience response to our theatrical interpretation of the issue.

Taking the view that we would be *animating* the research, we encouraged a more expressive and less-scripted form of theatre. Although our script features a powerful monologue that relays a personal experience with mental health issues, *The Other End of the Line* purposely includes dance, movement, and humour to develop its metaphorical interpretation. Like Brendan Arnott's theatrical approach, in *Haiti Held Hostage*, to the issue of Canada's interference in Haitian democracy, humour in *The Other End of the Line* "served a double purpose": it not only empowered our actors and extended hope to our audience, it also effectively highlighted the idea of dysfunction within the mental health system. To be sure, such an approach carries potential risks, which must be evaluated and re-evaluated over the course of the production phase; yet humour also creates an opportunity for the audience to experience a deep emotional connection to the issue. When used effectively, metaphor is another tool that opens the space up to innovative thinking. In our case, offering an informed metaphorical understanding gave new meaning to the problem and provided new points of engagement for action. Immediately after the performance at the conference, we were approached by several audience members who expressed an emotional response to our piece. One audience member confessed to having connected on such a deep personal level, she found herself crying during the performance. And for us, as graduate students, this moment speaks not only to the overall "success" of the live performance, but, more specifically, to the success of achieving connection in the community.

We had, to a large extent, overcome what bell hooks cautions against: "One of the dangers we face in our educational systems is the loss of a feeling of community, not just a loss of closeness among those with whom we work ... but also the loss of a feeling of connection and closeness with the world beyond the academy" (*Teaching Community* xv). Those within academe had connected with the larger community and vice versa; as several of the chapters in this book make clear, this is neither an easy nor a common accomplishment in the humanities classroom.

Evidently, from these immediate responses to *The Other End of the Line*, we got a sense of the overall success of the performance. As mentioned previously, to confirm this success, we asked audience members to fill out a short survey to focus their response. We also had the CURA partners and Professor Heble evaluate our project as a whole. Using these written evaluations to measure our success, we quickly developed an understanding of an afterlife emerging for *The Other End of the Line*.

From a single performance at a conference in Waterloo, Ontario to a series of performances at conferences and community events in ten cities across Canada, *The Other End of the Line* has become something of a catalyst for social change. Providing a different access point for engagement with the issue signals a commitment to change that translates as action in process. From using a live, mutable performance as a way to disseminate information to employing a dialogic model in the creation of the script to participating in self and peer-evaluative exercises at the end of our graduate course (rather than being assigned a grade by our professor), we sought to enact the very notion of process over product, process as significant as product, and, ultimately, process *as* product, a notion that, as Elizabeth Jackson and Ingrid Mündel point out in their chapter on "Access Interventions," is so often at the heart of what "really matters" in community-engaged teaching, learning, and scholarship.

As an adaptable production, *The Other End of the Line* represents a form of exchange between communities. Connections made between communities have heightened the potential for further innovation. The emotional resonances of individual communities become the field of meaning that is shared across space. Through an exchange of emotions, we can begin to develop compassionate communities that are quick to respond to dysfunctional systems. In a sense, *The Other End of the Line* fulfils a particular need, one for innovative arts-based practices within our social institutions to meet the demands of cultural diversity across Canada. As such, what *The Other End of the Line* suggests are possibilities for further university-community partnerships and for community-based forms of teaching and learning that combine research with creative expression.

Additional Thoughts and Further Work: Majdi

Community and connection are at the heart of why we do what we do at the MT Space Theatre. That was the spirit that we brought to the performance of *The Other End of Line.* It is the idea of defining or redefining ourselves in a new context, as immigrants, or as sons and daughters of immigrants, as people growing up in a totally different cultural environment from the one we now live in. It is an act of finding community again.

For me, leaving Lebanon and coming to live in another country, Canada, meant leaving behind family, the neighbourhood, the church or the mosque, essentially the community.

When we were working on this project, research and material from focus groups told us that immigrating to a new country was among the greatest sources of stress. One of the major stressors that can contribute to the manifestation of mental illness is the loss of support systems from one's homeland, and what arises as a result may be anxiety, depression, or another condition. In my opinion, in Canada, the mental health system is trying to fill that gap, to take the place of the community of origin.

We, as creators, as people who are working in theatre, are trying to tell our stories, trying to bring forward the voices that need to be heard by policymakers and experts in various fields. That's why people felt this work was genuine. It's not just a theatre piece: it is creating a community through theatre performance; it's bringing people together to talk about an issue.

Furthermore, these issues are urgent and relevant. If something is not dealt with, it will lead to disaster, some kind of explosion, even death. That's where these stories originate from, a sense of urgency. We take that urgency, and we use it to create dialogue. The first act of creating community is creating it in a small circle. In the studio, the stories we tell, and stories from artists, intersect and become one.

Immigration is a stressor, and we are trying to find ourselves in a diasporic experience. When we take the work to the stage, when people are watching the piece, they don't necessarily know what is acted and what is real; for example, performer Miroki Tong's monologue was her own, and dealt with her own experience. In this space, the mental health experts and researchers become participants, and we are all together in the present moment, engaged in creating the experience of telling others about ourselves. The mental health service providers reflect on themselves, and the people facing barriers see themselves, and the actors on stage, the storytellers, and those who were interviewed for the research also see themselves. Thus, everyone is reflected in the present moment, and this is how theatre becomes a collective act of being in a community.

The whole work is not just about teaching or performing theory, it is about defining ourselves and re-discovering ourselves as people. That's the spirit that we brought to the project, and it's a spirit that's absolutely central, as we learned in ENGL 6691, to the dialogic pedagogical processes that need to inform transformative models of community-based education.

Majdi's Story

My childhood was spent in Lebanon; I grew up in the mountains during the Lebanese civil war. I was born in 1974. The civil war started in 1975 and ended in 1989. During my entire childhood, the reality of life was war; we didn't know any other way. The whole purpose of life was to survive, but because we were children, it was like a big game of play-acting: as a child, you don't really feel fear the way adults do.

I have many memories of the shelter, a dark room underground. These shelters were like furnace rooms, and they were thought to be safer than anything above-ground. Each neighbourhood was assigned a shelter to go to during bombing or air raids. For us, as kids, it was entertaining to be together with all the kids in the neighbourhood in one room. There was an American warship on the shores of Beirut in

1984, targeting Palestinian troops and Syrian fighters. We could hear the missiles, deep and faraway. We could hear the missile emerge from its source, and we knew it had left the cannon and was coming. Everyone would hold their breath; everyone, collectively, was suspended in time. The missile would pass over our heads, whistling, and the explosion had a cracking sound. Based on where the sound of the explosion came from, we could estimate the location of the explosion. This came with the experience of years of listening. Sometimes the adults would go outside the shelter and look for the smoke to see where the missile had hit.

We would hear the whistling of the missile and feel relief. And after we heard the massive explosion, we would wonder where it had hit. Whose house? Whose neighbourhood? Who had been killed?

This is the experience that is always present for me when I make theatre. Love and bombs among people. That's the experience I always try to create. The bomb shelter is very similar to the theatre, because people come together and collectively experience suspense, fear, love, and laughter. The more relevant the theatre experience is, the more it is like the experience in the shelter.

In the bomb shelter we were such a close community. We shared everything: clothes, blankets, and food. Sometimes we were there for hours, sometimes for weeks. People became vulnerable. There was interdependence and love. Think of ten families sleeping in a small room for weeks. You interact with everybody, and for me, theatre is very much about this.

When I came to Canada, community relations were not there for me as they were in Lebanon, where my family has been living for generations. In Canada, I tried to recreate this sense of connection. Theatre is a fantastic tool for doing this. It starts with a smaller circle, involving the storytellers and the people who filter their tales through their own experience. Then you share the stories with the wider audience. It happens in a dark, intimate place. The seats, side by side, echo the closeness in a bomb shelter. Theatre is about creating intense, emotional responses, like those responses that happened in the shelter organically. For me, it's creating community.

Additional Thoughts and Further Work: Morvern

One of the practical requirements for my Bachelor of Education was to complete a three-week community placement. I chose to work at a local literacy centre, where I assisted adult learners on the computer and helped them with their English language skills. Some of the learners I worked with had mental health issues, which made their efforts to improve their literacy skills an even greater challenge. Yet they faced this challenge with a steady determination and clear vision of themselves as competent, literate community members. My experience at the literacy centre showed me how important it is for people with mental health issues to overcome their feelings of isolation and how a network of service providers can collaborate to empower individuals who are struggling to improve their lives. Years later, when I spoke to Majdi about the MT Space and the Centre for Community-Based Research's offer to commission a theatre piece focused on cultural diversity, mental health, and issues of accessibility, and his idea of pitching this as a community-facing project for our class, I knew I wanted to be involved.

It was a project that spoke to me on many levels. Until I applied for and got my Canadian citizenship in my late twenties, I had been a landed immigrant. I had also worked with people who dealt with mental health issues, and I strongly believed in the efficacy of theatre for social change. Majdi and I began to think about what this project meant to us as individuals, what human rights issues it addressed, and what it might do for Canadian society. I remember feeling energized by our conversation. I told myself that this project had to be done. It was a chance to intervene, to enter the discussion, to connect and initiate a path for change. For me, it held the excitement of application. Using our knowledge and creativity to connect people on an emotional level, I thought, would have a positive impact on the conference as a whole, its presentation and goals. In my mind, I wanted to believe that our theatre piece would help to end dysfunction within the mental health system and would lead to a system that would be more responsive to the needs of culturally diverse communities. I wanted, in short, to believe that the work I was doing as a graduate student in the humanities classroom could be a vital force for sparking social change in the broader community.

At some point during our process, I began to see how this project connected to other projects I had been involved in. As a graduate student, I was in a different position from that in which I had been as a writer and performer, but working for social change was still my motivation. Even though the risks seemed higher than usual in this project, there are always risks involved in taking a critical look at how we do things;

however, without this perspective, I decided, we risked not being able to change at all.

Initially, I felt unsure of my role in the process: how could I support the director and actors with their physical exploration of the topic? What experience of the intersection of cultural diversity and mental health could I draw on to bring more of my whole self to the project rather than just my academic self? I began thinking about my life as an immigrant to Canada and the friendships I had formed while growing up in Toronto. I realized that children who grow up in a new homeland struggle with their parents about how to act and live. To be sure, this antagonism is not uncommon between parents and children in general, but in immigrant families, parents often expect their children to act as if they had grown up in the original homeland. This is very stressful for children, because it negates their actual experience and forces them to live up to an imagined one. Through my personal reflections, I deepened my emotional commitment to our project. I looked forward to being a part of a university community project that focused on a human rights issue, yet I couldn't shrug off a feeling of danger.

Despite the existence of a body of research that already clearly marked the dysfunction within the Canadian mental health system, we were going to take a "critical" and "active" stance on the issue. We were going to create a piece of theatre to incite social change, and it was going to be presented at a conference for mental health professionals and community members. The danger was that we might get it wrong; we might either offend someone or be seen as mere entertainment. This was an important project. It had to *do* something. It was this pressure that I initially carried with me. I soon realized I had to push aside the fear and focus on our dialogic co-creative process. My work in ENGL 6691, in short, encouraged me to think deeply about collaborative work, shared intentions, and affecting people to motivate positive change. Although that feeling of danger never quite disappeared (I would push it aside, then it would come back), I decided that it was a part of the process; it was a source of energy, a check on risk, and a push for innovation.

Additional Thoughts and Further Work: Natalie

My experience in Ajay's class and involvement in our project, *The Other End of the Line*, inspired me to reflect more fully on the importance and power of stories and storytelling, in all forms, and to think deeply not only about stories that are told, but also those that remain untold, unshared, unheard – even lost. My experience with *The Other End of the Line* led me to explore other stories about health and illness and other personal medical narratives, especially those that focused on individual and collective agency.

In other graduate coursework, I looked at written and visual medical narratives (photographs, comics), and I examined how individuals ("patients") could enact agency by representing, re-signifying, and re-inscribing their own ill bodies through artistic acts. For example, I looked at photographic texts by the American photographer Matuschka, who underwent an unnecessary mastectomy in 1991 at the age of thirty-seven. Post-surgery, she photographed herself, breastless, purposefully using her scarred body as a site of inquiry around the objectification, commodification, and medicalization of the female body contextualized within "the politics of breast cancer." In an interview, Matuschka discusses how her art functions as a form of activism:

In the '90s, women were using their bodies as metaphors to address a variety of issues they were unhappy about. Some of us tried to break through social constructions of "woman as object." In a way, my breast cancer photos challenged an advertising-dominated world that believed only visually perfect bodies are proper subjects for artistic depiction, or appropriate vehicles for emotional and erotic experience. The idealized female body is simultaneously an object of adoration and abuse in our modern, male-defined world. For a long time it was taboo in artistic image-making to show a woman in my condition to the public. Many female artists were putting their diseases and discontent up on the wall before I came on the scene. They were doing it their way … It's just that my exposure was brighter for a period of time. When women use their experiences and their bodies to convey messages about society, they are also creating culture, and should not be viewed only as eternal victims or idealized female images. (qtd. in Petersen)

If Matuschka's self-portraits of her body, post-surgery, are visual medical narratives – that is, visual stories about her experience and her post-surgery self – could her act of self-portraiture also be considered a kind of narrative medicine?

If a medical narrative is a narrative about illness and health, what is narrative medicine? Physician Rita Charon defines narrative medicine as "medicine practiced with the narrative competencies to recognize, absorb, interpret, and be moved by the stories of illness" (262). She

also states that "many of us within medicine and within literary studies have realized the critical importance that writing – autobiography,
memoir, pathography, fiction, personal essay – has developed within
health care. Patients and their families are giving voice to their suffering, finding ways to write of illness and to articulate – and therefore
comprehend – what they endure in sickness. The therapeutic potential of narrative medicine expands when we encourage patients to join
us in writing their own medical charts, for patients are, or should be,
the co-authors and curators of whatever records are kept about them"
(Charon 262). While in graduate school, I also learned of the existence
of the journal *Ars Medica: A Journal of Medicine, The Arts, and Humanities,*
a literary journal focused on the arts and healing as well as the art of
medicine, that reflects Charon's observations about the links between
writing and treatment.

Recently, in thinking about the potential for social change through
storytelling (a topic, as we've seen, of significant concern to many of
the chapters in this book), especially as it applies to health and illness,
I was inspired to begin an online journal, like *Ars Medica*, that focuses
on intersections of medicine and narratives, visual and written, to provide a forum in which people could share their stories of illness and
healing from any perspective (from "patient" to "physician" to friend
to family member). I wanted to create a space in which stories could
be told, shared, heard, recovered and reclaimed, a place to build community and connection. Thus, *Narratio Medicina* came into being (www.
narratiomedicina.wordpress.com). I also wrote and read a short piece,
"Critical Care: The Importance of Narrative Medicine," at Phil Dwyer's
book launch of his non-fiction work, *Conversations on Dying*: "the story
of the end-of-life experience of Larry Librach, a palliative care pioneer
who helped thousands of patients to die well" (Dwyer). Looking back,
then, on my experiences with the creation of our play, *The Other End of
the Line*, I can see just how much I've been changed and inspired by the
work we did as part of Ajay's class, how my current commitments and
ongoing activism are testament to the vital lessons (about the power of
stories, about the importance of community, about dialogic pedagogies)
we learned all those years ago in the classroom and the community.

**Additional Thoughts: Miroki Tong (performer in *The Other End
of the Line*)**

As someone who has personally dealt with the Canadian mental health
system, and with mental health issues since my teens, working on *The*

5.1. A lonely immigrant waits at a bus stop on a cold, windy day and wonders: "What the hell am I doing here?!" Left to right: Badih AbouChakra, Amanda Paixao, Miroki Tong, Nicholas Cumming, Eva Labadi.

Other End of the Line was an opportunity to connect with something that was a part of my life. It was also a relationship that changed over the years as I experienced brutal mental health systems in countries other than Canada, and as I made my own journey towards better mental health.

Working on the project allowed me finally to have my say about everything I went through in my youth. It was a story that I often kept only between my psychologist and myself because of the stigma my culture has regarding people with mental health problems. The freedom gave me the courage to say my piece, and I am thrilled to see how much more exposure mental health issues now have in the community. I see it on billboards, pamphlets, and even recently in the Bell Media "Let's Talk" campaign.

I remember when I started the project, I was still going through a lot of troubles, and I came from a really angry place. After working on the project, and in my later years of performing, I grew as a person. I approached my performance with a greater maturity, and was able

5.2. The mental health system is overwhelmed by phone calls in multiple languages and from individuals of diverse cultural backgrounds. Left to right: Amanda Paixao, Badih AbouChakra, Nicholas Cumming, and Eva Labadi.

to disconnect my personal issues from the messages of the story. The disconnection, I believe, was necessary because, instead of projecting myself upon the audience, I gave the audience the story, and allowed audience members the freedom to express their own emotions, rather than what I thrust upon them.

Sometimes these projects seem small, or sometimes they seem insignificant, but most of the time that is because these projects are the trailblazers for something huge in the future. Hidden issues like mental health are not given a voice until there is that first small peep. Once the seeds have been sown, then the plants bear amazing fruit. It just takes a few years.

NOTES

1 In using "received," we want to emphasize the role of the listener as an active participant in storytelling, one who is potentially changed by the experience of reception.
2 "The World Conference on Human Rights in the Vienna Declaration and Programme of Action (in particular, para. 33 of Section I) stated that human rights education, training, and public information were essential for the promotion and achievement of stable and harmonious relations among communities and for fostering mutual understanding, tolerance and peace. The Conference recommended that States should strive to eradicate illiteracy and should direct education towards the full development of the human personality and the strengthening of respect for human rights and fundamental freedoms. It called on all States and institutions to include human rights, humanitarian law, democracy and rule of law as subjects in the curricula of all learning institutions in formal and non-formal settings." (http://www2.ohchr.org/english/issues/ education/training/decade.htm)
3 Interestingly, this course was offered through the department of English and Theatre Studies but was listed as an interdisciplinary course. Thus, to a certain extent, the course itself pushed the boundaries of what constitutes a graduate "English" course.

Coda: Sign Up Here

AJAY HEBLE

In the published version of *The Noam Chomsky Lectures*, playwrights Daniel Brooks and Guillermo Verdecchia include a series of endnotes that call attention to the ways in which the play itself changed depending on the contexts in which it was produced and received. "In order to give the reader an idea as to how *The Noam Chomsky Lectures* has developed over time," they write, "we offer some alternate readings. Each time we perform the show, we re-write certain sections in order to address current world events, changes in the local cultural scene, and the circumstances of production (the theatre in which we perform, the sponsors of the event, etc.) and, ultimately, the connections between all the above" (67). Now, the use of an academic convention such as endnotes may well seem out of place in the context of a published version of a play. After all, Brooks and Verdecchia go out of their way in the play to insist that *The Noam Chomsky Lectures* isn't some kind of academic paper, but rather part of the popular-theatre genre (67). But the endnotes here work productively to unsettle any orthodox assumptions we might have about the fixity of genres: *Isn't this a play we're supposed to be reading? Or are these really lectures after all?* Moreover, by offering us alternate readings and alternate versions of the production, the endnotes reinforce the claim, made at the play's outset, that *"The Noam Chomsky Lectures* is a perpetual workshop, an unfinished play, a fourth draft, a work in progress" (12). In short, the endnotes signal to us that, rather than a finished production or a fixed and finalized script, the play we are reading is, in fact, an incomplete, unfinished, and (to adapt Mikhail Bakhtin's terminology) unfinalizable text – one that's constantly being rewritten in response to the situations at hand.

In writing this coda, I'm tempted to take my cue from Brooks and Verdecchia's admission of their play's unfinalizability. I'd love to provide readers of this book with my own "alternate readings" that show the many different community-based projects that have emerged from my classes (not just the ones highlighted in the book's five chapters), as well as how these projects were shaped by, and responsive to, the particular situations and circumstances related to their time and place.[1] In some sense, I confess, I can't help but feel that this book on community-based education tells a story whose final chapter can't easily be written. It can't be written because human rights education has to be understood and contextualized as part of a lifelong and ongoing process of change and intervention. It can't be written because, as the contributors themselves suggest, human rights education doesn't simply end when the course is over, when the grades are in. It can't be written because there are so many alternate readings: other projects that have happened, that can happen, that will happen, as well as other perspectives on these cases (from audiences, community partners, the lobbied, and so forth) – and these are projects, and perspectives, that just can't be accounted for here. It can't be written because human rights education (despite the importance, in planning and designing community-facing projects, of working towards a final goal, a finished product) must, at its best, remain emergent, responsive, adaptive, unfixed, and improvisational.

Recall, too, the sustainability challenge I issue to my students: *find ways*, I tell them, *for others to take up the work you've done, find ways to put into place mechanisms that encourage replication of your efforts.* I'd love to track those efforts. Those efforts, after all, form a crucial part of the legacy of this work. They are important stories of impact. And when I reflect on the work that my students (many now working as professors in tenure-track positions, many working in non-academic contexts) are doing in their own classrooms and communities (and how they are training and mentoring their own students in community-based learning initiatives, or, in other ways, broadening the reach and scope of critical, community-based learning), I recognize that there's a kind of ever-expanding nature to this work that can't finally be fixed in the pages of the book you are holding in your hands. That too, I believe, needs to be understood as part of the legacy.[2]

What, then, might it mean to sign up for social change in a university-level classroom? What could (and should) an academic institution committed to community engagement look like, and what implications might this have for how universities formulate teaching and research agendas, for how institutions assess and value particular ways of knowing?

We live in troubled times. It's a time when, as one of the anonymous peer reviewers of an earlier version of the manuscript put it while encouraging me to write this coda, much of the world population seems to have been deemed disposable, when new and more virulent racisms rear their ugly heads as borders are closed or fortified against fleeing bodies, and when the struggles of trans and queer groups globally have raised key questions about limits to the notions of rights in relation to gender. We live in a time when "Black Lives Matter" and "I Can't Breathe" have become urgent rallying cries and part of a widespread conversation about police impunity. It's a time, in short, when the rights and dreams of aggrieved populations across the globe are constantly at risk of being abandoned, despite the ratification of various international declarations, covenants, and treaties. In this context, it can be difficult not to see the limitations of human rights education. Add to this what Deborah Barndt identifies as "the deepening contradiction of increasingly neoliberal market-driven universities that at the same time promote community engagement and knowledge production for autonomy and social justice" (132), and investing energy in pedagogy to pursue a transformative rights-based agenda might seem to make little or no difference in the world. How, then, can our teaching result in improvements in people's lives, in policy changes, in alterations in the distribution of power, in prevention of rights abuses? True, these sorts of changes can (and have) sometimes come about because of the work we do in our classrooms. But perhaps these are not really the most appropriate kinds of questions for us to ask. What I've learned from the projects initiated by my students is that it's better perhaps to explore and encourage pedagogical initiatives that engage with concerns anchored in the real communities in which we live and work. Better to reflect on the power of education to nourish the resources, to unleash the capacity, that will give rise to an informed citizenry. Better to seek to activate knowledge in ways that provide strength and inspiration for social movements. Better to reflect on how community-based learning can help us conceptualize opportunities for change, how it can provide a way to see possible futures more clearly, more vividly, more expansively. Better, in short, to focus on hope and opportunities for change, even as our projects may make apparent the contradictions, compromises, challenges, and accommodations that can accompany what the contributors to this volume acknowledge to be the often messy and complicated work of community-engaged learning. In an essay documenting urgent priorities conditioning the struggle for human rights, Juan Antonio Blanco suggests, "The challenge is to bring together all the wisdom, imagination and hope needed in order to correct in a timely fashion the self-destructive direction of our social history." He continues: "Advocates and activists for human rights ... are often told to resign themselves to the understanding that no other future is possible" (47–8). Pedagogy – and here I draw inspiration, once again, from Sun Ra and his Afro-futurist vision – needs to be insistent in its sounding of other possible futures.

Other possible futures. Alternate readings. Improvised, responsive, community-engaged pedagogy: such principles define a commitment to human rights education animated not only by issues of content (what we teach), but also by questions about how and why we teach. Now more than ever, it seems to me, we must engage in a serious rethinking of our educational practices and priorities. Now, more than ever, we need to loosen the grip of habitualized ways of doing things in the classroom, and to unsettle assumptions about the conventional (and institutionally determined) relationship between students and teachers (what Freire calls the banking concept of pedagogy). Now is the time to recognize how that relationship discourages the active public involvement of citizens. Now is the time to think rigorously about the kinds of strategies that can help foster links between what students learn and do at universities in their classrooms and how they come to understand themselves as engaged citizens in broader communities of involvement. Now is the time, in short, to develop a more robust and newly alert pedagogy that reaches outside the walls of the classroom as traditionally defined, in an effort to foster new institutional possibilities for the development of active and critical citizens. Now is the time to bring the things we, as teachers and students in the academy, know into dialogue with the knowledges that are emerging all around us from people and communities living the lives that happen to be open to them in these troubled times.[3]

What, then, does it mean to sign up for social change in a university-level classroom? It means being able to listen – really listen – to what's going on around us, and to respond accordingly. It means developing a capacity to adapt to unprecedented change. It means working with the situations in which we find ourselves, and doing so in the arenas that are open to us. It means creating sustained, meaningful collaboration between our classrooms and other sites of learning. It means practicing the craft of stewardship: what some of the contributors in this volume rightly identify as the need to set aside time to follow up with a project's participants after its primary material goals have been met. It means working with community partners, building trust, and learning from the internal education endeavours of community groups. It means participating in these partnerships in a spirit of humility, respect, and goodwill. Indeed, if struggles for social change often take as one of their most salient manifestations an allegiance to pedagogical forms that can't readily be scripted, predicted, banked, or accommodated within received, familiar, or habitualized frameworks of assumption, then our success in solving some of the most critical problems we're facing, now and in the future, may well depend on our ability to break out of conventional, recurrent solution patterns – may well depend, in short, on our ability to imagine, to hope, and to improvise. Now is the time for classroom action. Sign up here.

NOTES

1 While most of the projects highlighted in these chapters might appear to emphasize oppositional, rights-based activism as something that needs to be encouraged outside the academic institution (Elizabeth Jackson and Ingrid Mündel's chapter on Access Interventions is, of course, the notable exception, given its explicit focus on questions of education and access), and while the emphasis tends largely to fall (at least in these pages) on broader communities of practice and involvement that are made and negotiated outside the classroom – and, indeed, outside the hierarchies that increasingly manage university affairs – it's worth noting that each time I teach these courses, the projects that emerge are (as, indeed, they should be) very different. I can't and won't inventory them all here (to do so would fill the pages of another book), but I thought that it might be instructive (again, taking my cue, in part, from the endnotes in *The Noam Chomsky Lectures*) to zoom in for a moment on another rights-based project from my class. This one has explicitly taken up questions about how universities themselves are sites of struggles in which students can play important roles. Organized by Chris Cameron, Marc Cameron, Justin Frudd, Brandon Kidd, Megan-Fay Rothschild, and Scott Thomson, this collaborative initiative, entitled Advocates for Responsible Curricula, involved, among other areas of focus, efforts to lobby the newly formed College of Management and Economics at the University of Guelph to consider positioning ethics at the core of its business curriculum. From the project's conception and development through to its planned outcomes, the students involved in this initiative did tremendously impressive work that has, in concrete ways, continued to have a significant and

long-lasting impact in shaping curricular and policy decisions in the college. Particularly worthy of note in this case was how the students were successful in nuancing and contextualizing their work in such a way that it managed not only to forestall any perceived resistance or opposition that might come from those who saw them (as humanities students) as outsiders to the discipline (Business) and to the college (Management and Economics) that was being lobbied, but also to mobilize significant, long-lasting, and widespread support for their efforts. I've singled out this project here because, unlike most of the other initiatives described in this book, it explicitly calls attention to curricular and policy-oriented issues within the academy.

2 See Elizabeth Jackson and Ingrid Mündel's chapter in this volume for details about some of the ways in which other students from the class have continued to be inspired by and committed to the principles of community-based learning in their own classrooms and communities.

3 Thanks to George Lipsitz for the phrasing, which I've adapted from a grant application on which we collaborated.

Webography
Human Rights Education: Resources for Research and Teaching

COMPILED BY RACHEL COLLINS, AJAY HEBLE, CORY LEGASSIC, AND BART VAUTOUR

Activism/Organizing
ActionPA
Campus Activism
Global Youth Action Network
Human Rights Education
    Associates
Protest.Net
Public Citizen
The Ruckus Society
TakingITGlobal
Youth Activism Project

Alternative Media/Media Activism
Adbusters
Alternative Radio
AlterNet
BigMedia.org
ColourLines
The Corporation / Hello Cool
    World Media
Corp Watch
Democracy Now!
Disinformation
The Dominion
Earth First! Journal
Free Speech TV

Indigenous Action Media
InfoShop.Org
The Media Co-op
New Dimensions Radio
New Internationalist
    Magazine
One World
Press Progress
Protest.Net
The Real News Network
Reporters Without Borders
Z Communications

Anarchism
InfoShop.Org
Institute for Anarchist Studies

Animal Rights
Alliance for Animals and the
    Environment
Animal Liberation Front
Animal Welfare Institute
The Jane Goodall Institute
Last Chance for Animals
    (LCA)
People for the Ethical Treatment
    of Animals (PETA)

Sea Shepherd Conservation
Society
Vegan Action

Anti-Racism
The African American Policy
Forum (AAPF)
Black Lives Matter
(#blacklivesmatter)
ColorLines
Do Black Lives Matter? Robin
D. G. Kelley and Fred Moten
in Conversation
National Association for the
Advancement of Colored
People (NAACP)
Radical Women
Say Her Name
(#SayHerName)
TRIBES PROJECT

Corporate Accountability
Business & Human Rights
Resource Centre
The Corporation / Hello Cool
World Media
Corp Watch
International Labor Rights
Forum
The Leap Manifesto
Organic Consumers
Association

Democracy
The Alliance for Democracy
Canadian Centre for Policy
Alternatives
The Center for Responsive
Politics
The Council of Canadians
Democracy Now!

Fair Vote: The Center for
Voting and Democracy
Press Progress
Public Campaign
Public Citizen
Reclaim Democracy!
World Citizen Foundation

Economic Justice
AFL-CIO
Canadian Centre for Policy
Alternatives
Center for Economic and
Social Rights
Center for Social Justice
Economic Policy Institute
Global Exchange
International Forum on
Globalization
Jobs with Justice
Jubilee USA Network
The Leap Manifesto
Oxfam International
Union for Radical Political
Economics
United for a Fair Economy

Education/Critical Pedagogy
The Brecht Forum Archive
Centre for Commercial-Free
Public Education
Citizen Lab
Critical Pedagogy
The Encyclopaedia of Informal
Education
Institute for the Study of
Human Rights
Issues in Freirean
Pedagogy
Pedagogy & Theatre of the
Oppressed

The People's Movement for
  Human Rights Learning
Praxis Peace Institute
Public Citizen's Commercial
  Alert
Radical Teacher

Environmentalism
350.org
Action for Solidarity,
  Environment, Equality,
  and Diversity (A SEED
  Europe)
ActionPA
Alliance for Animals and the
  Environment
Bioneers
Center for Food Safety
The Council for Canadians
Earth First! Journal
Earth Island Institute
Food Not Bombs
Friends of the Earth
  International
Greenpeace International
Institute for Policy Studies
International Rivers
The Jane Goodall Institute
The Leap Manifesto
Native Forest Council
One Earth
Ontario Public Interest
  Research Group
Organic Consumers
  Association
People and Planet
Rainforest Action
  Network
Sierra Club
Worldwatch Institute

Fairness in Media
Organizations
Fairness and Accuracy in
  Reporting (FAIR)
Institute for Public Accuracy
Media Alliance
We Interrupt This Message

Feminism/Women's Issues
Feminist.com
Feminist Majority Foundation
National Organization for
  Women
Office on Violence Against
  Women
Radical Women
Say Her Name
  (#SayHerName)
Teen Talking Circles
Third Wave Fund
Women's Issues
Women Thrive Worldwide

Food & Farming
Center for Food Safety
Corporate Agribusiness
  Research Project
Food First
Food Not Bombs
Institute for Agriculture and
  Trade Policy
Organic Consumers
  Association

Globalization
Global Exchange
International Forum on
  Globalization
Jubilee USA Network
Oxfam International

Human, Labour, & Civil Rights
AFL-CIO
Amnesty International
Business & Human Rights
  Resource Centre
Carnegie Council for Ethics in
  International Affairs
Center for Economic and
  Social Rights
Center for Social Justice
Dignitas International
Ella Baker Center for Human
  Rights
Freemuse
Global Policy Forum
Human Rights Education
  Associates
Human Rights Interactive
  Network
Human Rights Internet
Human Rights Watch
Institute for Global Labour
  and Human Rights
Institute for Policy Studies
Institute for the Study of
  Human Rights
International Labor Rights
  Forum
Jobs with Justice
The Leap Manifesto
National Association for the
  Advancement of Colored
  People (NAACP)
National Network for
  Immigrant and Refugee
  Rights
Office of the High
  Commissioner for Human
  Rights

Pedagogy & Theatre of the
  Oppressed
The People's Movement
  for Human Rights
  Learning
Public Citizen
Social Watch
Union for Radical Political
  Economics
Young Democratic Socialists

Indigenous Rights
Idle No More
Indigenous Action Media
The International Leonard
  Peltier Defense Committee
The Leap Manifesto
Survival International

**Peace, Nonviolence, Anti-War,
& Anti-Militarism**
Fellowship of Reconciliation
Food Not Bombs
Institute for Policy Studies
International Campaign to Ban
  Landmines
Nonviolence International
Praxis Peace Institute
War Child
War Resisters League

Prison Industrial Complex
Critical Resistance
Do Black Lives Matter?
  Robin D. G. Kelley and
  Fred Moten in Conversation
October 22nd Coalition
Prison Activist Resource
  Center (PARC)

Queer Rights
Act Up (AIDS Coalition to Unleash Power)
Egale Canada Human Rights Trust
Gay, Lesbian, & Straight Education Network (GLSEN)
International Lesbian, Gay, Bisexual, Trans, and Intersex Association (ILGA)
Radical Women
YouthLine

Youth Movements & Organizing
ActionPA
Campus Activism
Canadian Federation of Students (CFS)
Global Youth Action Network
Ontario Public Interest Research Group
People and Planet
TakingITGlobal
Teen Talking Circles
Third Wave Fund
TRIBES PROJECT
Young Democratic Socialists
Youth Activism Project
YouthLine

350.org

www.350.org
team@350.org
(518) 635–0350
@350

"350.org is building a global climate movement. Our online campaigns, grassroots organizing, and mass public actions are coordinated by a global network active in over 188 countries.

"The number 350 means climate safety: to preserve a livable planet, scientists tell us we must reduce the amount of $CO2$ in the atmosphere from its current level of 400 parts per million to below 350 ppm.

"We believe that a global grassroots movement can hold our leaders accountable to the realities of science and the principles of justice. That movement is rising from the bottom up all over the world, and is uniting to create the solutions that will ensure a better future for all."

Environmentalism

Action for Solidarity, Environment, Equality, and Diversity (A SEED Europe)

www.aseed.net/en
info@aseed.net
31 20 668 2236 (Netherlands)

"A SEED Europe … is an international campaigning organisation, giving importance to involving youth in direct democracy activities. A SEED Europe targets the structural causes of environmental destruction and social injustice.
"We do this by campaigning on multinational corporations and their national and international influence spheres and control tools. At the same time we promote sustainable alternatives. Currently A SEED Europe focuses on issues related to the global food chain: the decline of biodiversity in agriculture and the availability of seeds, genetic engineering and power concentration by global agro/biotech giants."

Environmentalism

ActionPA

Pennsylvania's Environmental Justice Resource
www.actionpa.org
catalyst@actionpa.org
(215) 743–4884

"A Pennsylvania-based research, organizing, and networking center for the grassroots environmental justice movement." The site includes resources on activist training, student organizing, and community organizing, as well as on various social justice issues, primarily related to environmental justice. A site map is available here: http://www.actionpa.org/sitemap/ and gives links to all their available resources.

Activism/Organizing; Environmentalism; Youth Movements & Organizing

Act Up (AIDS Coalition to Unleash Power)

www.actupny.com
info@actupny.com

(212) 966–4873
@actupny

"ACT UP is a diverse, non-partisan group of individuals united in anger and
committed to direct action to end the AIDS crisis. We advise and inform. We
demonstrate. WE ARE NOT SILENT"

Queer Rights

Adbusters

Journal of the Mental Environment
www.adbusters.org
info@adbusters.org
(604) 736–9401
@Adbusters

"We are a global network of artists, activists, writers, pranksters, students,
educators, and entrepreneurs who want to advance the new social activist
movement of the information age. Our aim is to topple existing power
structures and forge a major shift in the way we will live in the 21st
Century.
"Ultimately *Adbusters* is an ecological magazine, dedicated to examining
the relationship between human beings and their physical and mental
environment. We want a world in which the economy and ecology resonate
in balance. We try to coax people from spectator to participant in this quest.
We want folks to get mad about corporate disinformation, injustices in
the global economy, and any industry that pollutes our physical or mental
commons."

Alternative Media/Media Activism

AFL-CIO

America's Unions
www.aflcio.org
@AFLCIO

"We are the umbrella federation for U.S. unions, with 56 unions representing
12.5 million working men and women. We work to ensure that all people
who work receive the rewards of their work – decent paychecks and benefits,

safe jobs, respect and fair treatment. We work to make the voices of working people heard in the White House, on Capitol Hill, in state capitals across the country and in corporate boardrooms. We provide an independent voice for working families and ways for working people to be actively engaged in politics and legislation. We also hold corporations accountable for their treatment of employees and ensure the voice of working people is heard in the financial system. We also work with federations of unions in other countries toward global social and economic fairness."

Economic Justice; Human, Labour, & Civil Rights

The African American Policy Forum (AAPF)

www.aapf.org
info@aapf.org
(212) 854–3049
@AAPolicyForum

"The African American Policy Forum (AAPF) is an innovative think tank that connects academics, activists and policy-makers to promote efforts to dismantle structural inequality. We utilize new ideas and innovative perspectives to transform public discourse and policy.

"We promote frameworks and strategies that address a vision of racial justice that embraces the intersections of race, gender, class, and the array of barriers that disempower those who are marginalized in society. AAPF is dedicated to advancing and expanding racial justice, gender equality, and the indivisibility of all human rights, both in the US and internationally."

Anti-Racism

Alliance for Animals and the Environment

Promoting Compassion and Respect for All Animals
www.allanimals.org
alliance@allanimals.org
(608) 257–6333
@All_Animals_org

"The Alliance for Animals and the Environment is a nonprofit animal and environmental organization promoting the ethical, compassionate treatment of all animals and care for the planet we share."

Animal Rights; Environmentalism

The Alliance for Democracy

Joining together to end corporate rule
www.thealliancefordemocracy.org
afd@thealliancefordemocracy.org
(781) 894–1179
@EndCorpRule

"The mission of the Alliance for Democracy is to free all people from
corporate domination of politics, economics, the environment, culture and
information; to establish true democracy; and to create a just society with a
sustainable, equitable economy."

Democracy

Alternative Radio

Audio Energy for Democracy
www.alternativeradio.org
info@alternativeradio.org
1–800–444–1977
@audioenergy

"Alternative Radio, established in 1986, is a weekly one-hour public affairs
program offered free to all public radio stations in the US, Canada, Europe
and beyond. AR provides information, analyses and views that are
frequently ignored or distorted in other media."

Alternative Media/Media Activism

AlterNet

Alternative News and Information
www.alternet.org
@AlterNet

"AlterNet is a program of the Independent Media Institute (IMI), a nonprofit
organization that empowers people with independent journalism,
information, and media tools.
"IMI is dedicated to strengthening and supporting independent journalism,
and to improving the public's access to independent information sources.

We believe democracy is enhanced and public debate broadened when more voices are heard and more points of view are made available."

Alternative Media/Media Activism

Amnesty International

Working to Protect Human Rights
www.amnesty.org
info@amnesty.ca
44 20 74135500 (UK)
@amnesty

"Amnesty International is a global movement of more than 3 million supporters, members and activists in over 150 countries and territories who campaign to end grave abuses of human rights.
"Our vision is for every person to enjoy all the rights enshrined in the Universal Declaration of Human Rights and other international human rights standards."

Human, Labour, & Civil Rights

Animal Liberation Front

Worldwide News and Information Resource about the A.L.F.
www.animalliberationfront.com

Mission: "To effectively allocate resources (time and money) to end the 'property' status of nonhuman animals."

Animal Rights

Animal Welfare Institute

www.awionline.org
awi@awionline.org
(202) 337–2332
@AWIOnline

"Since 1951, the Animal Welfare Institute has been dedicated to reducing animal suffering caused by people. We seek better treatment of animals everywhere – in the laboratory, on the farm, in commerce, at home, and in the wild."

Animal Rights

BigMedia.org

Home of the Rocky Mountain Media Watch Archive
www.bigmedia.org
tips@bigmedia.org
@BigMediaBlog

"Our goal at Bigmedia.org is to hold journalists and media figures to basic standards of fairness, accuracy, and decency."

Alternative Media/Media Activism

Bioneers

Revolution from the Heart of Nature
www.bioneers.org
info@bioneers.org
1–877-BIONEER
@bioneers

"Founder Kenny Ausubel coined the term Bioneers in 1990 to describe an emerging culture. Bioneers are social and scientific innovators from all walks of life and disciplines who have peered deep into the heart of living systems to understand how nature operates, and to mimic 'nature's operating instructions' to serve human ends without harming the web of life. Nature's principles – kinship, cooperation, diversity, symbiosis and cycles of continuous creation absent of waste – can also serve as metaphoric guideposts for organizing an equitable, compassionate and democratic society.
Mission: "Bioneers is a fertile hub of social and scientific innovators with practical and visionary solutions for the world's most pressing environmental and social challenges."

Environmentalism

Black Lives Matter (#BlackLivesMatter)

Freedom and Justice for All Black Lives
www.blacklivesmatter.com
@Blklivesmatter

"#BlackLivesMatter was created in 2012 after Trayvon Martin's murderer, George Zimmerman, was acquitted for his crime, and dead 17-year old Trayvon was posthumously placed on trial for his own murder. Rooted in the experiences of Black people in this country who actively resist our de-humanization, #BlackLivesMatter is a call to action and a response to the virulent anti-Black racism that permeates our society. Black Lives Matter is a unique contribution that goes beyond extrajudicial killings of Black people by police and vigilantes.

"It goes beyond the narrow nationalism that can be prevalent within Black communities, which merely call on Black people to love Black, live Black and buy Black, keeping straight cis Black men in the front of the movement while our sisters, queer and trans and disabled folk take up roles in the background or not at all.

"Black Lives Matter affirms the lives of Black queer and trans folks, disabled folks, black-undocumented folks, folks with records, women and all Black lives along the gender spectrum. It centers those that have been marginalized within Black liberation movements. It is a tactic to (re)build the Black liberation movement."

Anti-Racism

The Brecht Forum Archive

www.brechtforum.org
brechtforum@brechtforum.org
(212) 242–4201@BrechtForum

"From October, 1975 to May, 2014, the Brecht Forum/New York Marxist School was a place for people working for social justice, equality and a new culture that puts human needs first. Through its classes and events, the Brecht Forum brought people together across social and cultural boundaries and artistic and academic disciplines to promote critical analysis, creative thinking, collaborative projects and networking in an independent community-level environment. This site is being maintained as an archive. Over time, additional videos, podcasts and other archival materials will be posted. There are also materials that have been donated to New York University's Tamiment Library."

Education/Critical Pedagogy

Business & Human Rights Resource Centre

Tracking the Positive and Negative Impacts of Over 5100 Companies Worldwide
www.business-humanrights.org

contact@business-humanrights.org
(212) 564–9160
@BHRRC

"We work with everyone to advance human rights in business. We track the
human rights abuse and advances of companies around the world, and
help the vulnerable eradicate abuse. Our mission is to:

Build Corporate Transparency …
Strengthen Corporate Accountability …
Empower Advocates …

Taking international human rights standards as our starting point, topics
covered include labour rights, conflict over natural resources such as
land and minerals, internet freedom, privacy and freedom of expression,
children, pollution and climate change, discrimination, access to medicines,
security, tax avoidance, and trade and investment agreements."

Corporate Accountability; Human, Labour, & Civil Rights

Campus Activism

Tools for Activists
www.campusactivism.org | www.campusactivism.org/uploads/org
guide.pdf
aaron@campusactivism.org

"This interactive website has tools for progressive activists. You can use it
to start a campaign, share activism resources, publicize events, and build
networks. Or you can join an existing campaign, get resources, learn about
upcoming activist events, and let people find you."
Secondary link provided is a pdf guide on campus organizing for social justice.

Activism/Organizing; Youth Movements & Organizing

Canadian Centre for Policy Alternatives

www.policyalternatives.ca
(613) 563–1341
@CCPA

"The Canadian Centre for Policy Alternatives is an independent, non-
partisan research institute concerned with issues of social, economic and

environmental justice. Founded in 1980, the CCPA is one of Canada's leading progressive voices in public policy debates."

Democracy; Economic Justice

Canadian Federation of Students (CFS)

http://cfs-fcee.ca
info@cfs-fcee.ca
613.232.7394
@CFSFCEE

"The Canadian Federation of Students is Canada's largest student organization, uniting more than 600,000 students across Canada. The Canadian Federation of Students and its predecessor organizations have represented students in Canada since 1927 in their call for fully accessible public post-secondary education."

Youth Movements & Organizing

Carnegie Council for Ethics in International Affairs

www.carnegiecouncil.org
info@cceia.org
(212) 838–4120
@carnegiecouncil

"The mission of Carnegie Council is to enlarge the audience for the simple but powerful message that ethics matter, regardless of place, origin, or belief.
"Since our founding by Andrew Carnegie a century ago, we have been one of the world's top creators of nonpartisan educational resources on international ethics used by professionals, journalists, educators, students, and the greater public. Carnegie Council is a non-profit 501(c) (3) institution."
Human Rights Initiative Program: www.carnegiecouncil.org/programs/archive/67/resource.html

Human, Labour, & Civil Rights

Center for Economic and Social Rights

Social Justice through Human Rights
www.cesr.org

info@cesr.org
(718) 237–9145
@social_rights

"The Center for Economic and Social Rights (CESR) works to promote social justice through human rights. In a world where poverty and inequality deprive entire communities of dignity, justice and sometimes life, we seek to uphold the universal human rights of every human being to education, health, food, water, housing, work, and other economic, social and cultural rights essential to human dignity.

"Our mission is to work for the recognition and enforcement of economic and social rights as a powerful tool for promoting social justice and human dignity. CESR exposes violations of economic and social rights through an interdisciplinary combination of legal and socioeconomic research and analysis. Together with civil society groups around the world, CESR advocates for changes to economic and social policy at the international, national and local levels so as to ensure these comply with international human rights standards."

Economic Justice; Human, Labour, & Civil Rights

Center for Food Safety

Protecting Our Food, Our Farms, & Our Environment
http://www.centerforfoodsafety.org/
office@centerforfoodsafety.org
(202) 547–9359
@CFSTrueFood

"Center for Food Safety (CFS) is a national non-profit public interest and environmental advocacy organization working to protect human health and the environment by curbing the use of harmful food production technologies and by promoting organic and other forms of sustainable agriculture. CFS also educates consumers concerning the definition of organic food and products. CFS uses legal actions, groundbreaking scientific and policy reports, books and other educational materials, market pressure and grass roots campaigns through our True Food Network. CFS's successful legal cases collectively represent a landmark body of case law on food and agricultural issues."

Environmentalism; Food & Farming

The Center for Responsive Politics

Inform, Empower, & Advocate
www.opensecrets.org
info@crp.org
(202) 857–0044
@OpenSecretsDC

"The Center for Responsive Politics is the nation's premier research group
tracking money in U.S. politics and its effect on elections and public policy.
Nonpartisan, independent and nonprofit, the organization aims to create
a more educated voter, an involved citizenry and a more transparent and
responsive government."

Democracy

Center for Social Justice

Fighting against Inequalities in Income, Wealth, and Power
www.socialjustice.org
office@socialjustice.org
(416) 927–0777

"The Centre for Social Justice conducts research, education and advocacy in
a bid to narrow the gap in income, wealth and power, and enhance peace
and human security; brings together people from universities and unions,
faith groups and community organizations in the pursuit of greater equality
and democracy; supports social movements in the struggle for social justice;
offers a non-partisan perspective on political, social and economic issues; and
uses creative communications to educate Canadians about public policies."

Economic Justice; Human, Labour, & Civil Rights

The Centre for Commercial-Free Public Education

www.ibiblio.org/commercialfree
unplug@igc.org
(510) 268–1100

"The Centre for Commercial-Free Public Education is a national non-profit organization that addresses the issue of commercialism in our public schools. The Center provides support to students, parents, teachers and other concerned citizens organizing across the U.S. to keep their schools commercial-free and community-controlled. By providing our constituents with the information and the skills that they need to have a voice in the running of their schools, we facilitate leadership development and democratic participation at the local level."

Education/Critical Pedagogy

Citizen Lab

www.citizenlab.org
info@citizenlab.org
(416) 946–8903
@citizenlab

"The Citizen Lab is an interdisciplinary laboratory based at the Munk School of Global Affairs at the University of Toronto, Canada focusing on advanced research and development at the intersection of digital media, global security, and human rights."
Mission: "We are a 'hothouse' that combines the disciplines of political science, sociology, computer science, engineering, and graphic design. We undertake research that monitors, analyzes, and impacts the exercise of political power in cyberspace.
"The Citizen Lab accomplishes these goals through collaborative partnerships with leading edge research centres and individuals around the world and through a mixed methods approach that combines technical reconnaissance, field investigations, and data mining, analysis, and visualization."

Education/Critical Pedagogy

ColorLines

News for Action
www.colorlines.com
community@colorlines.com
(212) 513–7925
@Colorlines

"Colorlines is a daily news site where race matters, featuring award-winning investigative reporting and news analysis. Colorlines is published by Race Forward, a national organization that advances racial justice through research, media and practice.

"Colorlines is produced by a multiracial team of writers who cover stories from the perspective of community, rather than through the lens of power brokers."

Alternative Media/Media Activism; Anti-Racism

Corporate Agribusiness Research Project

www.thecalamityhowler.com
avkrebs@earthlink.net
(425) 258–5345

"The Corporate Agribusiness Research Project (CARP) was established to monitor corporate agribusiness from a public interest perspective through awareness, education, and action while at the same time advocating the importance of building alternative, democratically controlled food systems. By utilizing fact-based strategic research and the publishing of The AgriBusiness Examiner, a weekly e-mail newsletter, and The Agbiz Tiller, a periodic online news feature service, CARP seeks to serve family farmers, farm workers and consumers in their struggles for economic and social justice."

Food & Farming

The Corporation / Hello Cool World Media

www.thecorporation.com | www.hellocoolworld.com
(604) 251–5567
info@hellocoolworld.com

"As the grassroots team behind THE CORPORATION, we are dedicated to harnessing the power of this film to launch a campaign that will change the corporate form. Over the past 10 years, our approach has been to try to connect with as many individuals and groups as possible that have a stake in the issues the film raises. The film itself is a vehicle for creating a community ready to rethink the corporate form. "HelloCoolWorld.com is the network that ties the community to action.

"Ideas to Audiences > > Audiences to Action > > Action to Outcome

"More people are questioning the governing role corporations play in our societies and in our lives. Over and over, people have asked us: 'What can I do now?' Our answer has been: 'Spread the word, join our network and tell us what you think.' In other words, grow the community and together let's come up with a plan for action."

Alternative Media/Media Activism; Corporate Accountability

Corp Watch

Holding Corporations Accountable
www.corpwatch.org
cwadmin@corpwatch.org
(416) 226–6226
@CorpWatch

Mission: "Non-profit investigative research and journalism to expose corporate malfeasance and to advocate for multinational corporate accountability and transparency. We work to foster global justice, independent media activism and democratic control over corporations.
"We seek to expose multinational corporations that profit from war, fraud, environmental, human rights and other abuses, and to provide critical information to foster a more informed public and an effective democracy."

Alternative Media/Media Activism; Corporate Accountability

The Council of Canadians

Acting for Social Justice
www.canadians.org
info@canadians.org
1–800–387–7177
@CouncilofCDNs

"Founded in 1985, the Council of Canadians is Canada's leading social action organization, mobilizing a network of 60 chapters across the country.
"Through our campaigns we advocate for clean water, fair trade, green energy, public health care, and a vibrant democracy. We educate and empower people to hold our governments and corporations accountable.
"Join us and be part of a global movement working for social and environmental justice. We believe a better Canada and a fairer world are possible. Together, we turn that belief into action."

Democracy; Environmentalism

Critical Pedagogy (University of Colorado at Denver, School of Education)

http://users.monash.edu.au/~dzyngier/critical_pedagogy_read
ing_list.htm

Scholarly resource with many links put together by Martin Ryder of the
  University of Colorado at Denver, School of Education, encompassing a
  resource and reading list.

Education/Critical Pedagogy

Critical Resistance

A National Grassroots Organization Committed to Ending Society's
  Use of Prisons and Policing as an Answer to Social Problems
www.criticalresistance.org
crnational@criticalresistance.org
(510) 444–0484
@C_Resistance

"Critical Resistance seeks to build an international movement to end
  the prison industrial complex (PIC) by challenging the belief that caging
  and controlling people makes us safe. We believe that basic necessities
  such as food, shelter, and freedom are what really make our communities
  secure. As such, our work is part of global struggles against inequality
  and powerlessness. The success of the movement requires that it
  reflect communities most affected by the PIC. Because we seek to
  abolish the PIC, we cannot support any work that extends its life or
  scope."

Prison Industrial Complex

Democracy Now!

A Daily Independent Global News Hour
www.democracynow.org
(212) 431–9090
@democracynow

"Democracy Now! is a national, daily, independent, award-winning news program hosted by journalists Amy Goodman and Juan Gonzalez ...

"Democracy Now!'s War and Peace Report provides our audience with access to people and perspectives rarely heard in the US corporate-sponsored media, including independent and international journalists, ordinary people from around the world who are directly affected by US foreign policy, grassroots leaders and peace activists, artists, academics and independent analysts. In addition, *Democracy Now!* hosts real debates–debates between people who substantially disagree, such as between the White House or the Pentagon spokespeople on the one hand, and grassroots activists on the other."

Alternative Media/Media Activism; Democracy

Dignitas International

www.dignitasinternational.org
info@dignitasinternational.org
1–866–576–3100
@DignitasIntl

"Dignitas International is a medical and research organization dedicated to transforming patient health and health care systems for the most vulnerable people.

"Committed to innovation, Dignitas works in partnership with patients, health workers, researchers and policymakers to tackle the barriers to health care in resource-limited communities. Combining frontline expertise and rigorous research, Dignitas saves lives and upholds the right to health for the world's most vulnerable by treating patients, strengthening health systems and shaping health policy and practice."

Human, Labour, & Civil Rights

Disinformation

Everything you know is wrong.
www.disinfo.com
@disinfo

"The Disinformation Company is a dynamic, independent media company based in New York City. We are active in book publishing, film production and home video distribution, with well over 150 books and films in our catalog. We are known for working with filmmakers and authors to promote important political, social or cultural issues that are ignored by the mainstream media. "Disinfo.com, our web presence, collects the most shocking, unusual and quirkiest news articles, podcasts and videos on the web, most of which are submitted by the site's visitors. It is our intent that Disinformation becomes news that you did not know that you needed … based on the extent that anyone today can define what news is in our hyper-mediated, cyber-cultural environment."

Alternative Media/Media Activism

Do Black Lives Matter? Robin D. G. Kelley and Fred Moten in Conversation

https://vimeo.com/116111740

"On Dec. 13th [2014], Critical Resistance was honored to host Fred Moten and Robin D.G. Kelley for a conversation on the impacts of the prison industrial complex on Black communities. The conversation was a collaboration with Oakland's Bethany Baptist Church and was skillfully moderated by Maisha Quint."

Anti-Racism; Prison Industrial Complex

The Dominion

News from the Grassroots
www.dominionpaper.ca
info@mediacoop.ca
(514) 394–0623
@mediacoop

"*The Dominion* is a monthly paper published by an incipient network of independent journalists in Canada. It aims to provide accurate, critical coverage that is accountable to its readers and the subjects it tackles. Taking its name from Canada's official status as both a colony and a colonial force, the Dominion examines politics, culture and daily life with a view to understanding the exercise of power … *The Dominion* is a publication of the Media Co-op."

Alternative Media/Media Activism

Earth First! Journal

Media from the Frontlines of Ecological Resistance
www.earthfirstjournal.org
collective@earthfirstjournal.org
(561) 320–3840
@efjournal

"Earth First! formed in 1979, in response to an increasingly corporate,
  compromising and ineffective environmental community. It is not
  an organization, but a movement. There are no 'members' of EF!,
  only Earth First!ers. We believe in using all of the tools in the toolbox,
  from grassroots and legal organizing to civil disobedience and
  monkeywrenching. When the law won't fix the problem, we put our
  bodies on the line to stop the destruction. Earth First!'s direct-action
  approach draws attention to the crises facing the natural world, and it
  saves lives.
"The *Earth First! Journal* is the voice of the radical environmental
  movement. Published quarterly, it contains reports on direct action;
  articles on the preservation of wilderness and biological diversity; news
  and announcements about EF! and other radical environmental groups;
  investigative articles; critiques of the entire environmental movement;
  book and music reviews; essays exploring ecological theory and a
  sometimes-lively letters to the editor section."

Alternative Media/Media Activism; Environmentalism

Earth Island Institute

www.earthisland.org
erin@earthisland.org
(510) 859–9100
@earthisland

"Since 1982, Earth Island Institute has been a hub for grassroots campaigns
  dedicated to conserving, preserving, and restoring the ecosystems on which
  our civilization depends."

Environmentalism

Economic Policy Institute

Research and Ideas for Shared Prosperity
www.epi.org
epi@epi.org
(202) 775–8810
@EconomicPolicy

"The Economic Policy Institute's mission is to inform and empower
   individuals to seek solutions that ensure broadly shared prosperity and
   opportunity...
"The Economic Policy Institute (EPI) is a nonprofit, nonpartisan think
   tank created in 1986 to include the needs of low- and middle-income
   workers in economic policy discussions. EPI believes every working
   person deserves a good job with fair pay, affordable health care, and
   retirement security. To achieve this goal, EPI conducts research and
   analysis on the economic status of working America. EPI proposes public
   policies that protect and improve the economic conditions of low- and
   middle-income workers and assesses policies with respect to how they
   affect those workers."

Economic Justice

Egale Canada Human Rights Trust

www.egale.ca
egale.canada@egale.ca
1–800–204–7777
@egalecanada

"Founded in 1995, Egale Canada Human Rights Trust is Canada's
   only national charity promoting lesbian, gay, bisexual, and trans
   (LGBT) human rights through research, education and community
   engagement.
"Egale's vision is of a Canada free of homophobia, biphobia, transphobia and
   all other forms of discrimination so that every person can achieve their full
   potential, unencumbered by hatred and bias. Our mission and values help
   pave the way for our vision to become reality."

Queer Rights

Ella Baker Center for Human Rights

She led. So can you.
www.ellabakercenter.org
contact@ellabakercenter.org
(510) 428–3939
@ellabakercenter

Mission: "Through organizing, leadership development and advocacy, the
   Ella Baker Center unlocks the power of low-income people, people of color,
   and their allies to transform California and inspire the world."
About: "The Ella Baker Center is named for an unsung hero of the civil
   rights movement who inspired and guided emerging leaders. We build on
   her legacy by giving people opportunities and skills to work together to
   strengthen our communities so that all of us can thrive ...
"Through our people-powered campaigns, the Ella Baker Center offers smart
   solutions and uplifting alternatives to violence and incarceration. The safest
   neighbourhoods aren't the ones with the most prisons and the most police.
   They're the ones with the best schools, the cleanest environment, and the
   most opportunities for young people and working people. Instead of basing
   policies on fear, we're building a society where decisions and laws are
   based on love and common concerns."

Human, Labour, & Civil Rights

The Encyclopaedia of Informal Education

Exploring informal education, lifelong learning, and social action
www.infed.org
info@infed.org
44 020 7540 4929
@infed

"*infed* was established in 1995 at the YMCA George Williams College,
   London as an open and not-for-profit site. Put together by a small group
   of educators, it is now accessed over 6 million times a year ... Our aim is to
   provide a space for people to explore education, learning, and social action –
   and in particular the theory and practice of informal education, community
   learning and development, social pedagogy and lifelong learning."

Education/Critical Pedagogy

Fairness and Accuracy in Reporting (FAIR)

Challenging Media Bias & Censorship since 1986
www.fair.org
fair@fair.org
(212) 633–6700
@FAIRmediawatch

"FAIR, the national media watch group, has been offering well-documented
criticism of media bias and censorship since 1986. We work to invigorate
the First Amendment by advocating for greater diversity in the press and
by scrutinizing media practices that marginalize public interest, minority
and dissenting viewpoints. As an anti-censorship organization, we expose
neglected news stories and defend working journalists when they are
muzzled. As a progressive group, FAIR believes that structural reform
is ultimately needed to break up the dominant media conglomerates,
establish independent public broadcasting and promote strong non-profit
sources of information."

Fairness in Media Organizations

Fair Vote: The Center for Voting and Democracy

www.fairvote.org
info@fairvote.org
(301) 270–4616
@fairvote

"FairVote makes democracy fair, functional, and representative by developing
the analysis and educational tools necessary for our reform partners to win and
sustain improvements to American elections. We are a non-profit, non-partisan
organization with a history of working with people from across the spectrum."

Democracy

Fellowship of Reconciliation

Working for Peace, Justice, and Nonviolence Since 1915
www.forusa.org
(845) 358–4601

@FORpeace

Statement of Purpose: "The Fellowship of Reconciliation is composed of women and men who recognize the essential unity of all creation and have joined together to explore the power of love and truth for resolving human conflict. While it has always been vigorous in its opposition to war, FOR has insisted equally that this effort must be based on a commitment to the achieving of a just and peaceful world community, with full dignity and freedom for every human being."

Peace, Nonviolence, Anti-War, & Anti-Militarism

Feminist.Com

www.feminist.com
mail@feminist.com
@feministdotcom

"Feminist.com is a thriving online community fostering awareness, education and activism for women all across the world. We serve as the Internet's definitive hub for resources and information dedicated to women's equality, justice, wellness and safety. Like a "feminist Google," Feminist.com facilitates connections between women and the many, varied organizations serving their needs and interests worldwide."

Feminism/Women's Issues

Feminist Majority Foundation

Equality around the World
www.feminist.org
feedback@feminist.org
(703) 522–2214
@feministnews

"The Feminist Majority Foundation (FMF), which was founded in 1987, is a cutting edge organization dedicated to women's equality, reproductive health, and non-violence. In all spheres, FMF utilizes research and action to empower women economically, socially, and politically. Our organization believes that feminists – both women and men, girls and boys – are the majority, but this majority must be empowered."

Feminism/Women's Issues

Food First

Institute for Food and Development Policy
www.foodfirst.org
info@foodfirst.org
(510) 654–4400
@foodfirstorg

"The mission of the Institute for Food and Development Policy, better known as Food First, is to end the injustices that cause hunger…
"Food First envisions a world in which all people have access to healthy, ecologically produced and culturally appropriate food. After nearly 40 years of analysis of the global food system, we know that making this vision a reality involves more than technical solutions – it requires *political transformation*. That's why Food First supports activists, social movements, alliances and coalitions working for systemic change."

Food & Farming

Food Not Bombs

www.foodnotbombs.net
menu@foodnotbombs.net
1–800–884–1136
@Food_Not_Bombs_

Mission: "The mission of Food Not Bombs is to recover and share free vegan or vegetarian food with the public without restriction to protest war, poverty and the destruction of the environment. Each of our over 1,000 groups is independent making decisions using the consensus process. Food Not Bombs is also dedicated to taking nonviolent direct action to change society so no one is forced to stand in line to eat at a soup kitchen expressing a commitment to the fact that food is a right and not a privilege. With over a billion people going hungry each day how can we spend another dollar on war?"

Environmentalism; Food and Farming; Peace, Nonviolence, Anti-War, & Anti-Militarism

Freemuse

Freedom of Musical Expression
www.freemuse.org
(+45) 3332 1027 (Denmark)
freemuse@freemuse.org
@Free_Muse

> "Freemuse – The World Forum on Music and Censorship is an independent international membership organisation advocating and defending freedom of expression for musicians and composers worldwide."

Human, Labour, & Civil Rights

Free Speech TV

www.freespeech.org
viewercomments@freespeech.org
(303) 442–8445
@freespeechtv

> "Free Speech TV is an independent, 24-hour television network and multi-platform digital news source with news, stories and perspectives you won't find anywhere else. A non-profit, public interest network, FSTV is publically supported by its viewers and by philanthropic foundations. Television broadcasts are commercial-free."

Alternative Media/Media Activism

Friends of the Earth International

www.foei.org
31 (0) 20 6221369 (Netherlands)
@FoEint

> "Friends of the Earth International is a global network representing more than two million activists in 75 different countries.

"Our vision is of a peaceful and sustainable world based on societies living in harmony with nature.

"We envision a society of interdependent people living in dignity, wholeness and fulfilment in which equity and human and peoples' rights are realized.

"This will be a society built upon peoples' sovereignty and participation. It will be founded on social, economic, gender and environmental justice and be free from all forms of domination and exploitation, such as neoliberalism, corporate globalization, neo-colonialism and militarism."

Environmentalism

Gay, Lesbian, & Straight Education Network (GLSEN)

www.glsen.org
info@glsen.org
(212) 727–0135
@glsen

"At GLSEN, we want every student, in every school, to be valued and treated with respect, regardless of their sexual orientation, gender identity or gender expression. We believe that all students deserve a safe and affirming school environment where they can learn and grow.

"We accomplish our goals by working in hallways across the country – from Congress and the Department of Education to schools and district offices in your community – to improve school climate and champion LGBT issues in K-12 education."

Queer Rights

Global Exchange

Building People-to-People Ties
www.globalexchange.org
web@globalexchange.org
(415) 255–7296
@globalexchange

"Global Exchange is an international human rights organization dedicated to promoting social, economic and environmental justice since 1988 ...

"We're changing the rules across the globe from a profit-centred global economy to thriving people-centred local economies; from the politics of greed to a living democracy that respects the rights of workers and nature; and from currency to community."

Economic Justice; Globalization

Global Policy Forum

www.globalpolicy.org
gpf@globalpolicy.org
(212) 557–3161
@globalpolicy

"Global Policy Forum is an independent policy watchdog that monitors the work of the United Nations and scrutinizes global policymaking. We promote accountability and citizen participation in decisions on peace and security, social justice and international law.
"GPF gathers information and circulates it through a comprehensive website, as well as through reports and newsletters. We play an active role in NGO networks and other advocacy arenas. We organize meetings and conferences and we publish original research and policy papers."

Human, Labour, & Civil Rights

Global Youth Action Network

http://gyan.tigweb.org
gyan@youthlink.org
(416) 977–9363 (Canada)
@globalyouth

A part of TakingITGlobal, the GYAN was founded "to create a clearing house for today's youth movements, encourage collaboration and help maximize the collective impact of youth activism around the world."

Activism/Organizing; Youth Movements & Organizing

Greenpeace International

www.greenpeace.org
supporter.services.int@greenpeace.org (International)

31 (0) 20 718 20 00 (Netherlands)
@Greenpeace

"Greenpeace is an independent global campaigning organisation that acts to
change attitudes and behaviour, to protect and conserve the environment
and to promote peace by:
Catalysing an energy revolution to address the number one threat facing our
planet: climate change.
Defending our oceans …
Protecting the world's ancient forests and the animals, plants and people that
depend on them.
Working for disarmament and peace …
Creating a toxic free future with safer alternatives to hazardous chemicals …
Campaigning for sustainable agriculture …"

Environmentalism

Human Rights Education Associates

The Global Human Rights Education Network
www.hrea.org
(617) 301–4379
@HREAnews

"Human Rights Education Associates (HREA) is an international non-
governmental organisation that supports human rights learning; the
training of activists and professionals; the development of educational
materials and programming; and community-building through on-line
technologies. HREA is dedicated to quality education and training to
promote understanding, attitudes and actions to protect human rights, and
to foster the development of peaceable, free and just communities.
"HREA works with individuals, non-governmental organisations,
inter-governmental organisations and governments interested in
implementing human rights education programs. The services provided
by HREA are:

assistance in curriculum and materials development;
training of professional groups;
research and evaluation;
clearinghouse of education and training materials;
networking human rights defenders and educators."

Activism/Organizing; Human, Labour, & Civil Rights

Human Rights Interactive Network

Human Rights, Globalization, and Disaster Relief: The Internet Citizen's Guide and Directory
www.guidetoaction.org

"Human Rights Interactive Network is a public resource packed with links, articles and other information pertaining to human rights worldwide. In addition to the Internet Guide to Human Rights, Globalization and Humanitarian Relief, HRIN maintains a legal archive for the Association of Humanitarian Lawyers which also contains substantial data.

"Besides human rights and related endeavours, you'll find links and information about international development, disaster relief, consumer awareness, socially responsible investing and international law. There's a comprehensive listing of organizations, government agencies and academic institutions throughout the world."

Human, Labour, & Civil Rights

Human Rights Internet

Consulting and Capacity Building Organization Committed to Social Justice, Good Governance, and Conflict Prevention
www.hri.ca
info@hri.ca
(613) 789–7407

"Human Rights Internet (HRI) is committed to promoting human rights and social justice, through providing opportunities to prepare human rights leaders of the future, practicing 'quiet diplomacy', and preserving human rights documentation. HRI seeks to accomplish these goals through internships and intern training, promoting dialogue and 'quiet' diplomacy, and transferring knowledge of human rights documentation.

"Governed by a small, volunteer board of directors, we currently ensure that human rights is the central focus of intern training. We conduct international human rights projects and, through our relationships with human rights organizations around the world, we collect, catalogue and record human rights information from around the world."

Human, Labour, & Civil Rights

Human Rights Watch

Defending Human Rights Worldwide
www.hrw.org
(212) 290–4700
@HRW

Mission: "Human Rights Watch defends the rights of people worldwide. We
   scrupulously investigate abuses, expose the facts widely, and pressure those
   with power to respect rights and secure justice. Human Rights Watch is
   an independent, international organization that works as part of a vibrant
   movement to uphold human dignity and advance the cause of human
   rights for all."

Human, Labour, & Civil Rights

Idle No More

Turn the Tables: Self Determination, Not Termination
www.idlenomore.ca

"Idle No More has quickly become one of the largest Indigenous mass
   movements in Canadian history – sparking hundreds of teach-ins,
   rallies, and protests across Turtle Island and beyond. What began as
   a series of teach-ins throughout Saskatchewan to protest impending
   parliamentary bills that will erode Indigenous sovereignty and
   environmental protections, has now changed the social and political
   landscape of Canada.
"Idle No More calls on all people to join in a peaceful revolution, to honour
   Indigenous sovereignty, and to protect the land and water.
"INM has and will continue to help build sovereignty and resurgence of
   nationhood.
"INM will continue to pressure government and industry to protect the
   environment.
"INM will continue to build allies in order to reframe the nation to nation
   relationship, this will be done by including grassroots perspectives, issues,
   and concern."

Indigenous Rights

Indigenous Action Media

Action, Art, Strategic Communications, Workshops, & Support
www.indigenousaction.org
indigenousaction@gmail.org
@media_action

"Indigenous Action Media (IAM) was founded on August 25th, 2001 to
provide strategic media support and direct action to address issues
impacting Indigenous communities.
"IAM offers media strategy consultation and support in the face of
environmental and social injustices. We do this through direct support,
workshops, web and graphic design services, documentaries and youth
empowerment projects.
"We are a volunteer collective of experienced Indigenous media makers and
activists that work together on a project by project basis for media justice
from an anti-colonial and anti-capitalist framework."

Alternative Media/Media Activism; Indigenous Rights

InfoShop.Org

Anarchist news and information
www.infoshop.org
@InfoshopDotOrg

"Infoshop.org is an online resource of news, opinion and information
on anarchism and many other topics. We are one of the oldest political
websites, having been online since 1995. Around 50,000 people each month
use our services and read our pages.
"The Alternative Media Project is the umbrella nonprofit for Infoshop.org,
Practical Anarchy magazine, and several other publishing, journalism, and
information dissemination projects."

Anarchism; Alternative Media/Media Activism

Institute for Agriculture and Trade Policy

Where Global and Local Meet Sustainability
www.iatp.org

(612) 870–0453
@IATP

Mission: "IATP works locally and globally at the intersection of policy
  and practice to ensure fair and sustainable food, farm and trade
  systems.
"IATP works with organizations around the world to analyse how global
  trade agreements impact domestic farm and food policies. Alongside a
  global coalition, IATP advocates for fair trade policies that promote strong
  health standards, labour and human rights, the environment and, most
  fundamentally, democratic institutions."

Food & Farming

Institute for Anarchist Studies

www.anarchiststudies.org
anarchiststudies@gmail.com
@narchiststudies

"The Institute for Anarchist Studies (IAS), a nonprofit foundation
  established in 1996 to support the development of anarchism, is a grant-
  giving organization for radical writers and translators worldwide. To date,
  we have funded over a hundred projects by authors from countries around
  the world ... Equally important, we publish the Anarchist Interventions
  book series in collaboration with AK Press and Justseeds Artists'
  Cooperative, the print and online journal *Perspectives on Anarchist Theory*,
  and the new Lexicon pamphlet series as well as organize educational
  events such as Anarchist Theory Tracks, onetime talks, and in the past,
  the Renewing the Anarchist Tradition conference. The IAS is part of a
  larger movement to radically transform society as well. We are internally
  democratic and work in solidarity with people around the globe who share
  our values."

Anarchism

Institute for Global Labour and Human Rights

www.globallabourrights.org
inbox@glhr.org
(412) 562–2406
@IGLHR

"The Institute for Global Labour and Human Rights (the Institute) is a
non-profit ... human rights organization dedicated to the promotion and
defense of internationally recognized worker rights in the global economy.
Founded in 1981 as the National Labor Committee, the Institute's research,
in-depth reports, high profile public campaigns and widespread
media coverage have been instrumental in creating the anti-sweatshop
movement in the United States and internationally. The Institute is
headquartered in Pittsburgh with regional offices in Dhaka and San
Salvador and research/advocacy partnerships in China, Jordan, Central
America and South Asia."

Mission: "We believe that worker rights are human rights. The mission of the
Institute is to promote and defend human, women's and workers' rights
in the global economy. With a widespread and highly experienced team
of international advocates, the Institute responds to appeals for support
from exploited workers all over the developing world who produce goods
for export to the U.S. The Institute undertakes in-depth research, public
education and popular campaigns that empower the American people to
provide support and solidarity to workers struggling to defend their most
basic rights. As workers across the developing world fight for their right
to work in dignity, in healthy and safe workplaces, to earn a living wage
and to organize independent unions, the Institute will provide solidarity
and international visibility to support their efforts, and we will continue
to demand that corporations be held legally accountable to respect core
internationally recognized worker rights standards."

Human, Labour, & Civil Rights

Institute for Policy Studies

Ideas into Action
www.ips-dc.org
info@ips-dc.org
(202) 234–9382
@IPS_DC

"As Washington's first progressive multi-issue think tank, the Institute
for Policy Studies (IPS) has served as a policy and research resource for
visionary social justice movements for over four decades – from the anti-
war and civil rights movements in the 1960s to the peace and global justice
movements of the last decade ...

"Today the Institute's work is organized into more than a dozen projects, reflecting our public scholars' diverse areas of expertise. In practice, these projects collaborate strategically to pursue three overarching policy goals: peace, justice, and the environment."

Environmentalism; Human, Labour, & Civil Rights; Peace, Nonviolence, Anti-War, & Anti-Militarism

Institute for Public Accuracy

Reliable Independent Sources for Breaking News
www.accuracy.org
institute@igc.org
(510) 788–4541
@accuracy

"IPA increases the reach and capacity of progressive and grassroots organizations (at no cost to them) to address public policy by getting them and their ideas into the mainstream media. IPA gains media access for those whose voices are commonly excluded or drowned out by government or corporate-backed institutions. As a national consortium of independent public-policy researchers, analysts and activists, IPA widens media exposure for progressive perspectives on many issues including the environment, human rights, foreign policy, and economic justice."

Fairness in Media Organizations

Institute for the Study of Human Rights

http://humanrightscolumbia.org/
ishr@columbia.edu
(212) 854–2479

"The Institute for the Study of Human Rights (ISHR) was established in 1978 at Columbia University as the Center for the Study of Human Rights (CSHR). In Spring 2010, Columbia University elevated CSHR to the level of an institute. ISHR is committed to its three core goals of providing excellent human rights education to Columbia students, fostering innovative interdisciplinary academic research, and offering its expertise in capacity building to human rights leaders, organizations, and universities around the world."

Education/Critical Pedagogy; Human, Labour, & Civil Rights

International Campaign to Ban Landmines

www.icbl.org
41 (0)22 920 03 25 (Switzerland)
@minefreeworld

"The International Campaign to Ban Landmines (ICBL) is a global network
in over 90 countries that works for a world free of antipersonnel landmines,
where landmine survivors can lead fulfilling lives."

Peace, Nonviolence, Anti-War, & Anti-Militarism

International Forum on Globalization

www.ifg.org
ifg@ifg.org
(415) 561–7650
@IFGlobalization

"The International Forum on Globalization (IFG) is a North-South research
and educational institution composed of leading activists, economists,
scholars, and researchers providing analysis and critiques on the cultural,
social, political, and environmental impacts of economic globalization."

Economic Justice; Globalization

International Labor Rights Forum

Dignity and Justice for Workers Worldwide
www.laborrights.org
(202) 347–4100
@ILRF

"International Labor Rights Forum is a human rights organization that
advocates for workers globally.
"ILRF works with trade unions, faith-based organizations, and community
groups to support workers and their families. We lead on initiatives such
as making apparel factories safe in Bangladesh; stopping the exploitation
of children in the cotton fields of Uzbekistan; increasing the income of farm

workers in the cocoa fields of West Africa; developing labor law clinics in
China; and supporting threatened union leaders in Latin America's banana
sector."

Mission: "ILRF is dedicated to achieving dignity and justice for workers
worldwide."

Vision: "ILRF works for a world where workers have the power to speak out
and organize to defend and advance their rights and interests; a world
where workers have the right to form unions and bargain collectively to
secure a safe and dignified life for themselves and their families; and a
world where everyone is free from discrimination, forced labor and child
labor."

Corporate Accountability; Human, Labour, & Civil Rights

The International Leonard Peltier Defense Committee

www.whoisleonardpeltier.info
contact@whoisleonardpeltier.info
(505) 217–3612
@PeltierHQ

"The International Leonard Peltier Defense Committee (ILPDC) is a
project of the Indigenous Rights Center LLC. We are the hub of
communication between Leonard Peltier and his program coordinators,
the general public, government officials, political and tribal leaders,
the media, and his supporters worldwide. We are in daily contact
with Leonard who is currently imprisoned at USP Coleman,
Florida."

Indigenous Rights

International Lesbian, Gay, Bisexual, Trans and Intersex Association (ILGA)

www.ilga.org
information@ilga.org
+41 227313254
@ILGAWORLD

"ILGA, the International Lesbian, Gay, Bisexual, Trans and Intersex
Association, is the world federation of national and local organisations

dedicated to achieving equal rights for lesbian, gay, bisexual, trans and intersex (LGBTI) people ...

"Established in 1978, ILGA enjoys consultative status at the UN ECOSOC Council, publishes an annual world report and a map on legislation criminalising or protecting people on the basis of their sexual orientation or recognising their relationships.

"ILGA's aim is to work for the equality of lesbian, gay, bisexual, trans and intersex people and their liberation from all forms of discrimination. We seek to achieve this aim through the world-wide cooperation and mutual support of our members."

Queer Rights

International Rivers

Protecting People - Water - Life
www.internationalrivers.org
info@internationalrivers.org
(510) 848–1155
@intlrivers

"Since 1985, International Rivers has been at the heart of the global struggle to protect rivers and the rights of communities that depend on them.

"We work with an international network of dam-affected people, grassroots organizations, environmentalists, human rights advocates and others who are committed to stopping destructive river projects and promoting better options.

"We seek a world where healthy rivers and the rights of local communities are valued and protected. We envision a world where water and energy needs are met without degrading nature or increasing poverty, and where people have the right to participate in decisions that affect their lives.

"Based in four continents, our staff has expertise in big dams, energy and water policy, climate change, and international financial institutions. We support partner organizations and dam-affected people by providing advice, training and technical assistance, and advocating on their behalf with governments, banks, companies and international agencies. The focus of our work is in Latin America, Asia and Africa."

Environmentalism

Issues in Freirean Pedagogy (Tom Heaney)

http://www.well.com/user/willard/Heaney%20-%20Friere%20
&%20Thresholds%20in%20Education.htm

This document is a resource for those who do not have an extensive
knowledge of Freirean Pedagogy. It includes a glossary and helpful
background information.

Education/Critical Pedagogy

The Jane Goodall Institute

www.janegoodall.org
(703) 682–9220
@JaneGoodallInst

Mission: "Founded by renowned primatologist Jane Goodall, the Jane Goodall
Institute is a global nonprofit that empowers people to make a difference
for all living things. Our work builds on Dr. Goodall's scientific work and
her humanitarian vision. Specifically, we seek to:
Improve global understanding and treatment of great apes through research,
public education and advocacy
Contribute to the preservation of great apes and their habitats by combining
conservation with education and promotion of sustainable livelihoods in
local communities
Create a worldwide network of young people who have learned to
care deeply for their human community, for all animals and for the
environment, and who will take responsible action to care for them[.]"

Animal Rights; Environmentalism

Jobs With Justice

Fighting for workers' rights and an economy that works for everyone.
www.jwj.org
info@jwj.org
(202) 393–1044
@jwjnational

"At Jobs With Justice, we are leading the fight for workers' rights and an economy that benefits everyone. We are the only nonprofit of our kind leading strategic campaigns and shaping the public discourse on every front to build power for working people. Jobs With Justice is committed to working nationally and locally, on the ground and online. We win real change for workers by combining innovative communications strategies and solid research and policy advocacy with grassroots action and mobilization."

Economic Justice; Human, Labour, & Civil Rights

Jubilee USA Network

Building an economy that serves, protects, and promotes participation of the most vulnerable
www.jubileeusa.org
coord@jubileeusa.org
(202) 783–3566
@JubileeUSA

"Jubilee USA Network is an alliance of more than 75 US organizations, 400 faith communities and 50 Jubilee global partners. Jubilee is building an economy that serves, protects and promotes participation of the most vulnerable. Jubilee has won critical global financial reforms and more than $130 billion in debt relief for the world's poorest people.
"Our efforts build the political support needed to influence world-wide decision makers, the White House, Congress, the G20, International Financial Institutions and the United Nations to promote poverty reduction and move solutions to the international debt crisis. Ultimately, we work to create an international financial system that protects and ensures participation of the most vulnerable within the context of human rights. Our advocacy promotes responsible lending and borrowing, increasing debt relief for poor countries, curbing illicit financial flows and corporate tax avoidance, moving forward an international debt resolution process, pushing reforms in international financial institutions and protecting poor people from predatory financial behavior."

Economic Justice; Globalization

Last Chance for Animals (LCA)

www.lcanimal.org
campaigns@lcanimal.org

(310) 271–6096
@LC4A

Mission Statement: "Last Chance for Animals (LCA) is a national, non-profit organization dedicated to eliminating animal exploitation through education, investigations, legislation, and media attention. The organization believes that animals are highly sentient creatures who exist for their own reasons independent of their service to humans; they should not be made to suffer for the latter. LCA therefore opposes the use of animals in food and clothing production, scientific experimentation, and entertainment. Instead, it promotes a cruelty-free lifestyle and the ascription of rights to non-human beings."

Animal Rights

The Leap Manifesto

A Call for Canada Based on Caring for the Earth and One Another
https://leapmanifesto.org/
contact@leapmanifesto.org
(514) 436–7629

"We start from the premise that Canada is facing the deepest crisis in recent memory.
The Truth and Reconciliation Commission has acknowledged shocking details about the violence of Canada's near past. Deepening poverty and inequality are a scar on the country's present. And Canada's record on climate change is a crime against humanity's future.
"These facts are all the more jarring because they depart so dramatically from our stated values: respect for Indigenous rights, internationalism, human rights, diversity, and environmental stewardship.
"We are not living according to those values today – but we could be …
"So we need to leap." [Excerpted from the Leap Manifesto]

Corporate Accountability; Economic Justice; Environmentalism; Human, Labour, & Civil Rights; Indigenous Rights

Media Alliance

Action and Resources for a More Just, Accountable, and Diverse Media System
www.media-alliance.org
information@media-alliance.org

(510) 684–6853
@twrling

Mission: "MA was founded with the belief that in order to ensure the free
and unfettered flow of information and ideas necessary to maintain a truly
democratic society, media must be accessible, accountable, decentralized,
representative of society's diversity and free from covert or overt government
control and corporate dominance. MA dedicates itself to fostering a genuine
diversity of media voices and perspectives, holding the media accountable
for their impact on society and protecting freedom of speech.
"Media Alliance is a media resource and advocacy center for media workers,
non-profit organizations, and social justice activists. Our mission is
excellence, ethics, diversity, and accountability in all aspects of the media in
the interests of peace, justice, and social responsibility."

Fairness in Media Organizations

The Media Co-op

Local Independent News
www.mediacoop.ca
info@mediacoop.ca
(514) 563–1399
@mediacoop

"The Media Co-op is a coast-to-coast network of local media cooperatives
dedicated to providing grassroots, democratic coverage of their
communities and of Canada." The Media Co-op also has local co-ops in
Vancouver, Montreal, Toronto, and Halifax.

Alternative Media/Media Activism

**National Association for the Advancement of Colored
People (NAACP)**

www.naacp.org
1–877-NAACP-98
@NAACP

Mission: "The mission of the National Association for the Advancement of
Colored People is to ensure the political, educational, social, and economic
equality of rights of all persons and to eliminate race-based discrimination."

Vision: "The vision of the National Association for the Advancement of Colored People is to ensure a society in which all individuals have equal rights without discrimination based on race."

Anti-Racism; Human, Labour, & Civil Rights

National Network for Immigrant and Refugee Rights

www.nnirr.org
nnirrinfo@nnirr.org
(510) 465–1984
@NNIRRnetwork

"The National Network for Immigrant and Refugee Rights (NNIRR) works to defend and expand the rights of all immigrants and refugees, regardless of immigration status. Since its founding in 1986, the organization has drawn membership from diverse immigrant communities, and actively builds alliances with social and economic justice partners around the country. As part of a global movement for social and economic justice, NNIRR is committed to human rights as essential to securing healthy, safe and peaceful lives for all."

Human, Labour, & Civil Rights

National Organization for Women

Taking Action for Women's Equality Since 1966
www.now.org
(202) 628–8669
@NationalNOW

"As the grassroots arm of the women's movement, the National Organization for Women is dedicated to its multi-issue and multi-strategy approach to women's rights. NOW is the largest organization of feminist activists in the United States, with hundreds of thousands of contributing members and more than 500 local and campus affiliates in all 50 states and the District of Columbia."

Feminism/Women's Issues

Native Forest Council

Saving Nature, Preserving Life
www.forestcouncil.org

info@forestcouncil.org
(541) 688–2600

Mission: "to fully protect and preserve every acre of publicly owned land in
the United States."
"Native Forest Council is dedicated to the preservation and protection of all
publicly owned natural resources from destructive practices, sales, and
all resource extraction. Commercial timber sales, grazing, mining, and oil
and gas extraction all contribute to the destruction and degradation of air
quality, wildlife habitat, and of our wilderness areas. We believe a sound
economy and environment need not be incompatible, and that current land
management practices are devastating to both."

Environmentalism

New Dimensions Radio

Changing the World, One Broadcast at a Time
www.newdimensions.org
info@newdimensions.org
(707) 468–5215
@newdimensions

"New Dimensions Radio & Media produces the longest-running and most
successful independently produced interview program in the history of public
radio. We feature leading-edge thinkers, scientists, artists, healers, ecologists,
spiritual leaders, and social architects in award winning, deep dialogues. We
have over a thousand MP3 programs that you can purchase and download."
Purpose: "The specific and primary purpose of New Dimensions Foundation
is to develop and disseminate information and knowledge relating to
the human mind, body, spirit and the natural world, through broadcast
programming, public forums, seminars, books and other means to encourage
public awareness of various approaches and methods for expanding the field
of possibilities towards a world that works for everyone."

Alternative Media/Media Activism

New Internationalist Magazine

People, Ideas, and Action for Global Justice
www.newint.org

help@newint.org
@newint

Mission: "The New Internationalist workers' co-operative (NI) exists to
report on the issues of world poverty and inequality; to focus attention
on the unjust relationship between the powerful and powerless worldwide;
to debate and campaign for the radical changes necessary to meet the
basic needs of all; and to bring to life the people, the ideas and the
action in the fight for global justice. The New Internationalist
communications co-operative is based in Oxford with editorial and
sales offices in Toronto, Canada; Adelaide, Australia and Christchurch,
Aotearoa /New Zealand."

Alternative Media/Media Activism

Nonviolence International

Action towards Peace and Justice
www.nonviolenceinternational.net
info@nonviolenceinternational.net
(202) 244–0951
@NVIntl

Mission: "Nonviolence International researches and promotes nonviolent
action and seeks to reduce the use of violence worldwide. We believe that
every culture and religion can employ appropriate nonviolent methods for
positive social change and international peace."

Peace, Nonviolence, Anti-War, & Anti-Militarism

October 22nd Coalition to Stop Police Brutality, Repression, and the Criminalization of a Generation

www.october22.org
oct22national@gmail.com

"The October 22nd Coalition to Stop Police Brutality, Repression and the
Criminalization of a Generation has been mobilizing every year since 1996
for a National Day of Protest on October 22, bringing together those under
the gun and those not under the gun as a powerful voice to expose the
epidemic of police brutality."

Prison Industrial Complex

Office of the High Commissioner for Human Rights (United Nations Human Rights)

www.ohchr.org
infodesk@ohchr.org
41 22 917 9220 (Switzerland)
@UNrightswire

"As the principal United Nations office mandated to promote and protect human rights for all, OHCHR leads global human rights efforts [and] speaks out objectively in the face of human rights violations worldwide. We provide a forum for identifying, highlighting and developing responses to today's human rights challenges, and act as the principal focal point of human rights research, education, public information, and advocacy activities in the United Nations system.

"Since Governments have the primary responsibility to protect human rights, the High Commissioner for Human Rights (OHCHR) provides assistance to Governments, such as expertise and technical trainings in the areas of administration of justice, legislative reform, and electoral process, to help implement international human rights standards on the ground. We also assist other entities with responsibility to protect human rights to fulfil their obligations and individuals to realize their rights."

Human, Labour, & Civil Rights

Office on Violence Against Women

http://www.justice.gov/ovw
ovw.info@usdoj.gov
(202) 307–6026
@TheJusticeDept

"The mission of the Office on Violence Against Women (OVW), a component of the U.S. Department of Justice, is to provide federal leadership in developing the nation's capacity to reduce violence against women and administer justice for and strengthen services to victims of domestic violence, dating violence, sexual assault, and stalking."

Feminism/Women's Issues

One Earth

Rethinking the Good Life
www.oneearthweb.org
info@oneearthweb.org
(604) 813–3361
@OneEarthWeb

"One Earth connects the dots between who we are, what we buy, where we
  live, what we make, what we trade, and how we live together to create
  positive impact.
"One Earth is a nonprofit 'think and do' tank based in Vancouver, Canada.
  Our mission is to transform production and consumption patterns locally,
  nationally and internationally to be sustainable, healthy, and just within the
  limits of living systems.
"Our passion is bringing people, ideas and activities together to accelerate
  the transition towards sustainability – we catalyze networking and action
  on the issues we care about. One Earth adopts a systems approach to
  identify high-impact solutions, and engages the arts and citizens to create
  compelling visions of life in sustainable futures."

Environmentalism

OneWorld

Empathy in Action
www.oneworld.org
hello@oneworld.org
@OneWorld_News

"OneWorld is a non-profit UK-based organization which innovates new
  media, mobile and web technologies for social good, helping people across
  the world to improve their lives and become active citizens."

Alternative Media/Media Activism

Ontario Public Interest Research Groups

www.opirg.org
opirgprovcoordinator@gmail.com

"The OPIRG Provincial Network is made up of individual OPIRG chapters
from across the province of Ontario. OPIRGs are grassroots student
organizations that are committed to struggling for social and environmental
justice."

"Public Interest Research Groups (PIRGs) are campus-based social and
environmental justice organizations. PIRGs are non-hierarchical (they use
a consensus model of decision-making) and are rooted in a commitment to
anti-oppression. Individual PIRG chapters are located at universities across
the province ... Outside of Ontario, PIRGs can also be found in Quebec,
Nova Scotia, Saskatchewan, Alberta, and British Columbia."

Environmentalism; Youth Movements & Organizing

Organic Consumers Association

Campaigning for Health, Justice, Sustainability, Peace, and Democracy
www.organicconsumers.org
info@organicconsumers.org
(218) 226–4164
@OrganicConsumer

"The Organic Consumers Association (OCA) is an online and grassroots
non-profit public interest organization campaigning for health, justice, and
sustainability. The OCA deals with crucial issues of food safety, industrial
agriculture, genetic engineering, children's health, corporate accountability,
Fair Trade, environmental sustainability and other key topics. We are the only
organization in the US focused on promoting the views and interests of the
nation's estimated 50 million organic and socially responsible consumers."

Corporate Accountability; Environmentalism; Food & Farming

Oxfam International

The Power of People against Poverty
www.oxfam.org
information@oxfaminternational.org
44 1865 339 100 (UK)
@Oxfam

"Oxfam is an international confederation of 17 organizations working
together with partners and local communities in more than 90 countries.

"One person in three in the world lives in poverty. Oxfam is determined to change that world by mobilizing the power of people against poverty.

"Around the globe, Oxfam works to find practical, innovative ways for people to lift themselves out of poverty and thrive. We save lives and help rebuild livelihoods when crisis strikes. And we campaign so that the voices of the poor influence the local and global decisions that affect them.

"In all we do, Oxfam works with partner organizations and alongside vulnerable women and men to end the injustices that cause poverty."

Economic Justice; Globalization

Pedagogy & Theatre of the Oppressed

www.ptoweb.org
@PTOtweets

"Pedagogy & Theatre of the Oppressed, Inc. (PTO) supports people whose work challenges oppressive systems by promoting critical thinking and social justice through liberatory theatre and popular education.

"Our approaches stem from the theories and practices of Paulo Freire and Augusto Boal. We foster collaborative connections to share, develop, promote, and document liberatory theatre, popular education, and other revolutionary actions. PTO serves as a resource for oppressed peoples and their allies in diverse communities, contexts, and traditions around the world."

Education/Critical Pedagogy; Human, Labour, & Civil Rights

People and Planet

Student Action on World Poverty and the Environment
www.peopleandplanet.org
people@peopleandplanet.org
44 (0) 1865 264 180 (UK)
@peopleandplanet

"People and Planet is the largest student network in Britain campaigning to end world poverty, defend human rights and protect the environment. People and Planet is a student-led movement that empowers young people with the skills, confidence and knowledge they need to make change happen, at home and globally."

Environmentalism; Youth Movements & Organizing

People for the Ethical Treatment of Animals (PETA)

www.peta.org
(757) 622–7382
@peta

Mission Statement: "PETA focuses its attention on the four areas in which the
  largest numbers of animals suffer the most intensely for the longest periods
  of time: on factory farms, in the clothing trade, in laboratories, and in the
  entertainment industry. We also work on a variety of other issues, including
  the cruel killing of beavers, birds, and other 'pests' as well as cruelty to
  domesticated animals.
"PETA works through public education, cruelty investigations, research,
  animal rescue, legislation, special events, celebrity involvement, and protest
  campaigns."

Animal Rights

The People's Movement for Human Rights Learning

www.pdhre.org
pdhre@igc.org
(212) 749–3156
@PDHRE

"PDHRE, People's Movement for Human Rights Learning, formerly
  The People's Decade for Human Rights Education, is an independent,
  international, non-profit organization promoting, enhancing and providing
  learning about human rights as relevant to people's daily lives at all levels
  of society, that leads to action. PDHRE was established in 1988 in an effort
  to respond to the unmet need for Human Rights Learning at the grassroots
  level that needed this knowledge and strategy the most as a powerful
  tool for action. Since then, PDHRE has conducted and/or facilitated
  Human Rights Learning and training at the community level in more than
  60 countries, and produced a unique range of written and audio-visual
  pedagogical materials to support learning and dialogue for socio-economic
  transformation. PDHRE was instrumental in the creation of the United
  Nations Decade for Human Rights Education (1995–2004) and is committed
  to create a process by which all will know human rights towards social and

economic transformation. PDHRE is convinced that imposed ignorance is a human rights violation and the learning about human rights as a way of life is an imperative for meaningful human, social and economic development. There is none other... to break through the vicious cycle of humiliation."

Education/Critical Pedagogy; Human, Labour, & Civil Rights

Praxis Peace Institute

Reconciling Theory and Practice
www.praxispeace.org
info@praxispeace.org
(707) 939–2973

"Praxis Peace Institute offers forums, workshops, and local and international conferences ... These events bring together leading facilitators and thinkers in the areas of conflict resolution, psychology, sociology, political science, economics, politics, history, philosophy, religion, gender studies, and the arts and sciences ... The ultimate goal is to make peacebuilding available to everyone – through education, media support, and community workshops."

Education/Critical Pedagogy; Peace, Nonviolence, Anti-War, & Anti-Militarism

Press Progress

www.pressprogress.ca
info@pressprogress.ca
@pressprogress

"PressProgress advances progressive solutions and challenges conservative ideas with hard-hitting news and analysis. PressProgress is a project of the Broadbent Institute.
"Mandate: PressProgress is editorially independent. It operates under the Broadbent Institute's mandate of advocating on issues that fall broadly within the following categories: social and economic equality; green economy; and democratic renewal.
"Commitment: All information presented by PressProgress is sourced and supported by links to credible and relevant online sources. Driven by facts, PressProgress takes strong editorial positions and is transparent about its advocacy for progressive issues."

Alternative Media; Democracy

Prison Activist Resource Center (PARC)

www.prisonactivist.org
info@prisonactivist.org
(510) 893–4648

"PARC is a prison abolitionist group committed to exposing and
challenging all forms of institutionalized racism, sexism, able-ism,
heterosexism, and classism, specifically within the Prison Industrial
Complex (PIC). PARC believes in building strategies and tactics that
build safety in our communities without reliance on the police or the
PIC. We produce a directory that is free to prisoners upon request, and
seek to work in solidarity with prisoners, ex-prisoners, their friends and
families. We also work with teachers and activists on many prison issues.
This work includes building action networks and materials that expose
the continuing neglect and outright torture of more than 2 million
people imprisoned within the USA; as well as the 5+ million who are
under some form of surveillance and control by the so-called justice
system."

Prison Industrial Complex

Protest.Net

www.protest.net
rabble-rouser@protest.net

"Protest.Net is a collective of activists who are working together to create our
own media. By publishing a public record of our political activities on the
web we are taking a stand against the established media. We are standing
up and showing that serious activism is alive and well at the dawn of the
21st century."

Activism/Organizing; Alternative Media/Media Activism

Public Campaign

Clean Money, Clean Elections
www.publiccampaign.org
info@publiccampaign.org

(202) 640–5600
@publiccampaign

"Public Campaign is a non-profit, non-partisan organization dedicated to
sweeping campaign reform that aims to dramatically reduce the role of
big special interest money in American politics. Public Campaign is laying
the foundation for reform by working with a broad range of organizations,
including local community groups, around the country that are fighting
for change and national organizations whose members are not fairly
represented under the current campaign finance system. Together we are
building a network of national and state-based efforts to create a powerful
national force for federal and state campaign reform."

Democracy

Public Citizen

Protecting Health, Safety and Democracy
www.citizen.org
member@citizen.org
(202) 588–1000
@Public_Citizen

"Public Citizen serves as the people's voice in the nation's capital. Since our
founding in 1971, we have delved into an array of areas, but our work
on each issue shares an overarching goal: To ensure that all citizens are
represented in the halls of power ...
"We have five policy groups: our Congress Watch division, the Energy
Program, Global Trade Watch, the Health Research Group and our
Litigation Group.
"Public Citizen is a nonprofit organization that does not participate in partisan
political activities or endorse any candidates for elected office. We accept
no government or corporate money – we rely solely on foundation grants,
publication sales and support from our 300,000 members."

Activism/Organizing; Democracy; Human,
Labour, & Civil Rights

Public Citizen's Commercial Alert

Protecting Communities from Commercialism
www.commercialalert.org

(202) 588–7741
@CommercialAlert

"Commercial Alert is a non-profit organization ... In 2011, Commercial Alert
became a project of Public Citizen. Our mission is to keep the commercial
culture within its proper sphere, and to prevent it from exploiting children
and subverting the higher values of family, community, environmental
integrity and democracy."

Education/Critical Pedagogy

Radical Teacher

Alternative Views on Teaching and Learning
www.radicalteacher.com
trking@radicalteacher.com

"Radicalteacher exists to bring alternative understandings and, more
important, alternative practices to undergraduate teaching."

Education/Critical Pedagogy

Radical Women

www.radicalwomen.org
radicalwomenus@gmail.com
(415) 864–1278
@RadicalWomenNYC

"A trailblazing socialist feminist organization, Radical Women is
the revolutionary wing of the women's movement and a strong feminist
voice within the Left. Immersed in the daily fight against racism,
sexism, homophobia, and labor exploitation, Radical Women believes in
multi-issue organizing around the needs of the most oppressed. We view
women's leadership as decisive to social change and train
women to take their place in the forefront of the struggle. Radical
Women is an autonomous, all-women's group, united on the basis
of shared socialist feminist ideals expressed in The Radical Women
Manifesto."

Anti-Racism; Feminism/Women's Issues; Queer Rights

Rainforest Action Network

www.ran.org
answers@ran.org
(415) 398–4404
@ran

Mission: "Rainforest Action Network campaigns for the forests, their
inhabitants and the natural systems that sustain life by transforming the
global marketplace through education, grassroots organizing and nonviolent direct action."

Environmentalism

The Real News Network

Independent News, Blogs, and Editorials
www.therealnews.com
contact@therealnews.com
(410) 500–5235
@TheRealNews

Mission: "The question we settle in an election is not whether elites shall rule,
but which elites shall rule," said conservative pundit George Will on ABC's
This Week.
"That's why we need daily television news that reports with ordinary
people's interests in mind. The Real News is such a network; it's the
missing link in the global media landscape …
"We cover the big stories of the day, but we broaden the definition of what's
important. The movements for working people's rights, for people, the
health of our planet and against racism – are news."

Alternative Media/Media Activism

Reclaim Democracy!

Restoring Citizen Authority Over Corporations
www.reclaimdemocracy.org

info@reclaimdemocracy.org
(406) 582–1224
@ReclaimDemo

"ReclaimDemocracy.org works to create a representative democracy
with an actively participating public, where citizens don't merely choose
from a menu of options determined by elites, but play an active role in
guiding the country and its political agenda. We believe that one's
influence should be a direct result of the quality of one's ideas and the
energy one puts into promoting these ideas, independent of wealth or
status."
Vision: "to create a society in which an informed and active citizenry
is sovereign and makes policy decisions based on the will of the
majority."
Mission: "to build democracy through activism, education, and
collaboration."

Democracy

Reporters Without Borders

For Freedom of Information
http://en.rsf.org
administration@rsf.org
33 1 44 83 84 84 (France - International Secretariat)
@RSF_RWB

Mission: "to continuously monitor attacks on freedom of information
worldwide; to denounce any such attacks in the media; to act in
cooperation with governments to fight censorship and laws aimed at
restricting freedom of information; to morally and financially assist
persecuted journalists, as well as their families; to offer material assistance
to war correspondents in order to enhance their safety."

Alternative Media/Media Activism

The Ruckus Society

Actions Speak Louder than Words
www.ruckus.org
ruckus@ruckus.org

(510) 931–6339
@ruckusociety

Mission: "The Ruckus Society provides environmental, human rights, and social
     justice organizers with the tools, training, and support needed to achieve their
     goals through the strategic use of creative, nonviolent direct action.
"Working with a broad range of communities, organizations, and movements –
     from high school students to professional organizations – Ruckus facilitates
     the sharing of information and expertise that strengthens the capacity to
     change our relationship with the environment and each other.
"We believe building partnerships with organizers and communities to create
     spaces for participatory learning, networking, and resource sharing is the
     most powerful way we as individuals can contribute to actualizing positive
     social change."

Activism/Organizing

Say Her Name (#SayHerName)

http://www.aapf.org/sayhernamereport/
info@aapf.org
@AAPolicyForum

"In honor of Sandra Bland, and to continue to call attention to violence
     against Black women in the U.S.... Say Her Name is intended to serve as
     a resource for the media, organizers, researchers, policy makers, and other
     stakeholders to better understand and address Black women's experiences
     of profiling and policing."

Anti-Racism; Feminism/Women's Issues

Sea Shepherd Conservation Society

www.seashepherd.org
info@seashepherd.org
(360) 370–5650
@seashepherd

Mission: "Established in 1977, Sea Shepherd Conservation Society (SSCS)
     is an international non-profit, marine wildlife conservation organization.
     Our mission is to end the destruction of habitat and slaughter of wildlife

in the world's oceans in order to conserve and protect ecosystems and species.

"Sea Shepherd uses innovative direct-action tactics to investigate, document, and take action when necessary to expose and confront illegal activities on the high seas. By safeguarding the biodiversity of our delicately-balanced ocean ecosystems, Sea Shepherd works to ensure their survival for future generations."

Animal Rights

Sierra Club

Explore, Enjoy, and Protect the Planet
www.sierraclub.org
information@sierraclub.org
(415) 977–5500
@sierraclub

"Founded by legendary conservationist John Muir in 1892, the Sierra Club is now the nation's largest and most influential grassroots environmental organization – with more than two million members and supporters. Our successes range from protecting millions of acres of wilderness to helping pass the Clean Air Act, Clean Water Act, and Endangered Species Act. More recently, we've made history by leading the charge to move away from the dirty fossil fuels that cause climate disruption and toward a clean energy economy."

Environmentalism

Social Watch

Poverty Eradication and Gender Justice
www.socialwatch.org
(598) 2403–1424 (Uruguay)
@socwatch

"Social Watch is an international network of citizens' organizations in the struggle to eradicate poverty and the causes of poverty, to end all forms of discrimination and racism, to ensure an equitable distribution of wealth and the realization of human rights.

"We are committed to peace, social, economic, environment and gender justice, and we emphasize the right of all people not to be poor.

"Social Watch holds governments, the UN system and international
organizations accountable for the fulfilment of national, regional and
international commitments to eradicate poverty.
"Social Watch will achieve its objectives through a comprehensive strategy
of advocacy, awareness-building, monitoring, organizational development
and networking. Social Watch promotes people-centred sustainable
development."

Human, Labour, & Civil Rights

Survival International

The Movement for Tribal Peoples
www.survivalinternational.org
info@survivalinternational.org
+44 (0)207 687 8700 (UK)
@Survival

"We're the only organization that champions tribal peoples around the world.
We help them defend their lives, protect their lands and determine their
own futures.
"Tribal peoples have developed ways of life that are largely self-sufficient and
extraordinarily diverse. Many of the world's staple crops and drugs used
in Western medicine originate with them, and have saved millions of lives.
Even so, tribal peoples are portrayed as backward and primitive simply
because their communal ways are different. Industrialized societies subject
them to genocidal violence, slavery and racism so they can steal their lands,
resources and labor in the name of 'progress' and 'civilization'.
"Our work is preventing the annihilation of tribal peoples. We give them
a platform to speak to the world. We investigate atrocities and present
evidence to the United Nations and other international forums. We support
legal representation. We fund medical and self-help projects. We educate,
research, campaign, lobby and protest. And we won't give up until we all
have a world where tribal peoples are respected and their human rights
protected."

Indigenous Rights

TakingITGlobal

Inspire, Inform, Involve
www.tigweb.org

(416) 977–9363
@takingitglobal

"TakingITGlobal is one of the world's leading networks of young people
learning about, engaging with, and working towards tackling global
challenges."
Vision: "Youth around the world actively engaged and connected in sharing a
more inclusive, peaceful and sustainable world."
Mission: "TakingITGlobal empowers youth to understand and act on the
world's greatest challenges."

Activism/Organizing; Youth Movements & Organizing

Teen Talking Circles

http://www.teentalkingcircles.org/
info@teentalkingcircles.org
(206) 842–3000
@talkingcircles

"The Daughters Sisters Project, Teen Talking Circles, was conceived in 1993
to help young women navigate the teen years and has since expanded to
include teen boys, and adults. Our first Girl's Circle started in March, 1994,
on Bainbridge Island.
"We are organically grown; founded on the principle that both a mature self-
identity and healthy relationships develop naturally when we feel free to
speak our truth from our hearts and hear the truth of others with our hearts.
"Talking Circles give teens an opportunity to strengthen their feelings of
self-esteem, self-worth, authenticity, and resilience, and practice skills
that contribute to making wise and healthy choices. Youth in TTC circles
learn Compassionate Listening and non-violent communication practices
to create sustainable and thriving relationships with self and others. TTC
fosters a deeper understanding of the values that unite us as a human
community: a critical component for creating meaningful lives, responsible
citizenship, and an empowered sense of self in an interdependent world."

Feminism/Women's Issues; Youth Movements & Organizing

Third Wave Fund

http://www.thirdwavefund.org/
info@thirdwavefund.org

(917) 387–1262
@3wave

"Third Wave Fund is the only national fund that supports and strengthens youth-led gender justice activism focusing on efforts that advance the political power, well-being, and self determination of communities of color and low-income communities in the US. We partner with institutions and individual donors to invest resources in under-funded regions and social justice youth movements."

Feminism/Women's Issues; Youth Movements & Organizing

TRIBES PROJECT

Multicultural Performing Arts
www.tribes-project.com

"TRIBES PROJECT is dedicated to multicultural perspectives and representation through the performing arts. We produce evocative original works and adaptations as forums for exploring race, culture, and issues of the human condition.
"TRIBES PROJECT brings together diverse groups of people to create performances that empower them to intensely investigate the complexity of race and cultural issues through the solidarity of an ensemble production process. Tribes members research, write, and perform their original and adapted productions for audiences of all ages and backgrounds ...
"By giving people a platform to voice their unique perspectives on race and culture, we strive to become an international model for multicultural awareness, education and understanding – through the arts."

Anti-Racism; Youth Movements & Organizing

Union for Radical Political Economics

www.urpe.org
urpe@urpe.org
(413) 577–0806
@urpe_

"The Union for Radical Political Economics (URPE) is an interdisciplinary association devoted to the study, development and application of radical political economic analysis to social problems. Founded in 1968, URPE presents a continuing critique of the capitalist system and all forms of exploitation and oppression while helping to construct a progressive social policy and create socialist alternatives. URPE members, often in cooperation with other organizations, organize local study groups, speaking and writing projects, and political events. URPE's international members in Latin America are involved in discussions, visits, and exchanges."

Economic Justice; Human, Labour, & Civil Rights

United for a Fair Economy

We support and help build social movements for greater equality.
www.faireconomy.org
info@faireconomy.org
(617) 423–2148
@UFE

"United for a Fair Economy challenges the concentration of wealth and power that corrupts democracy, deepens the racial divide and tears communities apart. We use popular economics education, trainings, and creative communications to support social movements working for a resilient, sustainable and equitable economy."

Economic Justice

Vegan Action

Change for a Better World
www.vegan.org
info@vegan.org
(804) 577–8341
@VeganActionOrg

"Vegan Action works to reduce animal suffering, minimize environmental impact, and improve human health.
"Our efforts over the past 19 years include certifying hundreds of vegan products with our logo through our Vegan Certification Campaign, introducing humane organizations to veganism with our Humane Outreach Campaign, bringing vegan food into public and private facilities nationwide with our Food Service Campaign, and sharing the compelling

ideas behind veganism with thousands of people with our Share Vegan Campaign and additional tabling events. We also raise awareness to over a quarter of a million people a year through [our] website."

Animal Rights

War Child

www.warchild.ca
info@warchild.ca
1–866-WARCHILD
@WarChildCan

"War Child's mission is to work with war-affected communities to help children reclaim their childhood through access to education, opportunity and justice. War Child takes an active role in raising public awareness around the impact of war on communities and the shared responsibility to act.
"War Child's vision is for a world where no child knows war."

Peace, Nonviolence, Anti-War, & Anti-Militarism

War Resisters League

Resisting War at Home & War Abroad since 1923
www.warresisters.org
wrl@warresisters.org
(212) 228–0450
@resistwar

WRL Pledge: "The War Resisters League has been resisting war at home and war abroad since 1923. Today, as one of the leading radical voices in the antiwar movement, we challenge military recruitment and war profiteering, organize nonviolent direct action, and offer on-the-ground tools to end the current war and all wars. The War Resisters League affirms that all war is a crime against humanity. We are determined not to support any kind of war, international or civil, and to strive nonviolently for the removal of all causes of war, including racism, sexism and all forms of exploitation."

Peace, Nonviolence, Anti-War, & Anti-Militarism

We Interrupt This Message

www.interrupt.org
we@interrupt.org

Mission: "We Interrupt this Message is an activist project dedicated to
    building the capacity of public interest advocates to conduct traditional
    media work, reframe public debate, and interrupt media stereotypes.
"Interrupt provides on-line media tools and access to a network of media
    consultants and trainers.
"Interrupt was founded on the belief that marginalized communities and
    their advocates need to be able to *change* media coverage as well as *get*
    media coverage in order to promote the well-being of their communities."

Fairness in Media Organizations

Women in Black

For Justice. Against War.
www.womeninblack.org

"Women in Black is a world-wide network of women committed to peace
    with justice and actively opposed to injustice, war, militarism and other
    forms of violence. As women experiencing these things in different ways
    in different regions of the world, we support each other's movements.
    An important focus is challenging the militarist policies of our own
    governments. We are not an organisation, but a means of communicating
    and a formula for action."

*Feminism/Women's Issues; Peace, Nonviolence,
Anti-War, & Anti-Militarism*

Women Thrive Worldwide

Because When Women Thrive, the Whole World Thrives
www.womenthrive.org
thrive@womenthrive.org
(202) 999–4500
@WomenThrive

"We are the leading nonprofit organization bringing the voice of women around the world directly to decision-makers in Washington, D.C."
Vision: "Women Thrive Worldwide works to create a world in which women and men work together as equals so that they, their families and their communities can thrive."
Mission: "Women Thrive Worldwide advocates for change at the US and global levels so that women and men can share equally in the enjoyment of opportunities, economic prosperity, voice, and freedom from fear and violence."

Feminism/Women's Issues

World Citizen Foundation

www.worldcitizen.org

"The World Citizen Foundation is a nonprofit nonpartisan think-tank dedicated to the design of solutions to international problems based on the fundamental principles of equal human dignity, liberty, democracy and constitutionally protected basic rights of all.
We are dedicated to the proposition that all levels of political authority can only derive their legitimacy from the fundamental sovereignty of the people. This is widely accepted at local and national levels but not internationally or globally. This contradiction is the ultimate source of the corruption of democracy at local and national levels, as the non-democratic paradigm which rules in international relations corrodes the paradigm of individual rights and freedom which is used domestically."

Democracy

Worldwatch Institute

Vision for a Sustainable World
www.worldwatch.org
worldwatch@worldwatch.org
(202) 745–8092
@Worldwatch

Mission: "Through research and outreach that inspire action, the Worldwatch Institute works to accelerate the transition to a sustainable world that meets human needs. The Institute's top mission objectives are universal access to renewable energy and nutritious food, expansion of environmentally sound jobs and development, transformation of cultures from consumerism to sustainability, and an early end to population growth through healthy and intentional childbearing."

Environmentalism

Young Democratic Socialists

The Youth Section of Democratic Socialists of America
www.ydsusa.org
info@dsausa.org
(212) 727–8610
@ydsusa

"We are a national organization of 20 campus chapters and several hundred activists, and we are the student section of the Democratic Socialists of America. We are proud of our unique status as one of the few national, multi-issue left-wing student organizations in the United States. Twice a year we meet at our winter outreach conference and summer leadership retreat in order to share our experiences and build a national community. We also work together to put forward our political perspective on our blog, The Activist.

"The Young Democratic Socialists is part of the international struggle to build a better world. We organize on college and high school campuses to fight for the immediate needs of workers and students, while building our capacity to fight for more radical and structural changes in the long term. We call the better society we are fighting for democratic socialism."

Human, Labour, & Civil Rights; Youth Movements & Organizing

Youth Activism Project

www.youthactivismproject.org
info@youthactivismproject.org
(301) 929–8808, (301) 929–8808
@activism_wendy

"The Youth Activism Project was founded ... as a non-partisan organization to encourage young people to speak up and pursue lasting solutions to problems they care deeply about. This national nonprofit clearinghouse strives to:

Promote youth civic engagement …;

Provide free advice to young people to help them transform their ideas into proposals …;

Train adults on how to collaborate and co-pilot successfully with young people;

Convince nonprofits, schools and government to engage young people in meaningful roles and the decision-making process;

Partner with organizations on upcoming visits to Congress to create hands-on training to increase the impact of young advocates …;

Share promising practices and strategies for lasting change through our online resources, training manuals and consulting;

Serve as a network, connecting like-minded individuals who are tackling similar youth empowerment and public policy issues in the United States and internationally."

Activism/Organizing; Youth Movements & Organizing

YouthLine

Confidential, free, and nonjudgmental peer support.
www.youthline.ca
askus@youthline.ca
1–800–268–9688 (YouthLine hotline)
@LGBTYouthLine

"The Lesbian Gay Bi Trans Youth Line is a toll-free service provided by youth for youth. We're here to offer support, information and referrals specific to your concerns. We are here because we want to be there for you – to be part of your community. We may not have lived your experiences exactly, but we can probably relate. We too, are lesbian, gay, bisexual, transgender, transsexual, two-spirit or queer."

Queer Rights; Youth Movements & Organizing

Z Communications

A Community of People Committed to Social Change
www.zcomm.org
zmag@zmag.org
(508) 548–9063

"Z Communications is the overarching name for all of Z's various projects and activities. It includes Z Magazine, ZNet, Z Media Institute, Z Video Productions, ZSpace, and ZBooks, and diverse components of each.

"Z Magazine is a print monthly periodical devoted to addressing class, race, gender, and power issues in contemporary society and social life ...

"ZNet is primarily a repository of thousands of text articles, video, audio and other links, and other content for general viewing. It is updated daily."

Works Cited

Ahmed, Sara. *The Promise of Happiness*. Durham: Duke UP, 2010. Print.

Archibold, Randal C. "Arizona Enacts Stringent Law on Immigration." *The New York Times*. New York Times, 23 Apr. 2010. Web. 13 Aug. 2010.

Bakhtin, Mikhail. *Problems of Dostoevsky's Poetics*. Ed. and trans. Caryl Emerson. Minneapolis: University of Minnesota Press, 1984. Print.

Barboza, David. "China Passes Japan as Second-Largest Economy." *The New York Times*. New York Times, 15 Aug. 2010. Web. 23 May 2011.

Barndt, Deborah, ed., with ¡VIVA! Project Partners. *¡VIVA! Community Arts and Popular Education in the Americas*. Albany, NY and Toronto: State University of New York Press and Between the Lines, 2011. Print.

Benjamin, Walter. *Illuminations: Essays and Reflections*. Trans. Harry Zohn. Ed. Hannah Arendt. New York: Schocken, 2007. Print.

Benzie, Robert, Bruce Campion-Smith, and Les Whittington. "Ordinary Folks Don't Care About Arts: Harper." *thestar.com*. Toronto Star, 24 Sep. 2008. Web. 13 Aug. 2010.

Blanco, Juan Antonio. "Natural History and Social History: Limits and Urgent Priorities which Condition the Exercise of Human Rights." *The Poverty of Rights: Human Rights and the Eradication of Poverty*. Ed. Willem van Genugten and Camilo Perez-Bustillo. London: Zed Books, 2001. 40–8. Print.

Brand, Dionne. *What We All Long For*. Toronto: Knopf, 2005. Print.

Brooks, Daniel, and Guillermo Verdecchia. *The Noam Chomsky Lectures: A Play*. Toronto: Coach House Press, 1991. Print.

Butler, Johnnella E. "Democracy, Diversity, and Civic Engagement." *Academe: Bulletin of the American Association of University Professors* 86.4 (Jul/Aug 2000): 52–5. Print.

Centre for Community-Based Research. 1 Apr. 2009. Web. 6 Jan. 2011.

– *Community University Research Alliance*. Centre for Community Based Research. 2008. Web. 6 Jan. 2011.

– *Leaders Mobilizing Change*. n.d. Web. 6 Jan. 2011.

– "Taking Culture Seriously in Community Mental Health." 2008. Web. Jan. 2011.

Chamberlin, J. Edward. *If This is Your Land, Where Are Your Stories? Finding Common Ground*. Toronto: Vintage Canada, 2004. Print.

Chang, Jeff. *Can't Stop Won't Stop: A History of the Hip Hop Generation*. New York: Picador, 2005. Print.

Charon, Rita. "Narrative Medicine: Attention, Representation, Affiliation." *Narrative* 13.3 (2005): 261–70. Print.

Chomsky, Noam, and Edward S. Herman. *Manufacturing Consent: The Political Economy of the Mass Media*. New York: Pantheon Books, 1988. Print.

Coates, Ta-Nehisi. *Between the World and Me*. New York: Spiegel & Grau, 2015. Print.

Conference Evaluation Forms. *Towards Cultural Empowerment*. Unpublished. Waterloo. 7 Dec. 2006. Print.

Cooper, David D. "Can Civic Engagement Rescue the Humanities?" *Community-Based Learning and the Work of Literature*. Eds. Susan Danielson and Ann Marie Fallon. Boston: Anker, 2007. 1–25. Print.

Cunsolo Willox, Ashlee, Paul Danyluk, Allison Dean, Julio Diaz, Colin Holland, Benjamin Walsh, and Robert Zacharias. Introduction. *Guelph Speaks! Re-Storying the City*. Eds. Ashlee Cunsolo Willox et al. Guelph, ON: Guelph Narrative Collective, 2007. 1–4.

Curry-Stevens, Ann. "New Forms of Transformative Education: Pedagogy for the Privileged." *Journal of Transformative Education* 5.1 (2007): 33–58. Print.

Dabulskis, Susanne E. "Outsider Research: How White Writers 'Explore' Native Issues, Knowledges and Experiences." Diss. University of Toronto, 1997. Print.

Davis, Lennard. *Resisting Novels: Ideology and Fiction*. New York: Methuen, 1987. Print.

Dean, Amber. "Colonialism, Neoliberalism, and University-Community Engagement: What Sorts of Encounters with Difference Are Our Institutions Prioritizing?" *Encounters Across Difference in a Neoliberal Context*. Eds. Caitlin Janzen, Donna Jeffery, and Kristin Smith. Waterloo: Wilfrid Laurier UP, forthcoming.

Diaz, Junot. "Keynote Speech at Facing Race Conference." Online Video Clip. *YouTube*, YouTube, 29 Nov. 2012. Web. 3 Dec. 2012.

Di Leo, Jeffrey R., ed. *On Anthologies: Politics and Pedagogy*. Lincoln, Nebraska: University of Nebraska Press, 2004. Print.

Ellsworth Elizabeth. "Why Doesn't This Feel Empowering? Working Through the Repressive Myths of Critical Pedagogy." *Harvard Educational Review* 59. 3 (August 1989): 297–324.

Fallon, Ann Marie. Preface. *Community-Based Learning and the Work of Literature*. Eds. Susan Danielson and Ann Marie Fallon. Boston: Anker, 2007. 1–25. Print.

Findlay, Stephanie, and Nicholas Köhler. "Too Asian?" *Macleans.ca*. Rogers, 10 Nov. 2010. Web. 16 Nov. 2013.

Freire, Paulo. *Pedagogy of the Oppressed*. Thirtieth Anniversary Edition. Trans. Myra Bergman Ramos. New York: Continuum, 2008. Print.

Giroux, Henry A. Foreword. Contending Zones and Public Spaces. *Zones of Contention: Essays on Art, Institutions, Gender, and Anxiety*. By Carol Becker. Albany: State University of New York Press, 1996. ix–xii. Print.

– *On Critical Pedagogy*. New York: Continuum, 2011. Print.

– *Youth in a Suspect Society: Democracy or Disposability?* New York: Palgrave, 2009. Print.

Goldberg, David Theo. *The Threat of Race: Reflections on Racial Neoliberalism*. Malden: Wiley-Blackwell, 2010. Print.

Haraway, Donna. "Situated Knowledges: The Science Question in Feminism and the Privilege of Partial Perspective." *Feminist Studies* 14.3 (1988): 575–99. Print.

Heble, Ajay. *Landing on the Wrong Note: Jazz, Dissonance, and Critical Practice*. New York: Routledge, 2000. Print.

– "'Why Can't We Go Somewhere There?' Sun Ra, Improvisation, and the Imagination of Future Possibilities." *Canadian Theatre Review* 143 (2010): 98–100. Print.

Hollander, Elizabeth L., and John Saltmarsh. "The Engaged University." *Academe* 86.4 (Jul/Aug 2000): 29–32. Print.

hooks, bell. "Performance Practice as a Site of Opposition." *Let's Get It On: The Politics of Black Performance*. Ed. Catherine Ugwu. Seattle: Bay Press, 1995. 210–21. Print.

– *Teaching Community: A Pedagogy of Hope*. New York: Routledge, 2003. Print.

– *Teaching to Transgress: Education as the Practice of Freedom*. London: Routledge, 1994. Print.

Hutcheon, Linda, and Michael Hutcheon. "A Convenience of Marriage: Collaboration and Interdisciplinarity. *PMLA* 116.5 (Oct 2001): 1364–76. Print.

Hyde, Catherine Ryan. *Pay It Forward*. Toronto: Pocket Books, 1999. Print.

Jefferess, David. "The 'Me to We' Social Enterprise: Global Education as Lifestyle Brand." *Critical Literacy: Theories and Practices* 6:1 (2012): 18–30.

Kelley, Robin. *Freedom Dreams: The Black Radical Imagination*. Boston: Beacon, 2002. Print.

King, Thomas. *The Truth About Stories: A Native Narrative*. Toronto: House of Anansi, 2003. Print.

The Kino-nda-niimi Collective, ed. *The Winter We Danced: Voices from the Past, the Future, and the Idle No More Movement*. Winnipeg: ARP Books, 2014. Print.

Klein, Naomi. *This Changes Everything: Capitalism vs. the Climate*. New York: Knopf Canada, 2014. Print.

Lewin, Tamar. "China Surges Past India as Top Home of Foreign Students." *The New York Times*. New York Times, 15 Nov. 2010. Web. 3 Feb. 2011.

Lewis, Stephen. *Race Against Time*. Toronto: Anansi, 2005. Print.

Lipsitz, George. *American Studies in a Moment of Danger*. Minneapolis: University of Minnesota Press, 2001. Print.

"Making a Run 'til November." *Economist.com*. The Economist, 4 Aug. 2010. Web. 6 Aug. 2010.

Martin, J. Paul. "Epilogue: The Next Step, Quality Control." *Human Rights Education for the Twenty-First Century*. Ed. George J. Andreopoulos and Richard Pierre Claude. Philadelphia: University of Pennsylvania Press, 1997. 600–9. Print.

McIntosh, Peggy. "White Privilege: Unpacking the Invisible Knapsack." *Race, Class, and Gender in the United States*. 6th ed. Ed. Paula S. Rothenberg. New York: Worth Publishers, 2004. 188–92. Print.

MT Space. "About Us," "Vision," and "Mission Statement & Mandate." MT Space, n.d. Web. 23 May 2011.

Nelson, Cary, and Stephen Watt. *Office Hours: Activism and Change in the Academy*. New York: Routledge, 2004. Print.

"No abortion in Canada's G8 Maternal Health Plan." *CBC News*. Canadian Broadcasting Corporation, 26 Apr. 2010. Web. 13 Aug. 2010.

Nussbaum, Martha. *Not for Profit: Why Democracy Needs the Humanities*. Princeton, NJ: Princeton UP, 2010. Print.

– "The Professor of Parody." *The New Republic Online*. N.p., 28 Nov 2000. Web. 22 Feb. 1999.

Nutt, Samantha. *Damned Nations: Greed, Guns, Armies & Aid*. Toronto: McClelland and Stewart, 2011. Print.

Ontario Council of Agencies Serving Immigrants. 10 March 2011. Ontario Council of Agencies Serving Immigrants. Web. 6 Jan. 2011.

Osnos, Evan. "Ai Weiwei Detained." *The New Yorker*. Condé Nast, 3 Apr. 2011. Web. 24 Apr. 2011.

– "The Grand Tour." *The New Yorker*. Condé Nast, 18 Apr. 2011. Web. 24 May 2011.

Petersen, Jennifer. "Case Re-Examined," 2003. Interview with Matuschka. < https://www.researchgate.net/publication/232874635_Interview_with_Matuschka_breast_cancer_art_sexuality_and_activism1>. Web. Accessed 2007.

Plan of Action, United Nations Decade for Human Rights Education (1995–2004), GA 49/184 of 23 Dec. 1994. Web. 16 Feb. 2012.

Poletta, Francesca. *It Was Like a Fever: Storytelling in Protest and Politics*. Chicago: University of Chicago Press, 2006. Print.

"The Power 100." *Art Review* (2011): 108–54. Print.

Ra, Sun. *The Immeasurable Equation: The Collected Poetry and Prose*. Eds. James L. Wolf and Hartmut Geerken. Wartaweil: Waitawhile, 2005. Print.

– Liner notes. *Sun Song*. By Sun Ra. Transition, 1957. LP.

Razack, Sherene H. *Looking White People in the Eye: Gender, Race, and Culture in the Courtrooms and Classrooms*. Toronto: University of Toronto Press, 1998. Print.

Robeson, Paul. "Robeson Calls for Aid to Negroes Defending Democracy in Spain." *Paul Robeson Speaks: Writings, Speeches, Interviews, 1918–1974*. Ed. Philip Sheldon Foner. New York: Brunner/Mazel, 1978. Print.

Rushdie, Salman. "Dangerous Arts." *The New York Times*. New York Times, 19 Apr. 2011. Web. 19 Apr. 2011.

Schaffer, Kay, and Sidonie Smith. *Human Rights and Narrated Lives: The Ethics of Recognition*. New York: Palgrave Macmillan, 2004. Print.

Scheppele, Kim Lane. "Foreword: Telling Stories." *Michigan Law Review* 87 (1989): 2073–98. Print.

Scholes, Robert. "Presidential Address 2004: The Humanities in a Posthumanist World." *PMLA* 120.3 (2005): 724–33. Print.

Shor, Ira. *When Students Have Power: Negotiating Authority in a Critical Pedagogy*. Chicago: University of Chicago Press, 1996. Print.

Shukaitis, Stevphen. "Space is the (Non)Place: Martians, Marxists, and the Outer Space of the Radical Imagination." *Sociological Review* 57.1 (2009): 98–113. Web. 15 Jan. 2010.

Simon, Roger. *Teaching Against the Grain: Texts for a Pedagogy of Possibility*. New York: Bergin & Garvey, 1992. Print.

Singh, Ajay. "The Education of a Radical." *UCLA Today*. UCLA Newsroom, 11 April 2006. Web. 5 August 2011.

Solinger, Rickie, Madeline Fox, and Kayhan Irani. Introduction. *Telling Stories to Change the World: Global Voices on the Power of Narrative to Build Community and Make Social Justice Claims*. Eds. Solinger et al. New York: Routledge, 2008. 1–11. Print.

Sommer, Doris. *The Work of Art in the World: Civic Agency and Public Humanities*. Durham, NC: Duke UP, 2014. Print.

Sousa Santos, Boaventura de, ed. *Another Knowledge is Possible: Beyond Northern Epistemologies. (Reinventing Social Emancipation: Toward New Manifestos)*. London: Verso, 2007. Print.

Spivak, Gayatri Chakravorty. *The Post-Colonial Critic: Interviews, Strategies, Dialogues*. New York: Routledge, 1990. Print.

Steiner, George. "The Muses' Farewell." *Salmagundi* 135/36 (2002): 148–56. Print.

Stoecker, Randy and Mary Beckman. "Making Higher Education Civic Engagement Matter in the Community." *Campus Compact*. N.p., 2 September 2010. Web. 5 Aug. 2011.

Strand, Kerry, Nicholas Cutforth, Randy Stoecker, Sam Marullo, and Patrick Donohue. *Principles and Practices: Community-Based Scholarship and Higher Education*. San Francisco, CA: Jossey-Bass, 2003. Print.

Tracey, Scott. "Tom King Likely to be NDP's Federal Candidate for Guelph." *Guelph Mercury* 26 March 2007: A3. Print.

United Nations General Assembly (2 March 2005). Revised Draft Plan of Action for the First Phase (2005–2007) of the World Programme for Human Rights Education. A/59/525/Rev.1 Web. 16 Feb. 2012.

United Nations General Assembly. (14 July 2005). United Nations World Programme for Human Rights Education. RES/59/113. Web. 16 Feb. 2012.

United Nations General Assembly. (6 March 1995). United Nations Decade for Human Rights Education. A/RES/49/184. Web. 16 Feb. 2012.

Volunteering Eh! Kitchener Waterloo Multicultural Centre, 2010. Web. 6 January 2011.

Wallerstein, Nina, and Bonnie Duran. "The Theoretical, Historical, and Practice Roots of CBPR." *Community-Based Participatory Research for Health: From Process to Outcomes*. Eds. M. Minkler and N. Wallerstein. San Francisco, CA: Jossey Bass, 2008. 25–46. Print.

Westheimer, Joel, and Joseph Kahne. "What Kind of Citizen? The Politics of Educating for Democracy." *American Education Research Journal* 41.2 (2004): n. pag. Web. 16 Feb. 2012.

Contributors

Brendan Arnott lives, works, and writes in the traditional territory of the Mississauga of the New Credit First Nations. His current work focuses on dance music's intersections with gender, race, politics, history, and identity.

Majdi Bou-Matar is a theatre practitioner residing in Waterloo, ON. Majdi founded the Multicultural Theatre Space after he immigrated to Canada in 2004, and IMPACT, an international theatre festival, in 2009. The MT Space is a growing professional company committed to cultural diversity.

Rachel Collins lives, works, and plays in Guelph, Ontario. She works for the International Institute for Critical Studies in Improvisation and Project Re·Vision: Revisioning Differences Mobile Media Arts Lab. She is an active volunteer for Girl Guides of Canada.

Ashlee Cunsolo is the Director of the Labrador Institute of Memorial University, and a former Canada Research Chair in Determinants of Healthy Communities. As a community-engaged social science and health researcher, working at the intersection of place, culture, health, and environment, she has a particular interest in the social, environmental, and cultural determinants of Indigenous health, capacity development, environmental ethics, and the social justice implications of social and health inequality. As a community-based researcher, Ashlee works collaboratively with Indigenous colleagues through community-led participatory research approaches and methods to identify community needs and priorities and work towards locally-appropriate and culturally-relevant adaptation strategies. She is a passionate researcher and environmental advocate, and has been recognized nationally and internationally for her community-based research and science outreach, and is one of Nature Canada's 75 Women for Nature.

Paul Danyluk has a Master's degree in English from Simon Fraser University and completed work towards a PhD at the University of Guelph, where he was a Doctoral Fellow at TransCanada Institute. His research focused on Canadian performance poetries and academic structure. Paul's work, "'everything wants to hang together': Re-Imagining Roy Kiyooka's Academic Subjectivities" was published in *Retooling the Humanities: The Culture of Research in Canadian Universities*, edited by Daniel Coleman and Smaro Kamboureli. Paul lives in Toronto, where he is actively involved in the cooperative movement as a member, director, and employee.

Gregory Fenton is a PhD candidate at McMaster University in Ontario, Canada, supported by a Joseph-Armand Bombardier Canada Graduate Scholarship (CGS) from the Social Sciences and Humanities Research Council (SSHRC). A resident of Toronto, his primary field of study is Asian North American literary and cultural studies. He currently works as Managing Editor of the journal *Critical Studies in Improvisation/Études critiques en improvisation* and serves as President of the Canadian Applied Literature Association (2015-Present) His artistic work has been displayed at Factory Media Centre in Hamilton, Ontario, and at the Ontario Science Centre in Toronto. He completed an M.A. in Cultural Studies and Critical Theory at McMaster University in 2012. From 2009 to 2011, he worked as a high school English teacher in Tianjin and Shanghai, China.

Ajay Heble is Professor of English in the School of English and Theatre Studies at the University of Guelph, and Director of the International Institute for Critical Studies in Improvisation. He is the author or editor of several books and the Founder and Artistic Director of the award-winning Guelph Jazz Festival. Recent projects include *People Get Ready: The Future of Jazz is Now* (co-edited with Rob Wallace), *The Fierce Urgency of Now: Improvisation, Rights, and the Ethics of Cocreation* (co-authored with Daniel Fischlin and George Lipsitz), and *The Improvisation Studies Reader: Spontaneous Acts* (co-edited with Rebecca Caines). He is also a founding co-editor of the journal *Critical Studies in Improvisation/Études critiques en improvisation* (www.criticalimprov.com), and Project Director for Improvisation, Community, and Social Practice, a large-scale

Major Collaborative Research Initiative, funded by the Social Sciences and Humanities Research Council of Canada. As a pianist, his recordings include *Different Windows*, a live recording of improvised music with percussionist Jesse Stewart (on the IntrepidEar label), *Hold True (Accroche-Toi)* and *Time of the Sign* with his quartet, The Vertical Squirrels (both on Ambiances Magnétiques).

Elizabeth Jackson's research interests include ethical models of community-engaged scholarship, the political implications of literary representation and criticism, critical pedagogy, and the often vexed relationship between formalized education and movements for social justice. Her work in non-profit, activist, and academic contexts has addressed a range of inter-connected themes – including environmental justice, human rights, the social impacts of artistic representation, and alternate conceptualizations of temporality – all of which inform her commitment to ethical and sustained engagement with communities. She is Community Engagement Officer with the SSHRC-funded International Institute for Critical Studies in Improvisation, where she works to support, develop, and implement community-engaged, arts-based research projects with a range of community-based, artist, and academic partners. Elizabeth holds a PhD (English & Cultural Studies) from McMaster University, and completed her BA and MA at the University of Guelph. Her academic publications include articles in *Studies in Canadian Literature, Postcolonial Text*, and *The Journal of West Indian Literature*.

Cory Legassic is part of the Sociology and Humanities faculty as well as the New School coordinator at Dawson College in Montreal. His teaching focuses on social movements, anti-racism, gender/sexuality, and media. He is also an active community organizer around migrant justice struggles.

Brendan Main lives in Peterborough, Ontario. He is currently working on a PhD at Trent University's Frost Centre, considering community and new media in a Canadian context.

Morvern McNie received her B.A. in English and M.A. in English and Theatre Studies from the University of Guelph, and her B. Ed. from Brock University.

Ingrid Mündel is a community-engaged researcher, facilitator, and educator with a particular interest in art-based approaches to community dialogue and social change. Ingrid holds a PhD in Literature and Performance Studies from the University of Guelph and is currently Managing Director of Re·Vision, an Ontario-based expressive arts institute that uses art to address social inequities. She has worked at the University of Guelph in a range of roles, including as the Acting Director of the Institute for Community Engaged Scholarship, and is invested in generating critical dialogue on engaged scholarship, arts-based methods, and innovative approaches to pedagogy. Her current research examines both the need for and challenge of telling stories from marginalized voices and perspectives in the current neoliberal "moment" in Canada. She has had articles published in *Theatre Research in Canada, Canadian Literature*, and *Postcolonial Text*, and a chapter in *Popular Political Theatre and Performance*. She has also co-edited a journal special issue of *The Review of Pedagogy, Education, and Cultural Studies* on social change and academia and has co-edited a book with Ric Knowles entitled *"Ethnic," Multicultural, and Intercultural Theatre in Canada*.

Natalie Onuška is a poet, fiction writer, and photographer. Her literary and photographic work has been published in *Descant, Prairie Fire, Prism International, Room of One's Own, Canadian Geographic Magazine, Huffington Post Canada, Huffington Post Hawaii*, and by the *CBC*. She holds a Masters degree in English from the University of Guelph where she served as part of the editorial team for the online academic journal *Critical Studies in Improvisation/Études critiques en improvisation*. She is a member of PEN Canada and an associate member of The League of Canadian Poets.

Bart Vautour is Assistant Professor of English at Dalhousie University. He is a scholar of Canadian literature, with a particular interest in transnational Canadian cultural production and social justice movements. He is co-editor, with Erin Wunker, Travis V. Mason, and Christl Verduyn, of *Public Poetics: Critical Issues in Canadian Poetry and Poetics*, and with Emily Robins Sharpe he is co-director of *Canada and the Spanish Civil War* (spanishcivilwar.ca)

Robert Zacharias is Assistant Professor in the Department of English at York University. He is editor of *After Identity: Mennonite Writing in North America* (2015) and, with Smaro Kamboureli, *Shifting the Ground of Canadian Literary Studies* (2012), and author of *Rewriting the Break Event: Mennonites and Migration in Canadian Literature* (2013).

Index

Cultural Spaces

Cultural Spaces is an interdisciplinary book series that examines cultural practices and social relations through bold new investigations of the contemporary world. Authors are invited to explore themes and subjects including, but not limited to, citizenship, indigeneity, migration, ecology, environment, violence, difference, and desire. Studies may take the form of cultural, literary, visual, political, sociological, or ethnographic analyses.

General Editor: Jasmin Habib, University of Waterloo

Editorial Advisory Board

Lauren Berlant, University of Chicago
Homi K. Bhabha, Harvard University
Hazel V. Carby, Yale University
Richard Day, Queen's University
Christopher Gittings, University of Western Ontario
Lawrence Grossberg, University of North Carolina
Mark Kingwell, University of Toronto
Heather Murray, University of Toronto
Elspeth Probyn, University of Sydney
Rinaldo Walcott, OISE/University of Toronto

Books in the Series

Peter Ives, *Gramsci's Politics of Language: Engaging the Bakhtin Circle and the Frankfurt School*
Sarah Brophy, *Witnessing AIDS: Writing, Testimony, and the Work of Mourning*

Shane Gunster, *Capitalizing on Culture: Critical Theory for Cultural Studies*

Jasmin Habib, *Israel, Diaspora, and the Routes of National Belonging*

Serra Tinic, *On Location: Canada's Television Industry in a Global Market*

Evelyn Ruppert, *The Moral Economy of Cities: Shaping Good Citizens*

Mark Coté, Richard J.F. Day, and Greg de Peuter, eds., *Utopian Pedagogy: Radical Experiments against Neoliberal Globalization*

Michael McKinnie, *City Stages: Theatre and the Urban Space in a Global City*

David Jefferess, *Postcolonial Resistance: Culture, Liberation, and Transformation*

Mary Gallagher, ed., *World Writing: Poetics, Ethics, Globalization*

Maureen Moynagh, *Political Tourism and Its Texts*

Erin Hurley, *National Performance: Representing Quebec from Expo 67 to Céline Dion*

Lily Cho, *Eating Chinese: Culture on the Menu in Small Town Canada*

Rhona Richman Kenneally and Johanne Sloan, eds., *Expo 67: Not Just a Souvenir*

Gillian Roberts, *Prizing Literature: The Celebration and Circulation of National Culture*

Lianne McTavish, *Defining the Modern Museum: A Case Study of the Challenges of Exchange*

Misao Dean, *Inheriting a Canoe Paddle: The Canoe in Discourses of English-Canadian Nationalism*

Sarah Brophy and Janice Hladki, eds., *Embodied Politics in Visual Autobiography*

Robin Pickering-Iazzi, *The Mafia in Italian Lives and Literature: Life Sentences and Their Geographies*

Claudette Lauzon, *The Unmaking of Home in Contemporary Art*

Kyle Conway, Little Mosque on the Prairie *and the Paradoxes of Cultural Translation*

Ajay Heble, ed., *Classroom Action: Human Rights, Critical Activism, and Community-Based Education*

www.ingramcontent.com/pod-product-compliance
Lightning Source LLC
Chambersburg PA
CBHW021859020426
42334CB00013B/404